Family Life, Trauma and Loss
in the Twentieth Century

Carol Komaromy • Jenny Hockey

Family Life, Trauma and Loss in the Twentieth Century

The Legacy of War

palgrave
macmillan

Carol Komaromy
The Open University
Milton Keynes, UK

Jenny Hockey
The University of Sheffield
Sheffield, UK

ISBN 978-3-319-76601-0   ISBN 978-3-319-76602-7 (eBook)
https://doi.org/10.1007/978-3-319-76602-7

Library of Congress Control Number: 2018939758

© The Editor(s) (if applicable) and The Author(s) 2018
This work is subject to copyright. All rights are solely and exclusively licensed by the Publisher, whether the whole or part of the material is concerned, specifically the rights of translation, reprinting, reuse of illustrations, recitation, broadcasting, reproduction on microfilms or in any other physical way, and transmission or information storage and retrieval, electronic adaptation, computer software, or by similar or dissimilar methodology now known or hereafter developed.
The use of general descriptive names, registered names, trademarks, service marks, etc. in this publication does not imply, even in the absence of a specific statement, that such names are exempt from the relevant protective laws and regulations and therefore free for general use.
The publisher, the authors and the editors are safe to assume that the advice and information in this book are believed to be true and accurate at the date of publication. Neither the publisher nor the authors or the editors give a warranty, express or implied, with respect to the material contained herein or for any errors or omissions that may have been made. The publisher remains neutral with regard to jurisdictional claims in published maps and institutional affiliations.

Cover illustration: Left hand photo: Nellie Davis, Carol Komaromy's mother, in WAAF uniform; Right hand photo: Bert and Ella Manning, Jenny Hockey's grandparents, with their elder son, Arthur
Cover design by Emma Hardy

Printed on acid-free paper

This Palgrave Macmillan imprint is published by the registered company Springer International Publishing AG part of Springer Nature.
The registered company address is: Gewerbestrasse 11, 6330 Cham, Switzerland

This book is dedicated to the memory of Carol's dad, James Gilmore, in gratitude for his legacy of unconditional love.

Foreword

This book is a testament to friendship and its enactment in the decision to co-mingle family stories in a joint writing project about war, trauma, memory, love and death. There is something distinctive about a book in which it is friendship that is the thread that binds different families and life histories in conversation and analysis. It is a generous endeavour full of heart, intellect, truth and depth. Feeling an affinity with these authors, their sensibilities speak to mine. At its heart, it addresses the human condition of mortality brought to writing in its painful beauty. Indeed, there is much to admire and appreciate about the way in which the mundane and extraordinary is given attention by Jenny Hockey and Carol Komaromy in order to faithfully render (as far as possible) the lives of family members who lived before, through and after World War One and World War Two, inheriting the emotional and material legacies of these wars. There is also something fearless about the way they take us into their family histories, the kinds of relationships they had with their mothers and fathers, especially trusting that the reader will grasp and understand what they have chosen to tell and represent.

This book comes from the lives of two women now officially in retirement from academia. Since the 1990s Carol and Jenny have been key figures in establishing a vibrant academic research agenda in Death Studies within the UK. Indeed, their friendship and intellectual connection emerged from their respective attendance at the second Death,

Dying and Disposal Conference initiated at the University of Bath, which has a dedicated research centre for the study of death and dying. It has become a key conference for international scholars, like myself, in which attendees find and connect with their tribe in an environment where the subject of death and dying is actually *normal*. I remember the first time I went to this conference at Bath in 2007—DDD8. Oddly enough it was a conference that initiated an incredibly important intellectual and personal friendship for me with academic and artist Polly Gould. After travelling over 24 hours non-stop on the plane, arriving at Heathrow and waiting in a long queue to get through security, I finally stepped up to the passport control counter where a man routinely asked my purpose in coming to the UK. I remember deciding that I would mention the conference matter-of-factly—it gave me a certain pleasure. And so I said, 'I am attending the Death, Dying and Disposal conference at Bath'. He gave me a look somewhere between amusement and disbelief and, duly stamping by passport for clearance, I was on my way.

By taking us into their working lives, and movement into higher education, first as students and then academics, we come to understand why this area of research on family, war and trauma might have come out of their respective backgrounds and especially their relationship to their fathers and mothers. Carol spent many years working as a nurse and some of this time in the aged care sector. This put her right at the centre of where death and dying are routine occurrences but nevertheless managed in ways that hide the death of residents from other residents by choreographed manoeuvrings of the deceased through rooms and corridors when residents are asleep, dozing, watching television or in some other activity. Carol's description of this task and her role in it has an absurdly humorous quality even though hiding and euphemising death is a deadly serious business.

Carol has been an important critic of the sequestration of the dying in places and amongst people who most need it to be communalised in discourse and ritual. What kind of suffering is inflicted on the ageing and the dying when death's reality is atomised as the province of each individual in their private consciousness, thereby creating barriers to witnessing and entry into conversation? The accusation when someone talks or just wants to talk about death that it is an unnecessary morbid thing to do is a profound indictment of societies that have lost their way, arrogant and dishonest about what truly matters and drives us as human beings. In middle-class social economies, particularly in the global north, there is a normalisation of unconscious, sedated dying, the medicalization of the life course and the sequestration of the ageing, the dying and the deceased from communal spaces of care and witnessing.

Carol's research and writing has resonated profoundly with my own father's experience in a hospice, which had a supportive, kind culture. I want to briefly tell the story of a stage in my father's dying in this hospice in Brisbane (Australia) and his witnessing, in the early hours of the morning when no one was around, the death of the man in the bed across from him. The next day he told me and perhaps other members of the family that he was greatly relieved to have had his chance of witnessing because he experienced this death as not frightening. It was, he said, comforting. I have thought about this story and of my father's exposure to a scene of dying as a man deeply aware of his own mortal trajectory well before his cancer diagnosis. If that man across from him had died in the light of day where his dying was exposed to management, would the curtain of privacy been drawn against this fleeting temporality and space of witnessing? I do not know, but if he and my father were in aged care, rather than a hospice facility of shared rooms, I am quite certain no witnessing would have been permissible either spatially or culturally.

The lack of intergenerational intimacy in witnessing death is part of this story of the unfamiliarity of death within life. In centuries past in Europe and other broadly 'Western countries' (one has to be careful of these naming practices and the imagined geographies of coherent self-contained culture they imply, wary too of overgeneralising or ignoring cultural and geographical diversities within these names), children watched parents and grandparents die and were able to touch and spend time with the deceased. It was not shamefully hidden nor treated as a potential trauma that children should be shielded from.

In contemporary thought, we have to think about trauma as an idea (with a reality) quite carefully because it has become one of those words that can be used loosely and sometimes without consideration of where, what and to whom it is applied historically for socio-political recognition and support. It has taken some time for family violence and particularly violence against women to be recognised in terms of trauma discourse raising important questions about the political invisibility of trauma histories that are gendered and nested in the private sphere. In the context of death and grief there are specific questions too around trauma. For example, if intergenerationally it becomes normal to shield children from the real aspects of human existence such as witnessing loved ones die, isn't there a danger that witnessing death becomes perceived as dangerous, even trauma inducing? Trauma at its most serious is a physically embodied disturbance that delimits the capacity to work, to form and to sustain loving relationships and strips life of value and meaning. Trauma is real, but it can be a word that is used too loosely and applied where it might not belong.

We know, from a great deal of war documentaries, memoir, biographies, journalism and cinematic representations, that (mostly) men went to war as one person and came back as someone else. Broken-inside returned servicemen and servicewomen now, and in the past, have felt betrayed and demoralised by 'get over it mentalities' enveloping their trauma forcing them into a code of privacy and self-management. And civilian populations caught up in the horrors of war are often an even more invisible group whose care needs and stories fall outside of government responsibility and official histories. The war histories of this book capture a distinctively British period of stoicism (although it undoubtedly has a very long historical trajectory of cultivation) in which men and women were culturally conditioned to cope and get on with things however difficult. The *Keep Calm and Carry On* mantra identified as a very British message has become commercialised in home décor and particularly wall decorations. I've seen it everywhere in shops in Australia and online. Pride in this Anglo-stoicism was, and perhaps to some extent still is, culturally imbued as valuable despite its sometimes painful and destructive potential. In practice it means holding one's pain inside as a burden to be weathered and internally managed. But stoicism as a cultural value, a way of being, also means that you know you are doing this like other people around you, so it is also shared in an unspoken way, and there is probably a comfort in this too. Today, it is fashionable to speak of resilience as something to instil in young children as a form of inoculation against whatever life might throw at you.

Jenny also has her own experience of death's cultural sequestration. She grew up in a middle-class English family where she was not taken to visit her maternal grandfather in hospital while he was dying. She could send him notes and things but that was the extent of her contact. She was emotionally very close to him—the family actually lived with him in his house. This exclusion of her nine-year-old self from witnessing his dying and thereby making sense of his death in a real way was just not the way it was done in her family. When her mother had just learned of her father's death, a firm squeeze of Jenny's hand before she left the house to go to the hospital was how this vague knowledge of his death was communicated. She was also given instruction to contain her emotion, as a mark of respect for her grandfather who, she was told, would not want her to cry too much. This was the intergenerational passage of a death and grief cultural way. Carol also recalls her mother's explicit exclusion of her attendance at funerals well into teenage years. Trying to understand this forbidden access to death and the funeral rite, she speculates that it may not just have been a peculiar aspect of her family but rather an expression of a larger post-war cultural attitude when it was possible to more easily shield the reality of death from children's everyday consciousness. If adults had had enough of death and grief from the trauma of war in their own childhood or adult life, then at least their children might enjoy the benefit of keeping it at a distance by not going to funerals. This might be part of what lies behind this shielding. The purpose of this book then is partly to explore and analyse aspects of family culture within this broader context of the historical conditions that produce or enable certain mentalities and practices, anchoring them in family life. Jenny's exclusion from death rites of course had the opposite effect, as one might expect, evidenced in her intellectual curiosity and career path into Death Studies.

This is also a book about ghosts and their accumulation as loved ones die and we ourselves grow older, haunted by their memory, thinking about how we too might be remembered and will eventually pass into forgetting. It also addresses the fragility of memory in the survival of family stories and remembered conversations and in the fragments of objects belonging to deceased family that manage to survive in attics, in drawers, on shelves, in garages, in wicker baskets and in boxes. Fragments of material life—personal diaries, family photographs, household objects, clothing, remembered conversations and events—enable the dead to remain connected to us and us to them as their memory custodians. In reading *Family Life: Trauma and Loss in the Twentieth Century. The Legacy of War*, I was delighted by the frankness of thought and feeling about this question of custodianship—an issue long part of my own research on *Objects of the Dead*. Jenny Hockey's (and Elizabeth Hallam's) groundbreaking scholarship on death and material culture, particularly the idea of the agency of things, opened up an important avenue of research in death and bereavement studies.

And yet we live in a time (particularly in the global north) where a prevailing popular culture figure is the hoarder who has a pathological relationship to the things they own and an inability to let go of even the most trivial of items. While not discounting the reality and indeed suffering of hoarding individuals and their families, I am also wary of the popularity of such a figure in throwaway capitalism that imposes a relentless logic of accumulation and disposal without much regard for either end of the equation. Might not the hoarder be seen as a representation and symptom of capitalist accumulation whose *social understanding* should not be individualised as a personal, idiosyncratic mental health issue? Another cultural expression that is part of the zeitgeist is the decluttering movement popularised in lifestyle television shows, magazines and book publishing. The international bestseller *The Life-Changing Magic of Tidying Up* raised a certain suspicion in me. It does have relevance and value because it speaks to a distinctly urban Japanese lifestyle issue of managing small living in terms of one's possessions. It is also mindful of mindless accumulation. However, in its international popularity, it has moved beyond any distinct cultural geography where space is a real issue. While it advises thoughtful, considered disposal of possessions where time is taken to arrive at decisions about what to keep into the future, it privileges certain moods and sensibilities with terms like 'joy' as criteria for decision-making. Immediately my thoughts go to the question of why not keep things that evoke melancholy and ways of owning and keeping loss and sadness? Owning sadness and indeed embracing the beauty and balance of a range of emotions should be foremost in social thinking and values around material culture and its continuity over time.

Of course nothing lasts forever—a cliché, which, like all clichés, is a truism. But, at the same time, sensitivity to material memories ground us in our connections to family and legacies in meaningful and enduring ways across generations, providing solace, materials for conversation and storytelling.

However, people can be hapless in this role of custodians of material memories, not knowing what to do with inherited personal objects and stories about deceased relatives. Also, so much just goes missing without us even realising that stories have been forgotten and things that might be clues to a life have disappeared, discarded in the mobility of modern life. In *Family Life: Trauma and Loss in the Twentieth Century. The Legacy of War*, Jenny Hockey and Carol Komaromy have done this work of looking at the traces they have left of family members' lives, the material fragments which give clues to the thinking, emotions and experiences of these deceased relatives. But this is done not for its own sake, but in order to map how their families are part of a larger social story of the lives of British people before, between and after the first and second World Wars. This book then embodies American sociologist C. Wright Mills' idea of the sociological imagination as the task of using personal and private life as a prism and jumping point for insight and examination of larger social patterns, forms of culture, value systems and historical events. But this book is more adventurous and affecting than mainstream approaches to sociology in its method of life writing, modes of address, reflexive awareness and source of documents.

In many ways Carol Komaromy and Jenny Hockey ask the reader to think about what can and cannot be known in the passage of intergenerational relationships and the formations and ongoing transformations of family cultures. They take us into that territory of imagination where we wonder about the people that make up our families and might have shaped our personalities, influencing perhaps vaguely or more obviously the direction of our lives and way of being the world. In its embrace of the work of imagination, this book is equally about lost and absent knowledge—the dead whose secrets, hidden lives, unspoken thoughts and desires are gone from any living memory or recorded trace. And so we might well ask: is there an unconscious thread of imperceptible affect and effects that we all inherit across the generations without ever really being able to pinpoint what these might be and how they are part of us?

We live in a time in which the figure of the ghost is largely the idea of a persistent memory—the trace of something or someone that haunts our consciousness, for better or worse. Hauntology is a concept that captures a turn in academic research and creative works towards questions of loss, trauma and memory in relation to a range of issues—adoption, dementia, trauma, bereavement experience and so on. For many of us, it is deceased loved ones that may happily haunt our lives as invisible companions. Trauma too is a form of haunting often expressed in anxiety, addiction, depression and violence. The relationship between war and trauma is now commonly recognised although it may remain hidden and unresolved in the lives of individuals and families who do not or cannot access and channel their pain in more life-affirming ways.

Many families shaped by the horrors of war have hidden or unspoken traumas mediating relationships and influencing the quality and form of emotional attachment and communication particularly between parents as couples, and between parents and children. Holocaust survivors and their families are where trauma histories have had an important and a profound focus in socio-historical research and published memoir. Through examining the war experience of her family, Carol Komaromy takes us on a journey into a particular trauma that lived within her father until the day he died. It is the story of her father's encounter with the stench of death and the remaining skeletal survivors of the concentration camp of Bergen-Belsen. As one of a few soldiers asked to deliver supplies to the camp, then already abandoned by German forces, it was a horror that he could never have anticipated nor could ever expunge. Carol's deep love and profound attachment to her father took her on a journey to Europe in order to walk the ground of the territories of war where she knew he had been and managed to survive. Her accounts are not only deeply affecting in their detail and quality of feeling, but also marked by insights and reflections on the nature of memorials—what can and cannot be achieved in bringing to witness and imagination the horrors of war and other mass tragedies?

While I do not come from a generation in which my father or grandfather went to war, as Carol and Jenny's did, I do recall the story of my father's uncle Jamey, a gentle soul shamed into signing up to World War One by that secret, cruel act of sending white feathers in the mail.

He went to war as a cook knowing he was incapable of killing. Anzac Day in Australia has become so sacred in political discourse and media culture that it is sacrilegious to even question why Australians were fighting in Europe. In the last five years or so, the political backlash against journalists or other public commentators who have dared to critically engage with the legacy of British imperialism and colonial history in Australian's war history has been deeply concerning. While the European world wars were mostly outside my intergenerational family history, reading this book printed up in my mind an image that took hold in me as a child of perhaps only six or seven years of age. It was the day in which I first set eyes on a returned World War One soldier in the small town I grew up—Kyogle, in the State of New South Wales, Australia. I remember the shock and bewilderment of seeing a man walking about town with severe burns on his face and missing both ears. Realising my shock, my mother or father—I can't recall which—explained to me that he was an Anzac veteran wounded by mustard gas.

This man's embodied trauma not only entered my childhood memory but lives in me today as a middle-aged woman. It is easy to forget that this is how histories and war images take shape, live, circulate and die as often invisible and private unless shared and brought to documentation in narrative. Writing about war and trauma in intimate biographical ways is an important part of official and unofficial war history and trauma testimony.

In reading *In Family Life: Trauma and Loss in the Twentieth Century. The Legacy of War*, I felt the newness of its inventive form. Jenny Hockey and Carol Komaromy have elegantly produced a co-authored memoir—a form in which the first-person narrative is accorded to each without resorting to some seamless fiction of one voice. To support this joint memoir, they have invented a technique of introducing and signalling each other's return of voice as themes, war histories and family life stories shift, unfold, echo and return. An analogy that comes to mind is the handing over of the baton in a relay race with each spurring the other onto the final page, sentence and word. This back-and-forth storytelling works because it is just like a conversation where each person takes turn to speak and listen. There is an intimacy and regard in this conversational style between Jenny and Carol that extends towards the reader, as if drawing them into a confidence. Indeed, the book brought me into a space of imagined community where my own family relationships and memory objects of deceased loved ones were activated like companions travelling along, coming and going through the weft and weave of the book's stories and sensibilities.

February 2018   Margaret Gibson

Acknowledgements

This book is a joint endeavour which has arisen from a collaborative working partnership. It was born out of a shared desire to tell the story of our personal legacies of war.

Jenny counts herself lucky to have had so many chances to work with Carol during their academic careers. This book was another opportunity and she was not going to pass it up. It has helped her get a whole lot closer to a branch of her family whose lives were cut short by war. At last she has done proper justice to the legacy of their memorabilia, stowed away for far too long.

Carol's motivation is to return the gift of her father's love and compassion for her and the people close to him and highlight how someone could maintain his integrity and humanity despite all that he saw and experienced in World War Two. James made a difference to the lives he touched, through humour and kindness. What greater legacy could there be than this?

We would like to thank the following people for all the help they have given us along the way. First of all, grateful thanks to Sharla Plant, publisher at Palgrave, who recognised the valuable contribution of personal memoir and life writing to Palgrave's expanding military sociology and Death Studies programmes. And to Amelia Derkatsch, commissioning editor, for her excellent support throughout the process of writing this book.

Acknowledgements

Carol would like to acknowledge the support and help she received in this endeavour from family and friends. In particular, her nephew Anthony Dolphin, who recorded James's family history, and her partner, Peter Miles, who accompanied her in retracing some of James's steps and who helped her to find Mala Tribich when James was dying and suffering such emotional pain related to the holocaust. George Gilmour, James's brother, showed typical Irish hospitality and tireless patience in answering Carol's many questions about her dad's childhood and who brought comfort through both his likeness and closeness to James. Barrie Davis helped to trace the details of the Davis family tree and offered help whenever requested. Thanks also to the many RAF and history groups who have helped to find and make sense of what information exists about ordinary airmen and airwomen and to close Death Studies colleagues, Arnar Arnasson, Glennys Howarth, Elizabeth Hallam and Douglas Davies who gave immense encouragement during the development of this book. And of course, Jenny Hockey has been a delight and great fun to work with, as well as being hard-working and dedicated to the task.

Jenny would like to express her gratitude to the following: Catriona Batty, Documentation Officer, Topsham Museum, for copies of her grandparents' adverts in the parish magazine and oral history recollections of their shop; Benedicta Makin for the benefit of her experience of compiling the Berryman letters; Anthony Bolton, Branch Chair of the Western Front Association in Chesterfield, for maps and references; Jonathan Brayshaw for his legal insight into family wills; Sally Cholewa, archivist, Royal Bank of Scotland, for pursuing and providing information about Arthur Manning; AnneLaure Gheerbrant, Archives Centrales, Centre Hospitalier Philippe Pinel, for helpful correspondence; Margaret Gibson for taking on the foreword to the book with such warmth and enthusiasm; my cousins Chris and Heather Gould of Exeter for information about Donald Gould; the manager of the NatWest Bank, Langport, Somerset, for putting me in touch with Sally Cholewa at the Royal Bank of Scotland; Gareth Hockey, my son, for information about military matters and the loan of relevant material; Jo Hockey, my daughter, for looking after the family photos, always encouraging me and putting me in touch with Benedicta Makin; Margot and Jeff Lock of Drayton, Somerset, for their kindness in copying letters written by the Mannings that were stored in their box of memorabilia; Julia Powell, Old Russellian Correspondent and archivist for the Royal Russell School, for her warmth and helpfulness; Jonathan Rayner, Reader in Film Studies and liaison officer for Yorkshire Universities' Royal Naval Unit for follow-up on excellent, relevant films he has screened; Jennifer Smith, local historian, for her excellent research on Baker Baker, Bristol, and her subsequent correspondence; Kirsty Surgey, post-graduate student in English at Sheffield University for her stimulating performance piece on absence and family history and for the very useful references she supplied; Greg Webb, from the Great War Forum, who went to endless trouble to provide extraordinary personal detail about Bert Manning; and everyone who has encouraged me with their excitement about this project, especially Val Binney, Lesley Glaister, Cora Greenhill, Nicky Hallett, Richard Jenkins, Stuart Oglethorpe, Victor Sage and Yvie Wetzel. I owe my partner, Bob Hockey, a big debt of gratitude for taking such an interest in the project, for driving half across France to visit World War One sites near Amiens at the end of a strenuous cycling holiday, for reading drafts, for drawing the map and the timeline and for cooking his wonderful dinners. And finally, a massive thank you to Carol Komaromy for coming up with such a brilliant idea in the first place.

Contents

1	**Recovery, Retrieval and Healing**	1
	1.1 Reflexivity	7
	1.2 Recovery	11
	1.3 Our Fathers' Deaths	14
	1.4 Writing a Life	16
2	**Missing Persons**	21
	2.1 Picking Up the Pieces	23
	2.2 Selective Memory	28
3	**Changing Perspectives on Death, Dying and Loss**	47
4	**World War One and its Transformations**	61
	4.1 A Farming Family	65
	4.2 The Arrival of Children and War	70
	4.3 Living with the Legacy of Conflict in Ireland	96
	4.4 Life in the Industrialised West Midlands	100
5	**Family Life Between the Wars: 1918–1931**	105
	5.1 The Armistice and its Aftermath	108

	5.2	The School Magazine and the Diaries	112
	5.3	The Pathe News Film	117
	5.4	Family Life in the Gilmore Household	119
	5.5	The Route to Brighton	122
6	**War in Prospect, 1930–1939**		123
	6.1	The Great Outdoors	123
	6.2	Leaving School, Leaving Topsham	124
	6.3	Reading Between the Lines	128
	6.4	The Mannings at Home	129
	6.5	Out to Work	131
	6.6	Mother and Son	134
	6.7	Transitions to Adulthood (1): Sketching	136
	6.8	Transitions to Adulthood (2): Walking	138
	6.9	At Home in a Group	142
	6.10	Brother and Mother	143
7	**At Home and Abroad**		147
	7.1	War in Prospect	148
	7.2	Living with War	151
	7.3	Arthur on Active Service	153
	7.4	The Italian Campaign	159
	7.5	The Aftermath	160
	7.6	Enlistment	164
	7.7	Enlistment and Training for the Normandy Landings	169
	7.8	Seven Years of Change	176
8	**Experiencing the Horror of World War Two**		179
	8.1	The Bigger Picture	180
	8.2	The Allied Advance	181
	8.3	Personal Journey	186
9	**Growing Up Post-War: All Over Now?**		211
	9.1	Home Life	221
	9.2	Fathering	225

9.3	Social Life	229
9.4	Leaving Home	233
9.5	Bringing the Threads Together	235
9.6	The Impact of War	236
9.7	The End of Family Life	240

10 Endings and Beginnings — 245
- 10.1 L'Osteria Restaurant, London — 246
- 10.2 The Rutland Arms, Bakewell — 247
- 10.3 Form, Content and Style — 248
- 10.4 John Lewis, Birmingham — 249
- 10.5 Death Studies — 250
- 10.6 Journey's End? — 253
- 10.7 Legacies We Take Forward — 257
- 10.8 The Personal and the Professional — 260

Index — 263

About the Authors

Carol Komaromy is a medical sociologist and worked at The Open University for over 20 years on distant learning teaching in death and dying, and on several funded research projects in end-of-life care. Latterly, she was a Media Fellow for the Health and Social Care Faculty as part of the OU/BBC partnership.

Jenny Hockey trained as an anthropologist and worked extensively on death, memory and material culture, the life course, gender and loss. She was president of the Association for the Study of Death and Society (2009–2013). Now Emeritus Professor of Sociology at Sheffield University, she is also a published poet.

List of Figures

Fig. 1.1	Timeline showing the relationship between individual lives and the two World Wars. Overall, it shows the short duration of time in both world wars compared with peace-time and highlights their enduring impact over the period considered	2
Fig. 2.1	The headstone of Carol's paternal grandparents' grave, at Garvagh, Coleraine	41
Fig. 4.1	Jenny's grandmother, Ella, with her elder son, Arthur, on the left of the photo and David, her younger son (Jenny's father), on the right	64
Fig. 4.2	Marjorie and David Manning on the beach at Sidmouth, South Devon, in about 1926	67
Fig. 4.3	Christopher Gould and Jenny Hockey (nee Manning) on the beach at Dawlish, South Devon, in about 1956	68
Fig. 4.4	The second Devonshire Royal Garrison Artillery Territorial Force camping near Topsham, South Devon. Bert Manning is fourth from the left	74
Fig. 4.5	Bert Manning in the uniform of the Royal Garrison Artillery, taken in about 1917	81
Fig. 5.1	Ella, Jenny's grandmother, with her son David (Jenny's father) on the steps of the Drapers' School	115

List of Figures

Fig. 7.1	Arthur Manning in Egypt	156
Fig. 7.2	David and Lorna Manning, Jenny's parents, as a young couple	169
Fig. 7.3	Nellie Davis and James Gilmore. Marriage at Croydon Registry Office, England. February 5, 1944	174
Fig. 8.1	Retracing Carol's father's journey from Arromanches to Belsen	188
Fig. 8.2	The remains of Mulberry Harbour, Arromanches, Normandy, France, 2017. Photo taken by Carol Komaromy.	189
Fig. 8.3	A photo of Mr. and Mrs. Peel, Valkenswaard, given to Dad in 1944	194
Fig. 8.4	A standard-issue RAF Christmas card sent from James to his wife and daughter, 1944	197
Fig. 8.5	Individual graves in the grounds of Bergen-Belsen, Memorial. Photo taken by Carol Komaromy, 2017	203
Fig. 8.6	Studio photograph of Nell with Pauline taken in, Wolverhampton, 1946	207
Fig. 9.1	The war memorial in Kilrea where Dad's name appeared when he was recorded as 'missing believed killed' (Taken by Carol Komaromy, 2017)	228
Fig. 9.2	David and Lorna Manning walking by the river	230

1

Recovery, Retrieval and Healing

It all began in 1995. We were excited to be participants at what was only the second of the International Death, Dying and Disposal Conferences.[1] The academic work on death and dying we had each been carrying out in relative isolation now seemed to be acquiring a place in the scheme of things. There, at the University of Sussex, circumstances drew us together for the first time. This book is a piece of collaborative writing that explores the different routes each of us had taken to that conference. It is a memoir, but rather than the story of an individual, it explores our shared background of two world wars and the distinctive ways in which family life, for each of us, was affected. At its heart are six key members of our families: Bert and Arthur Manning, Jenny's paternal grandfather and his son, both of whom died in military action; Bert's wife, Ella, and their second son, David, who became Jenny's father; and James Gilmore, Carol's father, who participated in the liberation of Belsen, and his wife Nell (Fig. 1.1).

The project of researching and assembling their lives in this book reflects the spirit of creative partnership that has guided our careers so successfully as women—in an academic world where the heroic (often male), single-authored output retains its currency. The book is therefore

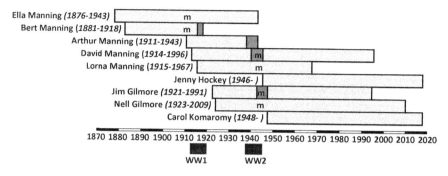

Fig. 1.1 Timeline showing the relationship between individual lives and the two World Wars. Overall, it shows the short duration of time in both world wars compared with peace-time and highlights their enduring impact over the period considered

made up of passages we have each written in the first person, as well as those which reflect joint authorship. Carol begins with her personal history and how it led her to the 1995 International Death, Dying and Disposal Conference at the University of Sussex.

Carol I began to study part-time for a degree in 1984, when I was getting frustrated by the lack of intellectual stimulation in my work. I was doing agency nursing and also hospital bank nursing to fit around the needs of my son and daughter's childcare but felt I needed something more. Over the next seven years, I studied a variety of courses part-time to fit in with paid work and childcare. These included the social sciences, technology, development studies and philosophy. Although I had received high marks and lots of praise during my assessment for nursing studies, I was still haunted by my school experiences and the dread of exams. (I did very well and gained a first class open, honours degree through The Open University.) Of course my thinking was changing and my ideas were being challenged. Alongside taking a module on beliefs and ideologies—having studied feminist ideas—and during the midwifery training I undertook near the end of my health-care career, I became horrified by the medicalization of childbirth and the power imbalance in a system through which this control was achieved. My new awareness was later deepened by my experiences among people nearing the end of their lives.

But at this stage, as a trained midwife, my primary concern was with what had happened to women and how wrong it was. Although I could make a difference at an individual level, I felt powerless to challenge the system as a whole. At a psychodynamic level, as I recognised in my personal psychoanalytic analysis, it seems I was trying to uncover what went wrong for my mother and how it could have been prevented. In other words, I was doing my bit to rescue other women who, like my mother, might be damaged by the experience of childbirth, in her case, partly as a result of World War Two. More fundamentally and on reflection through analysis, it seems that I was trying to rescue the damaged infant 'me'. This is something I discuss further in Chap. 9.

Encouraged by my partner and thinking that the best way to change things was through research and teaching, I went to the University of Warwick to do a full-time Master's in 'Sociological Research in Health Care'. Fortunately, my fear of being a mature student in a group of 'bright young things' was unfounded, and I spent a very stimulating year luxuriating in full-time study and holding my own intellectually. During my first degree, I had studied a course about social welfare and social problems and been bowled over by the theory of social construction and how 'things could be otherwise'. I chose to do a dissertation on 'The perceived risk of HIV infection in a labour ward setting' where I had noted the contradictions in practising *universal* precautions when some midwives perceived particular women to pose a higher risk than others and modified their practice as a result.

After gaining an MA, I applied for a fixed-term six-month research contract at The Open University, designing a research survey and analysing the data. It was the first part of a larger, three-stage study of end-of-life care for older people, to be submitted to the Department of Health. During this first phase, the project's principal investigators were successful in getting Department of Health funding to complete the next two stages of the study. I was recruited as the full-time Research Fellow, and my training as a counsellor and my health-care practice background and interest in palliative care helped me enormously in conducting interviews and with observational fieldwork. Thus began my entry into academia and, in particular, the arena of death and dying.

It was agreed that I should do a part-time PhD alongside the fieldwork—and I approached Jenny Hockey and asked her if she would like to collaborate on the project in some way. This was the beginning of what became a strong friendship in which we often wrestled with ideas about 'what is really going on here'. Jenny for her part arrived in Brighton by a different route.

Jenny In 1965 I abandoned Art College and took 'shelf-stacking' jobs in libraries at the University of Cambridge. Ten years later, when my children started school, I began an undergraduate degree in social anthropology. It involved a dissertation based on data we had gathered ourselves. The deaths of my mother and grandfather led me to traditional anthropological accounts of non-western societies which often give considerable space to descriptions and interpretations of ritual practices around the time of death. They are likely to be the most elaborate of any enacted at times of change and transition. Yet the deaths in my family were surrounded by silences and absences that stood out in marked contrast to the apparently extravagant behaviours of many traditional peoples. Those family deaths provided me with 'data', a point of comparison.

What became known as 'anthropology at home'—the study of one's own society—inspired me to begin investigating the taken-for-granted world of my everyday life and its brushes with death. I started with an undergraduate dissertation in 1977 and at first concluded that earlier forms of knowledge and ways of behaving had been forgotten, that death and the dead had become disgracefully neglected. I collected data by asking people around me for their 'death histories', accounts that often began with the first deaths they could remember, perhaps a grandparent, maybe the cat. I was interested in what appeared to make self-evident sense in my own society, the kind of knowledge often thought of as 'common' sense. It could, I believed, reveal fascinating systems of meaning if I interrogated it with enough care. Core to what busied me between 1977 and 2002 was therefore the sequestration or sidelining of death, the way its occurrence and aftermath were absent from everyday experience. But I was also curious to understand what these avoidances were *about*. In other words, I was trying to explain something that was *not happening*, particularly the relationships that living people might (not) have with the dead. Certainly I had considerable experience of silences and avoidance, and my relationships with dead family members were almost non-existent. I had sidestepped the end of my mother's life, and even my initial anthropological fieldwork in a care home for elderly people and a hospice introduced me to only a tiny number of corpses.

When I wrote up that fieldwork in the form of a PhD and later a book,[2] I prefaced it with childhood memories of the night my grandfather died: 'Suffering from heart trouble, he remained in hospital for more than a week. Though I sent in cards and presents for him, as a nine-year old child I was excluded from visiting. Within ten days of his admission, while lying awake, I overheard my father answering the front door. His "Oh Lor!" and my mother's unusually firm squeeze as they left the house evoked no conscious suspicion on my part – but I remember them still.'

Though exclusion seems to characterise this event, a set of practices were still being brought into play. Once my grandfather was dead, visiting his body in hospital was an immediate priority for my parents. For me, as a child, this visit and indeed the news that he had died were something I had to be protected from. Yet other people in other places do these things differently. Even in the UK, 50 years later, parents are unlikely to leave a nine-year-old child in the house alone. The absences and exclusions of my 1950s' Cambridge childhood are the outcome of particular beliefs and practices; they are not simply failures or voids.

These two examples illustrate this point.

In the residential home for elderly people where I began research in 1980, the apparent invisibility of death was the outcome of procedures that served to divide the living and dead people who shared the confines of the institution. I described these as follows:

> Though properly managed deaths take place in the sickbay, ambiguities are still encountered in that the corpse must then pass through the space of the living on its journey to the mortuary. An impromptu transformation of this space is effected through the deliberate closure of lounge and bedroom doors en route, and the strategic positioning of staff members between the 'frail' who doze in the open alcove and the passing corpse.[3]

Carol described similar practices after a death in the hospital where she worked as a nurse in the 1960s. 'The screens were pulled around the beds of living patients, side rooms were closed and all ambulant non-medical people were stopped and placed out of sight of the departing corpse.'[4] What she is saying is that for a death to be non-apparent, things have to be *done*. From her direct observations following death in the care home setting, Carol noted that the removal of the corpse was concealed, often with difficulty:

> *Fieldnotes: Leaving the home at 6.15 pm, shortly after being called, the undertakers arrived at Regis House to remove Alice's body. Matron and I went with them and on the way through the lounge to the bedroom, matron closed the curtains in the dining room, so that the residents would not see the hearse. I helped matron to move furniture around so that they could access the French doors. The room was very small and making room for the mortuary trolley was difficult. At one point the commode that was in the room toppled over onto the dressing table and made a loud crash. I wondered how much of this noise the surviving residents were able to hear and what they thought we were doing. The undertakers took Alice's body out in a body bag on a trolley through the French doors of her bedroom unseen by other residents, who were still having tea as part of the normal routine.*

Our very different routes to the University of Sussex conference had converged within care homes for older adults and the ways in which institutions managed death 'on the premises'. As we go on to describe, we brought different histories and questions to this environment of ageing and deterioration. Both of us had entered university as mature students with particular life experiences behind us. Alongside our personal trajectories, a wider world had begun to question the ways in which western societies were dealing with death. The academic insights we contributed to Death Studies derive from a period of profound change and diversification within the human encounter with mortality. Bereavement counselling; hospice care; the provision of niche funerals, for example for the members of minority ethnic groups; the removal of ashes from crematoria for personal disposal; the introduction of natural burial; the growth of DIY funerals and informal memorialisation at grave sites; the radical revision of theories of grief—these are all late twentieth-century innovations. They have evolved against the background of what the historian Jay Winter, writing about the World War One in 1995, called 'the cataclysmic record of European history in this century'.[5] In no sense, then, can our contribution to Death Studies be isolated from a whole series of political and personal upheavals, many of which have brought profound change in the way we experience dying, death and loss. Here, in this book, it is their implications for family life, particularly in relation to war, that we focus on.

1.1 Reflexivity

Both of us have developed our knowledge and understanding of death, dying and loss by speaking to people and watching what they do. Rather than statistical methods which are often used to predict what might happen in future circumstances, we have engaged with people's experience and tried to understand what is happening and the kind of beliefs and values they are drawing on. This makes us qualitative rather than quantitative researchers. Since we ourselves are part of the picture we are exploring, it would distort that picture to pretend that we were somehow devoid of ideas, emotions and agendas that were personal to us. Reflexivity is the term used to describe the way in which qualitative researchers reflect upon and write themselves into the work they are doing, taking account of how their data and their interpretations are both enabled and also constrained by who they are. The University of Toronto provides this definition of the term:

> Reflexivity is the process of examining both oneself as researcher, and the research relationship. Self-searching involves examining one's 'conceptual baggage', one's assumptions and preconceptions, and how these affect research decisions.[6]

As we look back over our years spent working in the field of Death Studies, a deeper form of reflexivity becomes possible. What are the histories that have shaped not only our own biographies but also the lives of our families in the twentieth century? What are the values and assumptions that led us to make particular choices within this broad field of research? Between us we have explored dying, death and loss within bereavement counselling organisations,[7] hospices and residential homes for older people[8]; in mortuaries[9]; among ministers of the church,[10] funeral directors and cemetery managers[11]; and within a variety of burial grounds.[12] In addition, as members of the growing international Death Studies community, we have become knowledgeable about dying, death and loss in a far wider range of settings. Yet as Carol explains in this chapter, Death Studies is a field which, more than most, has personal and emotional implications for researchers. It demands a reflexive approach that involves critical awareness of the distinctive identities of researchers, the subject positions from which they view the people, places and events they are finding out about. Without this kind of reflexive understanding, the data we gather assume a false objectivity that ignores the interpersonal dimension of social science research.

It was as early as the 1970s that qualitative researchers began to call for this kind of recognition of the presence of the researcher in research and so generated what became known as 'the reflexive turn'. Carol demonstrates this in a more personal way by reflecting on the beliefs she took forward from psychodynamic work into a sociological study within residential homes for older people.[13]

Carol Part of the ongoing dilemma, and one that arose in both my academic and (private) clinical supervision, was my tendency to take a psychodynamic approach to analysing my fieldwork data. I found myself asking *why* people did what they did and wondering about the individual psychodynamic motivations of those people in the study, as much as *what* people did and *how* events happened. This concerned me because I was taking a sociological approach to 'death and dying' in care homes for older people. I found it difficult to resolve this tension and experienced frustration throughout the fieldwork and the analysis. However, having analysed the data, the tension did not intrude into my writing up of this thesis. By being able to *write* about what I experienced as a dilemma, rather than suppress it, I argue that I was more able to focus on the sociological aspects of what was taking place. This is not to deny individual psychodynamic aspects that were also operating, but to recognise that I was taking one focus within a particular discipline. From this, I would argue that, while the aim of my thesis was to capture the social aspects of 'death and dying' in care homes for older people, there were many other interpretations that could have been made from different disciplinary perspectives. Indeed, this was consistent with my methodological approach of subtle realism. This approach is one that Martyn Hammersley[14] sees as helpful to researchers insofar as it acknowledges that objective reality is always subject to interpretation. At one extreme the way reality is interpreted can be constructed differently according to who has the power to define it—while at the other, there are many interpretations of reality with no single version holding a true reflection; there are multiple realities. A position between these two versions, which he calls subtle realism, allows researchers to offer valid versions of reality that are as close as possible to it, while also recognising the influence of the researcher's interpretation. Reflexivity is key to this position.

This tendency to want to analyse the data in different ways was not the only tension I felt when producing the thesis. I also found the analysis extremely painful. By this I mean that I was concerned about the way that I felt I was 'dissecting' the care home residents in order to be able to code my data and possibly make some generalised observations. However, after the analysis, I recognised that I could 'bring back' the residents as whole people in the interpretive vignettes, which I used as illustrations and which represented experiences and events that I had commonly witnessed. Therefore, the process of writing up was restorative for both those people who died, whom I called 'ghosts', and for me.

The experience of my fieldwork stayed with me long after the analysis of data was completed. I was self-evidently drawn to this type of work because I cared about the plight of older people in care homes. It was important for me to illustrate the way each individual resident had to be able to cope with his or her experience of the disintegration into death. Yet individual researchers who work in a sensitive area are also expected to be able to cope with 'death and dying' to the extent that he or she has to be able to make academic sense of what is taking place. I have discussed elsewhere what I put in place to help me to cope and how, from a psychodynamic perspective, I was able to explore 'death and dying' while keeping it at a safe distance academically (this was through clinical supervision as well as academic supervision). What I meant by this is that, in some ways, my 'ordering' of my thesis kept my distress bounded within an academic explanation of what was taking place. In this respect the thesis reflected the nature of the institutional life that I was recording, which itself also ordered and contained 'death and dying'. However, this strategy did not succeed entirely because I was emotionally distressed by much of what I saw and frustrated by the way that pain and suffering could be dismissed as a 'normal' part of ageing and dying. I would argue that people who carry out research in areas of society that are marginalised are more likely to be in need of support.

These issues recurred in my subsequent career. From my practice experience, I had expected that the issue of loss would be the aspect of death and dying that would interest and concern me most. However, it was what happened at the end of life and immediately after death that most intrigued me.

I stayed in academia—gaining a lectureship and moving into teaching. My focus was on death and dying but also included writing distance learning in the area of communication and dementia. My research interests, however, remained in end-of-life care across the life course. In particular, the way that people manage their emotions has held most fascination for me. Working with a colleague on a small funded project in a metropolitan hospital mortuary, we noted how the mortuary staff had to manage the spoiled identity associated with what is called 'dirty work'.[15, 16] This sociological term means that there are jobs in society which are not appealing because of their association with dirt and disgust—and those who perform these tasks are contaminated by their association. Part of the mortuary staff's role involved managing their feelings, particularly during post-mortems, but also the team we studied saw themselves as making a significant contribution to patient care and were trying to break down the barriers between their work and that of the rest of the hospital, with little success. Sadly, because of their association with corpses, they were perceived to be contaminated and therefore of a lower status than staff who cared for the living body.

In terms of the present project, reflexivity has been central to the process. Indeed, we are key actors in the accounts we explore. Examining the events that so affected the lives of our close family ancestors means also looking at how they affected us. Our presence and thoughts, including our speculations, are therefore made explicit as we tell our stories. In the final chapter, we reflect on how we have been changed by the experience of writing this book, reacquainting ourselves with and, to some extent, renegotiating our relationships with significant late family members.

1.2 Recovery

From Carol's example of reflexivity, we begin to get a sense of her values and her motivations. She describes wanting to make things 'better' for residents in care homes for older people. In the chapters that follow, she explores this orientation far more fully, and we begin to build a picture of the personal and family history from which it derives. The concept of recovery, as we go on to show, is an important theme here and in the rest of the book. For Carol it is closely associated with healing or restoration, the 'recovery' of justice for people whose needs are neglected, who are overlooked or indeed condemned.

It also has associations with bringing things back, lost objects, forgotten people. It has links with memory as well as loving care. If we were to differentiate between our underlying concerns and motivations, we might say that Carol is oriented more towards care, the recovery of well-being and justice, with making a difference; while Jenny is pre-occupied with restoring or recovering what has been lost.

Jenny In this chapter I focus on the deaths of my grandfather and my mother as sources of uneasiness and questioning, whereas Carol describes the dissatisfactions of her nursing career, the wrongs she was not in a position to right. Granddad died in 1955 and Mum died in 1967. I am an only child, and when my father died in 1996, nearly 30 years after my mother, I was the sole recipient—or custodian—of everything they and their families had owned.

When I began to work on this book I emptied out a wicker picnic basket that had contained most of what they had left by way of documents, letters, diaries and notebooks. In addition, there was a mighty collection of family photographs, and these I had already laboured over, extracting duplicates, jettisoning a very few—though my daughter, Jo, salvaged these—organising and fastening the remainder into a weighty family album. With my entire family of birth gone, I found myself 'a custodian of fragility'[17]—as both the materiality and the meaning of my legacy gradually lost substance. Like the sociologist Carol Smart, I also, 'want[ed] to step back to be near these people … because I believe them to be related to me and this sense of connectedness across the generations means I want to know more about them, their daily lives, their feelings, their views, their aspirations …'.[18]

My own 'people' proved elusive. Many of their photographs are undated and unlabelled; salient personal information is lost or hidden from view among years of bland diary entries—for example, 7 October 1945. *Sunny, quite warm. Father, Lorna and I went along by the river sketching in the morning. Got back about 3 o'clock. The Hitchin train has been altered to 8.40 pm now.* How might I achieve connection via these materials? I wanted to travel in two directions, backwards to relatives I had never met and forwards, to introduce them to family who will survive me: Jo, my quiet, arty daughter; Dennis, her big-hearted partner; and Blue, their goth-inspired teenage daughter, all living in Edinburgh, and, here in Sheffield, Gareth, my sporty, sociable son; Sally his warm, hard-working wife; and Rhys and Jess, their lively primary school-age children. If, as Smart says, 'dealing with family photos is not simply a hobby, but part of an active and culturally specific production of the self',[19] then the 'self' I want to produce not only looks back but also forwards to future connections with my younger family members.

Were I to throw all the photos and diaries and letters away, though, would anyone else know or care? Without siblings, aunts or uncles, with cousins I see rarely, my connections with my family of birth are fragile. Yet because of this and particularly as the only child of a father with no immediate family, I wanted some closeness with the paternal grandparents and uncles I had never met, the people whose images and diaries were now all mine. How they have frustrated my efforts. Why did they so often write in pencil? Did they know how fleeting its presence on the page would be? Would that the biro had been invented earlier.

And anyway, why *were* so many members of my family dead? Why was I not surrounded with a larger, living family? On my mother's side there are the children and grandchildren of her sister and her brother, people with whom I keep in touch. But on my father's side, there is no-one close. I envy my Welsh husband, Bob, his ranks of supportive, entertaining relatives, the siblings with whom he can reminiscence or reactivate old jokes. Not only were so many of my family dead, but their passing was profoundly unremarked. Faced with my mother's imminent demise, neither my father nor I, nor the medical practitioners who looked after her, spoke to my mother about her cancer and its evident implications. Though I have inherited 11 five-year diaries kept by my father from 1941 until a month before he died in 1996, there is only a brief entry for 25 October 1966, the day he was told by their GP that my mother had ovarian cancer. 'There's no hope', the doctor said, words my father quoted to me later that day in the Psychology Department library where I was employed. His diary entry, however, begins as always by recording the weather, 'Sunny periods. Cool', going on to say: 'I took Lorna to see her doctor in the morning and did not get to work until 11 am.' While the entry has been made in dark blue biro, the paler blue biro of the *following* year's entries has been used to add the words, 'The Doctor told me that she had an internal growth…'. So my father has almost certainly recorded her diagnosis after she was dead. Even though my parents had no practice of sharing the diary's contents, he had been careful to keep his news a secret. My mother died at home, in the front bedroom, six months later, in the early hours of 15 March 1967. My father sat up with her, leaving me asleep in the next-door bedroom. My head and hers were less than a yard apart. I was 20, in no way a child to be protected. Yet the next day I somehow did not go into the bedroom where her body lay. Nor did I see the funeral director come to collect it; I simply heard her coffin bumping against the stairwell walls. Her body was cremated after a minimal service. I have no idea what became of her ashes, nor can I remember what happened after we left the crematorium. Whatever impact these events had for me was muffled and has remained so. Recovering, revisiting, making sense of all this, has been an important stimulus in my academic work. It is also core to what we are doing here.

1.3 Our Fathers' Deaths

We both lost our fathers in the 1990s. Their deaths were in many ways the prompt for writing a reflexive account of the paths that had led to our meeting at the International Death, Dying and Disposal Conference. If this were a novel, rather than a memoir, those two deaths would be the inciting incidents. Carol lost her father to carcinomatosis in 1991. He was 70. The original cancer had not been diagnosed, and he had taken early retirement because of severe angina. His resulting income was so small that he and Carol's mother struggled to manage on a State Pension. Carol did what she could to help them financially—paying them a small regular amount, but she knew this was painful for her father who wanted to continue to be the breadwinner. Jenny's father was 82 when he died in 1996. She had experienced a difficult sense of responsibility for him ever since her mother's death in 1967. Aged 20, she was among his only close relatives. When she married soon after her mother's death and then left Cambridge for Durham in 1969, her father seemed very alone. Formality and a lack of emotional openness between them made his regular visits to her young family in Durham difficult. Neither of them found much to talk about beyond the itineraries of his latest walks.

As we go on to explain, it was these losses that inspired us to various tasks of recovery. And alongside a sense of loss, there were legacies. Carol has many personal memories, some very difficult given a childhood spent with parents who each, in their own way, had suffered enormously during and after World War Two. She also possesses an eyewitness account of the liberation of the Nazi concentration camp at Bergen-Belsen in North Germany that her father passed on only towards the end of his life, to help his nephew with a school project. In addition, she has access to a proliferation of publically available records and images which mark out the territory of suffering and death into which James, her father, was required to go. In 2007, for example, a film directed by Justin Hardy, *The Relief of Belsen*,[20] was first shown on Channel 4 television. It drew on first-hand testimonies from those who were there at the time. Children who survived the camp are also able to testify to what occurred, and Carol has been able to meet with a few of them.

Now, nearly 80 years later, the challenge is to piece together the relationship between personal biography and global history in order to understand the impact of these extraordinary events upon the ordinary lives of our families. Jenny also has personal memories—of her parents and of their recollections of her four grandparents, three of whom had already died when she was born. In addition, there are the photographs, letters, diaries and official documents that remained after her father died in 1996. For her it is a question of mining personal memories for clues as to the meaning of these materials, as well as finding out how they might be illuminated by published information about wars fought during the first half of the last century.

What we will be demonstrating, as our separate but intertwined stories unfold, are the demands that these legacies place upon us. Now retired, we have resolved to create a narrative from the disparate sources available to us. Its purpose is twofold. First, as explained, the making of such an account is a form of reflexivity that contributes to our existing bodies of academic work. Death Studies scholars like us have included material about their personal experiences and the emotional demands of research in their outputs.[21] But the field as a whole lacks an extended exploration that looks back across the whole century preceding the body of work now available. Questions about the personal implications of European and indeed global history for ourselves and our families have yet to be addressed. In academic jobs, few of us have time to write more than a few paragraphs about these issues. But retirement does offer us that opportunity to make a different kind of contribution.

Second, as we identify questions about our families' lives and how these have been shaped by recent history, we come to the questions we failed to ask our parents before they died. So common is this omission that it merits reflection in its own right. Realising what we would now love to know, it becomes imperative that we provide younger members of our families with the kind of account we lack. Certainly, if we chose not to carry out this work, the fragments that remain would mean almost nothing to our children and grandchildren.

It is this intertwining of personal and global histories that we lay out in this book. To the task we bring the research skills and knowledge we have built up across nearly 40 years. They cannot be separated from our more everyday thought processes. Instead, they contribute to the ways in which we make sense of our experiences, both present and past. It is their use here that enables us to reflect upon the society and the families that we were born into. As argued, then, the academic work we undertook in adult life cannot be viewed in isolation from social, economic and cultural environments we grew up in—and which shaped the lives and the consciousness of our parents and grandparents before us.

1.4 Writing a Life

What does this mean for the kind of book you are about to read? Both of us have published a variety of academic texts, some containing fragments of our personal histories. But these usually form a small part, a preface or a framing device. This book is not 'academic', even though it aims to inform readings of our academic publications and those of other researchers. The style and form we have chosen here fall within the frame of life writing. Marlene Kadar has produced extensive academic work on life writing and describes it as 'a genre of documents or fragments of documents written out of a life, or unabashedly out of a personal experience of the writer'.[22] Discussing Marlene Kadar's work, Christl Verduyn adds:

> Life-writing comprises many kinds of texts, both fictional and non-fictional. All are linked by a common concern with a life, or the self. While life-writing may comprise some of the elements of the more familiar genre of autobiography, it steps beyond genre boundaries and disciplines, particularly with regard to narrative unity, 'objective' thinking, and author/rity.[23]

Verduyn also refers to Kadar's argument that life writing allows dominant histories and received wisdom to be set alongside marginal, neglected or hidden areas of life. Our decision to explore the domestic lives of people in our own families seems to belong here. They lived through extraordinary times, especially when compared with the peace-time affluence of our own youth and adulthood, despite the presence of military conflicts in many other parts of the world. By retrieving different kinds of evidence—from public and private archives and from the memories of living relatives—we set out to recover and make available incidents that reveal our relatives' personal beliefs and values. These give us glimpses of what they might have been feeling when the world around them was undergoing radical change.

Rather than developing arguments that are enmeshed in swathes of academic theorising, then, we enter the territory of our personal or private lives. And, though informed by academic insights, our account utilises the language of everyday conversations and personal reflections. It is not overladen with academic references, though we do offer links to some of our sources. The writer, Alison Light, begins her family history, *Common People*, by saying: 'I … hoped my speaking voice would anchor the reader as we moved through time.'[24] By writing in this way, we not only provide a more personal, reflexive companion to the academic literature of Death Studies, but also offer a narrative which is accessible to a wider audience, one designed to include our children and grandchildren.

Notes

1. See the Association for the Study of Death and Society website for more information: www.deathandsociety.org/
2. Hockey, Jennifer. 1990. *Experiences of Death. An Anthropological Account.* Edinburgh: Edinburgh University Press. (P. 1).
3. Hockey, Jennifer. 1990. *Experiences of Death. An Anthropological Account.* Edinburgh: Edinburgh University Press. (P. 117).
4. Komaromy, C. 2000. The sight and sound of death: the management of dead bodies in residential and nursing homes for older people. Mortality, Vol. 5, No. 3, 299–315. (P. 4).
5. Winter, Jay. 1995. *Sites of Memory, Sites of Mourning.* Cambridge: Cambridge University Press. (P. 1).
6. A Process of Reflection. University of Toronto. http://www.utsc.utoronto.ca/~pchsiung/LAL/reflexivity. Accessed 11 December 2017.

7. Hockey, Jennifer. 1990. *Experiences of Death. An Anthropological Account.* Edinburgh: Edinburgh University Press.
8. Hockey, Jennifer. 1990. *Experiences of Death. An Anthropological Account.* Edinburgh: Edinburgh University Press.
9. Woodthorpe, Kate and Carol Komaromy. 2013. A missing link? The role of mortuary staff in hospital-based bereavement care services. *Bereavement Care* 32: 3.
10. Hockey, Jenny. 1993. The acceptable face of human grieving? Clergy's role in the management of funerals. In *The Sociology of Death*, ed. David Clark, 129–148. Blackwell Publishers, Oxford/Sociological Review Monograph.
11. Hockey, Jenny. 1996. Encountering the 'reality of death' through professional discourses: the matter of materiality. *Mortality* 1: 45–60.
12. Clayden, Andrew, Jenny Hockey, Trish Green, and Mark Powell. 2014. *Natural Burial: Landscape, practice and experience.* Abingdon: Routledge.
13. Komaromy, Carol. 2005. *The Production of Death and Dying in Care Homes for Older People: an ethnographic account.* PhD Thesis. Milton Keynes: The Open University.
14. Hammersley, Martyn. 1992. *What's Wrong with Ethnography?* London: Routledge.
15. Douglas, Mary. 1984. *Purity and Danger: an analysis of the concepts of pollution and taboo.* London: Routledge and Kegan Paul.
16. Goffman, Erving. 1963. *Stigma: notes on a spoiled identity.* Englewood Cliffs, NJ: Prentice-Hall.
17. Corman, Catherine. Ed. 2007. *Joseph Cornell's Dreams.* Cambridge MA: Exact Exchange. (P. ix)
18. Smart, Carol. 2007. *Personal Life.* Cambridge: Polity. (P. 2).
19. Smart, Carol. 2007. *Personal Life.* Cambridge: Polity. (P. 3).
20. *The Relief of Belsen.* Director, Justin Hardy. Produced in association with the Wellcome Trust. 2007.
21. Hockey, Jenny. 2007. Closing in on death? Reflections on research and researchers in the field of death and dying. *Health Sociology Review* 16:5, 436–446.
22. Kadar, Marlene Kadar. 1992. Essays in Life-Writing 5. Cited in Verduyn, Christl. Between the Lines: Marian Engel's *Cahiers* and Notebooks. In *Essays on Life Writing. From Genre to Critical Practice*, ed. Marlene Kadar, 29. Toronto: University of Toronto Press.

23. Verduyn, Christl. 1992. Between the Lines: Marian Engel's *Cahiers* and Notebooks. In *Essays on Life Writing. From Genre to Critical Practice*, ed. Marlene Kadar, 28–41. Toronto: University of Toronto Press.
24. Light, Alison. 2014. *Common People. The History of an English Family*. London: Penguin Figtree. (P. xxiv).

2

Missing Persons

As last chapter explained, the concept of recovery has been crucial to our academic work. Its associations with both retrieval and healing—and the relationship between them—also make it an apt focus for bringing together our different lives and the way they began to mesh, creatively, at the 1995 conference. Recovery has links with memory as well as loving care. Jenny's concern with the distances, if not secrecy, that surrounded the deaths of so many people in her family involves the recovery of both the relatives she grew up with and those who pre-deceased her birth. These lost or 'missing' persons are introduced more fully here, and we raise the question that Alison Light asks in her book, *Common People*: how does family history become a pre-occupation and why does the past matter? As she says: 'How much and what do we owe the dead?' Acknowledging that '[a]ncestor worship is common to all human cultures and as old as the hills', she becomes more specific when describing family historians as 'salvagers … motivated by a search for lost object. If family history is for some an extended mourning, they hope to recover and reuse the past, which otherwise seems like wreckage'.[1] For both of us, the notion of mourning and a sense of past 'wreckage' is resonant.

In the later part of this chapter, we learn about Carol's investigation of what was missing from the period surrounding her birth in 1948, three years after World War Two was supposedly over. She describes how her father was present around the time she was born, but not *at* the moment of her birth, and how for him this acted as a form of compensation for missing the birth and early infancy of his first daughter, Pauline. However, his was an intermittent presence as a result of circumstances such as working unsocial shifts while they were in lodgings and a brief but traumatic separation when Carol and her mother went into the workhouse because they were without anywhere to stay, effectively becoming homeless. A few years later, during the two weeks she spent in an isolation hospital with a form of atypical tuberculosis requiring emergency surgery, he felt unable to visit, for reasons Carol explains later. But no matter how significant his absences, his companionship and love represented a sustaining and nurturing presence that mitigated much of the damage caused by these separations for Carol. In adulthood, Carol learned of her parents' difficult times: of the way her mother was punished by Carol's grandfather for becoming pregnant before she got married and her mother's inadequacy as a parent in a situation where employment, financial support and even a home were missing and while she struggled with mental illness. All of these early foundations of family life seemed to be shaky and insecure. For Nell, Carol's mother, these early years of poverty and shame became a legacy that served as a constant warning of the dangers of losing 'everything'.

As we suggested, what each of us has inherited from the twentieth century differs in some significant ways. Jenny's sense of the past is couched in the material items that remained when her father died. They seemed to promise connection with people closely related to her in kinship terms, yet whose lives had been allowed to recede into pre-war obscurity. The optimism that pervaded Britain in the immediate aftermath of World War Two somehow marginalised the losses that preceded it. For Carol, whatever else might have been missing or lost, her family were alive and for her mother in particular, keeping up appearances within this optimism seemed to be a priority. Jenny's account of the missing persons in her life that follows highlights how central her family's residual material items were to her quest.

2.1 Picking Up the Pieces

> America is a place where the Old World shipwrecked, flea markets and garage sales cover the land. Here's everything the immigrants carried in their suitcases and bundles to these shores and their descendants threw out with the trash.[2]

Jenny These words from *Dime-Store Alchemy* are the American poet Charles Simic's response to the small boxed collages that the surrealist artist, Joseph Cornell, made between the 1920s and the 1960s. Cornell's materials were books and letters, curios and keepsakes, many of which he found in New York dime stores between the wars. Now, as I sit down to write, the dilapidated family diaries, personal letters, War Office correspondence, medals, certificates for birth, marriage and death certificates and photographs that I introduced in Chap. 1 cover a whole table in my workroom, all of them similarly 'shipwrecked'. Joseph Cornell saw himself as 'a custodian of fragility',[3] and a similar imperative was felt by the sociologist, Carol Smart, after she had inherited a carrier bag of family photos. Like her mother, from whom she had inherited the carrier bag, she 'could not throw them away either and so they lived for about two decades in the same plastic bag until [Smart] was left another batch from a maternal aunt'.[4] Smart not only felt the need to retain and sort the photographs; she also found herself embarking on 'a journey of the imagination, of memory, of emotion and of history'.[5] Simic connects Cornell's materials with an 'Old World', a landscape and a culture bundled across the Atlantic at the beginning of the twentieth century; Smart's connections are personal, familial, even though her photographs depict relatives she has never met and knows little about. However, her journey of the imagination, memory, emotion and history resonates with Cornell's description of his material as 'a clearinghouse for dreams and visions … childhood regained'.[6] *Navigating the Imagination* was the very apt title chosen for a retrospective of Cornell's work at the Smithsonian American Art Museum in 2006.[7]

What is it about such items that we safeguard? And what guides us to follow a particular set of clues about the past? Cornell *chose* his materials as he wandered New York's dime stores in his lunch breaks. My missing people—my paternal grandfather and grandmother and their son, my uncle—are accessible to me now only through the 'shipwrecked' fragments on my table. But theirs are not the only materials I have about me, and it is important to reflect on why I am concerned with my paternal family. For example, what did these items mean to their previous custodian, my father? That already is something unclear to me since he is not here to tell me why he kept the things he did, nor whether any of them were jettisoned over the years.

Now, over a hundred years after World War One broke out in Europe, there is a chasm between the small piles of envelopes and certificates that surround me, all grown fabric-soft from scrutiny, from the wear and tear of time—and the formal and informal military histories that provide a collective memory of two world wars. Isolated from their immediate contexts, my residual texts and images acquire a special poignancy. They are like the personal items returned to me after my father died in Castle Hill Hospital near Beverley, East Yorkshire, the town where my husband, Bob, and I were living in 1996. At the time of my father's death these were mundane objects—a black-faced watch with a steel bracelet strap, probably a bargain my father was proud of securing in a lost property sale, and £4.73p in loose change in a man's brown leather purse. Now that my father is gone, along with his home, his clothing and almost all his belongings, these items assume a new potency and cannot easily be returned to everyday use. They have come to share the same status as his earlier family's letters and certificates. For a long time, I stored them all in the same wicker basket.

When Joseph Cornell, the artist, gathered residual items in New York second-hand shops—his found objects and images—they too had come adrift from their original, often 'Old World' environments. Free-floating, they pointed towards the broad domains of travel, dance, romance and film that so enchanted Cornell. He acquired them simply because he liked them; for him they were objects of beauty possessed of highly charged resonances. As Simic says, 'The ideas of art came later, if they ever did come clearly.'[8] It was Cornell's closeness to the objects themselves, his love of classifying, cataloguing and storing them, that enabled him to think of himself as 'an armchair voyager'. The guide to 'Wanderlust', an exhibition of his work at the Royal Academy, London, in 2015, says:

> His remarkable works forge mysterious connections between distant places and eras – for Cornell's eclectic tendencies were paired with a highly elastic notion of time; each one is a window into the powerful wanderlust of an endlessly curious mind.
>
> Cornell's cellar studio became a personal museum, a microcosm of the wider world that brimmed with boxes of source materials and manila folders holding dossiers of paper ephemera.[9]

In assembling and thereby remaking the materiality of what he had stored in his cellar studio, Cornell 'performs his own poetic alchemy, transforming the humdrum into the marvellous' (guide). While the resonances of old theatre programmes, photographs of ballet dancers and film stars, exotic birds, advertisements for hotels in European capitals, fuel the final work, it is their juxtaposition that transcends more immediate points of reference.

Similarly, by taking in hand the materials I have inherited and drawing out their unapparent connections, both with one another and with a wider historical landscape, I am producing an account that is inevitably selective and will reshape rather than simply unearth the lives of my earlier family members. Their letters, certificates and medals have travelled across time, from one family member to another, from jewellery boxes and attaché cases stored in my parents' inaccessible attic, to my heavy photograph album and the wicker basket I had balanced on the bookcases in my workroom. In the process, the meaning of these items shifts. Putting them into the context of wars that took place in the last century encompasses the representations that my generation has created from film footage, official and personal diaries, military records and poetry. What we know as 'World War One' is the outcome of images and texts that are both factual and fictional. Historians such as David Reynolds[10] have pointed out that in academic work and popular culture, World War One is often seen through the narrow focus of trench warfare and a handful of poets. Other theatres of war and other soldiers, from Canada and Australia, for example, are somehow eclipsed. Even at the time, descriptions of life and death on the Western Front that men sent back to family in Britain were heavily edited. There are repeated examples of this on a website[11] that presents the letters that the five Berryman brothers wrote to their mother during this period:

> This war is too awful for words. This is only a scrawl, will write more when I have time. I am very fit and well and going strong. (13 March 1915 Ted Berryman)

This point is also made by Erich Maria Remarque in his account of trench warfare from the perspective of young German soldiers. His title, *All Quiet on the Western Front*, echoes one-line entries in British military diaries: 'All quiet on the front.' Speaking for his young characters, many of whom went to school together, Remarque describes their sense of disconnection from civilian life, their inability to make family and friends back home understand what was happening: 'Of course they understand, they agree, they think the same way, but it's only talk, only talk, that's the point – they *do* feel it, but always only with half of their being.'[12] Striking within representations of both world wars, among which the present book is included, are the parallel desires of combatants and civilians to make known and to know. Yet Remarque's account shows why any transparent telling is impossible. The mother of Kemmerich, a fellow soldier, is desperate to be told how he died. Yet the soldier narrator says: 'why can't she just accept it? Kemmerich is still dead whether she knows or not [the manner of his death].'[13]

As I research the period between Bert, my grandfather's departure from a World War One training camp at Codford in Hampshire and his death near Amiens, France, I too worry at the scraps of available information. I want to know. But when I eventually learn that he was 'mortally wounded in the head (shrapnel)', a darkened reality surfaces. That 'reality' has implications for my sense of myself in the here and now. It exposes me to an act of profound violence wrought upon someone who stands in the same relation to me as that between Bob, my husband and Jess, my granddaughter, watching *Peppa Pig* beside him on the settee.

Yet the link between Bert and me (as well as the links between me and his wife, Ella, and his son, Arthur) exists purely as a function of a kinship structure. Arguably they are not relationships, in the sense of a dynamic connection developed through practice. That said, through the *research* practices I have undertaken, it seems as if these connections are taking on qualities we associate with family relationships. Certainly, my grandparents and my uncle are not the people they were when I began this project. Indeed, after this book is finished, I already foresee that my relationships with them risk becoming less tangible, more 'past' than 'present' in the way they are for me now.

My desire to keep them alive raises the question of what they mean for my sense of self. The parts they played in my father's life are threads within the fabric of my own upbringing. Through him they contribute to the way my own sense of self developed. But what does it mean to retrieve these people, to raise them into the light for scrutiny? Is an acknowledgement of their suffering somehow a rationale or even an excuse for my pre-occupation with death and dying, my long-term interest in hauntings and the spiritual domain? Though I talk about these issues at greater length in the next chapter, it is pertinent to ask here how the fashioning of a particular kind of memory—or at least the making of a memoir that includes my paternal grandparents and their elder son—contributes to my sense of who I am and how I want to be known. As sociologist Carol Smart says, 'the past is part of the present; it permeates the present and helps to shape it both practically and conceptually'.[14] That said, my relationship with the past, with remembered or imagined family members, is not a process moving towards any kind of stability. As the historian Carolyn Steedman says, 'memory alone cannot resurrect past time because it is memory itself that shapes it, long after historical time has passed'.[15] As we age—and as we engage with the past—our memory of it shifts, like a story in the telling and retelling.

There is an analogy here in Geoffrey Batchen's[16] discussion of the photography of remembrance, where images are not only cherished but also *embellished* with paint, embroidery, texts, hair and other materials. He cites Richard Terdiman's discussion of a crisis of memory in nineteenth-century Europe that resulted from political revolution and industrial modernity. Europeans, Terdiman says, 'experienced the insecurity of their culture's involvement with its past'—a kind of detachment from what came before, with the result that 'the very coherence of time and of subjectivity seemed disarticulated'.[17] Batchen links this sense of dislocation with industrial production processes that distanced people from the way in which everyday objects were made. So while a photograph may stimulate memories of someone loved, it is a 'hollowed out' memory, 'disconnected from the social realities of its own production and also from those who are doing the remembering'.[18] In photographs of loved ones who have died, therefore, hand-made embellishments were some kind of response to the crisis of memory. Embellishing provided a way of taking part in the production of a memory that enriched it. Batchen describes photographs treated in this way as 'intensely social entities filled with emotion'.[19]

In our current exploration of two world wars and the family lives associated with them, we too are personalising a residue of remembered childhoods, adult testimonies, items of material culture and archival records. In so doing we are embellishing what we have inherited, making it 'unique and yet typical' in ways that indeed point to life's 'fractures, resistances and contradictions'.[20]

2.2 Selective Memory

Although we might feel that we have lost more than we have inherited, we should not overlook the selectivity of our remembering, and the uneven levels of curiosity we might feel about what remains, whether it is an event recalled or a photograph or a jotting in a diary. So the fashioning of memory, the embellishing of what might otherwise be 'hollowed out' objects or recollections, does not follow a random path but instead is guided by particular agendas and attachments. These might be personal losses or traumas that call for resolution; equally they may be the promise of pleasurable knowledge with the potential to inspire.

While these processes of recovery and remembering have a history, as Batchen describes for the nineteenth century, they sit oddly with academic arguments for a sequestration of death, its 'putting aside'—and certainly for its 'denial'.[21] On the one hand, these theories have now been reworked in more nuanced accounts. As an interpretation of late twentieth-century death ways, the idea that death is 'taboo' no longer holds up very persuasively. For example, since the 1990s many dying and bereaved people have played a much more active role in what happens when life comes to an end. Remembering the dead occurs through the mounds of floral tributes after a celebrity or violent death. Families now 'embellish' the marble gravestones that once stood in understated, uniform rows in municipal cemeteries. But on the other, I am still adrift in the silences that surround the tiny islands of information gleaned from restrained diary entries, all of which peter out as their stalwart writers weaken and die. Hence my quest to establish connections between them, to map out the obscured landscapes through which I move, uncertainly, stepping from one rock to the next. Somewhere along the way, there has been a sequestration of what became of my father's family.

These are the gaps and silences I will perpetuate if I abandon my table of shipwrecked fragments to my children for whom they will mean precious little. Is this situation despite or because of the fact that two members of my close family died violent deaths in war? Whatever remains of them is buried overseas. Before the late 1990s, when I searched for my paternal grandfather's grave in the military cemetery at Villers-Bretonneux, about 15 miles east of Amiens in Pas-de-Calais, their graves may never have been visited by anyone who knew them. Although my own post-war lifetime has unfolded within a few decades of the events of their deaths, and an EasyJet flight from the sites of their burial, these battlefield killings have indeed become sequestered. Both Bert, my grandfather and Arthur, his son, have retreated into a grainy past, represented only by unlabelled, often formal photographs and inscrutable diaries. They have become ancient, these two men. Yet when they died, they were more than ten years younger than my son is now. Maybe my mother, and her death immediately before my children were born, is similarly remote for them.

Still the question persists as to why these two men's deaths are important to me. If the last century's dead were often left to retreat into obscurity, I am also aware that distance can lend them an aura. Walter Benjamin[22] used the concept of an aura to describe the distinctive authenticity of an art object, as opposed to its subsequent manifestation as the subject of multiple, technical reproductions. The object itself remains embedded within its original context, the environment of tradition that surrounds it. Reproduction brings that object closer to hand, allowing it to be possessed in an apparently democratic fashion. But, brought closer, it is also stripped of its aura. As 'ancients' or ancestors, the distant dead are out of reach, embedded within the circumstances of their demise. As such, they potentially acquire an aura, a distinctive authenticity. Somehow they hover in a protected domain that is spared the stigmatising evidence of lost bodily control in old age. Their deaths do not evoke feelings of social embarrassment as when unexpected bereavements demand appropriate responses from friends and neighbours. Effectively, the distant dead are forever young. Even members of my family who suffered later life illnesses, for example, Ella, my paternal grandmother, live on through sepia photographs taken in their beautiful youth. I have never folded their wheelchairs into the back of a car or shared a meal that dribbles down their chins.

It was these ancient or celebrated dead who were welcomed when cemeteries began to supplant churchyards at the beginning of the nineteenth century. Luminaries such as Merimee, Chopin and Wilde were reinterred in Pere Lachaise Cemetery in Paris, for example. The aura that accompanied them had an allure sufficient to overcome any popular resistance to burial outside the hallowed ground of the churchyard—and their remains were relocated to achieve this end. Here, perhaps, lies the nub of the matter. Are the sufferings of the distant dead romanticised in a way that resembles the hurts and losses visited upon characters we 'experience' via fiction? In addition, as the historian Joanna Bourke says, '[i]n war, the mere fact of dying was ennobling'.[23] Mine is a generation for whom family members came to be 'ennobled' by two world wars. Yet they remain 'family', and the desire to get to know them, to feel for them, to perpetuate their memory for children and grandchildren, can be powerful. Maybe towards the end of our lives we look to them as ballast, an assemblage of forbears who will elevate and carry forward our own memory, along with theirs.

Despite living through a time when individual deaths remain difficult to speak about or indeed integrate into any satisfying system of meaning—a time when, for many, '"heaven" or "memory" has become an unbelievable or inadequate means of making sense of life and of death', as anthropologist Douglas Davies[24] explains—*some* of the dead acquire an allure. We search out these predecessors and are open to developing emotional ties with them, something we see in television programmes such as *Who Do You Think You Are?*. Here the calamities visited upon long dead and often previously unknown relatives evoke spontaneous tears from famous people researching their family history. Genealogy in general has become hugely popular among retired people, a 'hobby' extended and further commercialised by the scope for establishing genetic connections. Displays of old family photographs are even a fashionable aspect of home decoration—and Victorian photography, particularly images that depict the body of a dead relative, has become a focus for interest.

It can even be the case that relationships with certain of the dead take precedence over those with the living. At a cousin's 60th birthday party in the late 1990s, soon after I had compiled my hefty family album, I remember my cousins and I clustered together around the old photos it contains. Beyond these photos there was limited conversation between us. This was a rare opportunity to meet up with people with whom I had shared family holidays as a child, a chance to find out properly what had since gone on in their lives. Yet it was the dead members of our family with whom we were engaged. And I recall urging myself to try and rekindle the present-day relationships between us, to move beyond our shared roots in a period before any of us were born.

So family relationships are complicated and selective. We know this from studies of lived kinship systems, the academic turn towards seeing 'family' as the outcome of a set of practices, rather than a static network of linkages.[25] My father, for example, now dead for 20 years, was part of my children's growing up until they were well into their teens. Yet he was not a particularly significant figure for them. He lived at a distance and hedged himself about with set-piece conversations and an awkwardness with children. How this might reflect the events of his young adulthood is of course part of my project of unravelling what came before, of 'picking up the pieces'. The identity of 'Granddad', like other family ties, plays out in all kinds of ways.

My relationship with my maternal grandfather, Meredith Watling, for example, derived from the fact that he lived with me and my parents. Or more accurately, we lived with him—and he helped parent me from his fireside chair until I was nine. I retain clear sensory memories—of the roughness of his rust-coloured tweed jacket, the smoothness of his grey wool trousers, the curls of hair on his collar, the bulkiness of his back in a wing armchair when I scrambled up behind him, the elliptical Bakelite object he kept in his jacket pocket. When he unscrewed its embedded circular lid the pungent odour of tobacco was released. I still love that smell. Yet once Granddad was dead, his presence within the lives of my parents and me was all but extinguished. He died an 'absent' death, like my mother. I cried when my parents told me about it the next day—but stopped obediently when instructed: 'Don't cry. Granddad wouldn't want you to.' To upset Granddad so soon after he had died would be unkind.

In my father's tiny leather-bound appointment diary (eight centimetres by six with a press stud to hold it closed), I now find his record of Meredith's death: 'Father died' and 'Father funeral' are pencilled into the spaces for 3 April 1955 (Palm Sunday) and 7 April 1955. There are ticks through each of these entries. Tasks completed? The pages of this appointment diary are mainly empty, a few simply stating 'Branch Council' and 'Chipperfield Circus 4.45', entries again ticked through in pencil. If I turn to the dates of Meredith's death and funeral in my father's larger five-year diary for that year, I find the following:

Sunday April 3 1955.
  Bright intervals showers
  FATHER DIED THIS EVENING
  (caps in original)

In the days that follow, entries list the preparations for the funeral and the arrival of relatives, finishing on 7 April with 'Beautiful sunny morning. Rain in afternoon. FATHER'S FUNERAL 2 pm'.

So as I peruse these fragments, I become increasingly aware of the play of the imagination and of longing. Relationships never experienced in any face-to-face form can supersede those which might be pursued with more accessible *living* relatives—as I found at my cousin's birthday party. Some granddads may be forgotten or overlooked. Others may be sought after. This issue, of the elusiveness of the past and particularly of those who died 'ennobled' deaths, cannot be ignored as I begin fleshing out the shipwrecked items currently in my possession. I need to be aware that, like Joseph Cornell and many others, my sensibility 'thrives on contemplating the unattainable; [Cornell] loved moments of anticipation or nostalgia, reveries when he could "be" in two places at once. This duality is echoed in [his] seductive constructions. His arrangements offer viewers never-ending chains of associations enhanced by myriad kinships of texture, patterns and form, but always remain just out of reach, sealed and contained behind glass'.[26]

There is also the question of what kind of closeness I desire. In my jewellery box is my grandmother's rose gold bracelet—she wears it in studio photographs of herself in Edwardian dress, with her husband and two small sons. There are similar pieces that must have belonged to her family: a rose gold ring of entwined snakes, tiny jewelled lapel brooches. I also have the dog tag my father wore throughout World War Two, a beautiful cameo brooch of my mother's, with an owl and other symbols of the night, a rose gold watch chain. Though I keep these pieces, have had them repaired and even altered to fit me, I rarely wear them. Many are out of keeping with my choice of clothing, too formal, too small for an era of statement necklaces. But more than that, they promise a degree of closeness that unnerves me. This, I suspect, reflects their potency as remnants or traces. Like my father's bargain watch and loose change returned from the hospital where he died, they bear too much weight. As a consequence, my feelings about them are ambivalent. Maybe they risk unlocking the emotional distress my whole family believed they should deflect.

When legacies were referred to earlier, the related word heirloom did not come up. But it fits here. Usually taken to refer to something of value that must be passed from one generation to another, an heirloom carries within it the injunction not to sell or give it away. It belongs to the family, rather than the individual. When the public bring objects to be assessed by experts on the BBC's *Antiques Roadshow*, a high valuation elicits delight but also an assertion that an item will not, of course, be sold. Maybe this explains my ambivalence towards my own 'heirlooms'. On the one hand, they promise a relationship they cannot deliver; on the other, I must keep them, regardless of whether or not I can make use of them. If my children dispose of them, I have somehow failed to safeguard what belongs to previous generations. Writing this book, as an adjunct to these items, is partly an attempt to ensure that my children and grandchildren appreciate and so retain what has been left in our custody.

The imperative to recover my paternal grandfather and his son from obscurity, despite mixed feelings, might also reflect my own experience of grandparenting. This began in 2001 with the birth of Blue, my daughter's child, five years after my father died. Since then I have also regularly witnessed my husband, Bob, providing hours of childcare for two other grandchildren, Rhys and Jess, born in 2007 and 2011, respectively. These life-course transitions have shown me the scope for intense emotional connections between grandparents and grandchildren. So at about the time I became keeper of family memories, custodian of heirlooms, I also became a grandparent.

With a greater sensitivity, then, after becoming a grandparent myself, the curtailment of Bert and Arthur's lives impacts on me with new force. Ownership of the family papers is another element to all this. While the material resided with my father I had no ready access to it; it was not available for me to browse through. Now the violent deaths of Bert and Arthur at what can be seen as a tragically young age are making a call on me. For Carol, however, missing persons and their material traces stand in a different relationship with one another.

Carol Unlike Jenny, I have little material evidence of my past, but I have inherited a rich oral history of the war from my father who fought in Europe and who was involved in the D-Day landings and affected all his life by some of the sights of war. That story forms part of this book and was one of the key motivating factors for writing it. It is a form of recovery of what happened to ordinary people who enlisted to fight in the war, without knowing what the reality might be and whether and how they would survive. Unlike Jenny, there are no accounts of anyone in my family being killed in either of the two world wars. In that sense, my missing people are those who died from more natural causes—as well as those who were absent and did not feature, although aspects of their qualities feature strongly and leave a permanent legacy.

While my father missed the early years of my sister's life, by the time I was born, he had returned from the war and was very close to me.

Fathering at that time would not have involved him in any form of domestic or personal care; he was strictly forbidden from that 'unmanly' territory, as it was then viewed. But he did spend a lot of time with us as children. The serious fractures in that contact, already mentioned, are explored as part of our post-war life in Chap. 9. I remember clearly how Dad took Pauline and me out on walks and 'adventures'. His hobby of buying the occasional second-hand car, which would have been incredibly cheap and unreliable, meant we would sometimes go out for an evening drive. Occasionally the car would break down and we had to shamefacedly go home on the bus. Once this happened when Pauline and I were wearing house slippers. The horror and embarrassment haunts me still. I have lots of memories of spending time with my dad on my own, perhaps while Pauline who was four years older than me spent time with her friends. I helped him in the garden—he was a keen gardener; we went for walks together and, when possible, I went to work with him on trips in his delivery van. Indeed, I wanted to be with him all the time and missed him when I could not. As a child, if I did something of which he disapproved, just a firm look was enough to punish me. I have no memory of him ever shouting at me, although he and Mom regularly argued. Often, I suspect like many parents, they saved their rows until Pauline and I were in bed. As if hearing and not seeing made this acceptable. In my research I have tried to unpick this contradiction—expressing it as a collusion of silence. What 'we' are not allowed to see we assume we are not allowed to talk about.[27] But, I remember the threat of what the outcome of their fighting might be and how we might be abandoned by one or the other of them. For me, the ultimate terror was that Dad would leave.

Looking back, what was missing from my childhood was a stable mother. The times when she was happy and in a good mood served as a stark contrast to different and difficult times and provided a painful reminder of how wonderful life could have been; a recognition of this contrast as more damaging because of its inconsistency and unpredictability. As a family, we always had to be on guard for sudden mood changes. Also, my mother frequently reminisced about her life in ways that served as warnings to us all of what might happen if we were not careful. For example, she told us she had been caught out in a lie, had once been late and missed an important appointment, had been judged by not having clothes that were smart enough and so on. Indeed, she included speculative examples of how we might be judged if our shoes were not clean and if we had got our school uniform dirty—and that judgement would then, it seemed, reflect badly not only upon our character but upon her mothering skills.

Being so cautious is perhaps not surprising when my parents' lives involved times of poverty, brief homelessness and a continuous difficult struggle to manage financially. They owned nothing of much worth materially, certainly nothing that could be shown off on *Antiques Roadshow*. However, my mother left me with a few thousand pounds which she had saved in her later years, despite surviving on a state pension and living in a small council flat. As Chap. 1 relates, I had offered financial support to my parents when my father was too ill to work. After Dad died, Mom, who had learned to budget her money very carefully—and was terrified of being in debt—became even more frugal than before. She knew first-hand that debt brought with it suffering and deprivation and potential loss of home and family connection. Indeed, she paid for her funeral by weekly instalments into a co-op funeral plan and would show me the plan at regular intervals in her later years, as a reassurance that I would not be expected to pay. It mattered to her and her sense of pride that she could look after money and not get into debt. My father, who was less careful, was not given the choice of spending 'carelessly' since my mother always managed the finances. To that extent and from the emotional experience of the cost of being homeless, albeit briefly, I have inherited a sense of shame and dread about being poor.

As the only surviving family member, now my parents and sister are dead, I have inherited few family photographs, some of them taken professionally—I imagine at a time when it was an extravagance to own a camera. By contrast, my partner, who has a middle-class background, was given a large box of video recordings—made from cine films his father recorded, and which serve as a record of their childhood in action. He and his two siblings can be seen having great fun on boats on the Norfolk Broads and other sporting days out with lots of parental involvement and activity. I have joked about how films of my family would show comparatively less activity—but we did do things together—even though later photos, taken with a cheap camera, show us all in static poses, often on the edge of the photo, usually around or leaning on a car. Indeed, the car would take centre stage. For my dad, a car was a symbol of a secure life and freedom, a feeling I have inherited. As well as the family photos, a disordered collection and many of them undated, I also have a couple of letters my parents each wrote to me. One from my father when he knew he was dying and one from my mother in case of her death. My sister too wrote to me a letter to be opened after her death.

I smile every time I read Dad's letters because in the top right-hand corner he always put 'DAD'. In one letter just after he was given a terminal diagnosis in 1990, he said:

> I could not have wished for anyone as loving as you are to me. 'Your' all I ever dreamed of in a Daughter and I love you Dearly, as I also love your children.

In another letter, a month later, he said of the Remembrance Day memorial ceremony, 'There's no winners. I did nothing special during the war. I got home safe, as some of my good friends didn't make it.' I still find this sentiment extremely moving and profound, mostly in its simplicity and its 'mustn't grumble' tone. He ends the letter by telling me to be extra careful with the winter approaching: 'Hope you are all safe at all times now the Winter is Here. Be extra Careful now.'

We never openly declared love as a family, so this expression is unusual, even though I knew he loved me. Except with the grandchildren, and in exceptional times, there were no routine hugs or kisses as there are in some families, for example my current immediate family. It is as if the prospect of being without our dad helped my sister and me to overcome the embarrassment of expressing strong positive emotions. Pauline wrote to me when we were facing Dad's death and said:

> I love you and Dad so much. I feel you have a lot of his goodness in you. I see him in you, you are very caring, too.

I look back on the photos and these few letters now and realise how important they are to me. All else of their possessions was not of value in any material sense since they held neither sentimental nor financial value to me. When I read Margaret Gibson's *Objects of the Dead*, based on her exploration of how people manage the objects that those close to them leave behind after death, this sentence in particular resonated with me, '[d]eath reconstructs our experience of personal and household objects in particular ways; there is the strangeness of realising that things have outlived persons, and in this regard, the materiality of things is shown to be more permanent then the materiality of the body'.[28] For some time, I kept the caps that my father used to wear and one of his jackets so that I could hold something of him and still smell him on these items. But they gradually receded into the back of cupboards and I threw them away along with his sets of reading glasses when I moved house, on the basis that they no longer brought me comfort and consolation. When he died I cut off a piece of his hair and bought a small silver container in which to keep it with the words, 'Tread gently for you tread on my dreams', inscribed around the edge. But even that is lost which upsets me greatly and my carelessness concerns and puzzles me. By contrast, my mother got rid of his clothes within days of his death—and even gave away the cat I had given him when he longed for feline company near the end.

My material legacy also includes a china tea plate that belonged to my grandmother and which was part of the 'Sunday Best' tea set, saved for visitors. I think my mother inherited this—and most of the original tea set must have been either lost or given away. It is one of the few things of my mother's I have kept, others being her wedding ring, a watch and a necklace. I am not sure why I have kept the plate from my mother's belongings—it was peripheral in our various homes for several years and took on low-key duties, like being a plant saucer and a cat dish. In recent years, I have liberated the china I have collected from junk and antique shops into everyday use, realising that beautiful items need to be seen and used and not kept 'for best'. Casting off this indoctrination feels refreshing and daringly dangerous. I love the idea that my mother would have disapproved fiercely. However, despite my flippant, even careless disregard for such items as my dad's caps and glasses, I feel deeply jealous of Jenny's material inheritance of photos and diaries. Consequently, my contribution to the accounts of family that follow below and in other chapters is based on oral history, itself a rich and valuable form of inheritance but one that feels, by comparison, ephemeral or insubstantial.

Jenny reminds me that while it might seem to be the case, and while objects appear to be fixed points or anchors, they do not hold back the tide of time. But I am not consoled by this point, and realise that there is something else going on here which is partly around being able to get one's hands on something and to touch and feel it. I am reminded of the way that people in care homes and people in psychiatric hospitals find solace and comfort in objects. Memories might sustain and reassure us as we age, but they do not substitute for touching and holding. I have been reminded of how my mother needed to have money in her purse when she was in the care home at the end of her life. Indeed, I argue that it was essential to her well-being. On each visit, I would give her money and explain to the care staff that she had to be able to touch and feel money in her purse—that the evidence had to be tangible and just hers—but they kept locking it in the safe in case it was stolen, and at each visit she would express distress at not having any.

The need for hard material evidence, and perhaps being the only surviving member of the nuclear family of Gilmore, means I have no-one with whom to support or check my 'data'. Indeed, the family name is not being passed on. Choosing to change my name when I first married means that my children share this new surname. Further, it seems unlikely that my children will have children of their own, and while I have no conscious regrets, the Gilmore line ends at their death. Consequently, I have made much effort to validate the details of my accounts that feature in this book, going as far as to retrace my dad's steps across Europe. I have also visited his brother George and sister Gladys in preparation for this book—and also the graves of his parents. Indeed, I have photographed the memorial in Kilrea, County Antrim where Dad features as someone missing and believed killed in World War Two. This must have been on one of the occasions when he and his gunner were separated from the main convoy because of the impassable roads in Europe. As this book reaches completion, my Auntie Gladys has just died at the age of 90. In terms of this chapter's title, she is now a missing person from my life.

Likewise, I have consulted with my mother's remaining family, my cousins. Her family name was Davis, and with the help of Davis cousins,

I have managed to trace the family back to 1781. In 1901, my grandfather, Frederick William Davis, a 21-year-old bootmaker, married my grandmother, 21-year-old Louisa Harriet Appleby. She was a barmaid in the pub that her parents owned and lived next door. My granddad, Frederick, was the illegitimate son of Harriet Davis, who returned from domestic service to live with *her* parents, Edward and Jane Davis, when she was pregnant. The absence of his father seems to have instilled a sense of shame in the family—even though he was brought up as the son of his grandparents and given their name. Granddad died in 1953 when I was five. The memories that my mother shared with us as children of her father's violence towards his wife (her mother) make him despicable to me—and from her accounts he was clearly someone who had to be obeyed, a strict Victorian father who dominated the household. I have no memory of ever meeting him. My maternal grandmother, Louisa Appleby, by contrast, was kind and loving, and I grew extremely fond of her and saw her regularly, at least monthly during my childhood and remember her staying with us once. Grandma died in 1963 when I was 15.

I also have vivid memories of my paternal grandfather, James Gilmour, who was a very tall, handsome and slim man and extremely gentle and loving—and I feel sure my father took after him. For some reason my dad spelt his name differently, as Gilmore, and indeed the family name is spelt Gilmore on his birth certificate as well as his parents' surname on that certificate. I have no explanation other than the registrar changed the spelling. It became part of the family's story that we had a different spelling along with the fact that the actual date of Dad's birth was not entirely agreed and he could have been born earlier in June 1921, although his birth is registered as 11 June. Both grandfathers pre-deceased their wives and both died suddenly. My paternal grandfather, James Gilmour, as his name is spelt on the tombstone, died at the age of 78 years in 1959 when I was 11 years old. His death meant my father had to travel to Ireland suddenly in time for his wake and funeral. As one his sons, Dad had to be a coffin bearer which meant a long walk carrying the coffin from the house where he was waked to the church at Garvagh and then to the grave after the service, although it is likely that a hearse would have taken them as far as the last mile (Fig. 2.1).

Fig. 2.1 The headstone of Carol's paternal grandparents' grave, at Garvagh, Coleraine

The next grandparent to die was my maternal grandmother, Louisa Davis (nee Appleby), who died after a second severe stroke on 9 October 1963 when I was 15. She died at home before my mother was due to do her duty of night sitting, and I discuss the circumstances of her death and her dying in Chap. 3. I remember my feelings clearly of awkwardness in not knowing how I should feel. Consequently, my sense of being unable to comfort my mother remains a clear memory. I loved Grandma dearly, but did not feel anything at all when she died and was worried about my lack of emotion at a time when my mother was so very distressed.

Finally, in 1966, when I was an 18-year-old student nurse training in the mental hospital in Stafford, I have a distinct memory of my paternal grandmother, Margaret Gilmour, dying. I travelled part of the journey to her funeral with my dad on the train. He was going to Liverpool and taking the overnight boat to Belfast, Ireland. On reflection, I have no sense of mourning any of my grandparents. Somehow, they did not feel part of my life. Pauline and I just witnessed some of our parents' emotions. Dad was clearly distressed but not tearful—and anxious about how he would get to Ireland in time on both occasions. My mom cried a lot when her mother died but it seemed to be short-lived distress.

Interestingly, it was a 'rule' in the Davis family that children did not attend funerals—which felt as if it was something we might be privileged to be able to do at some stage—a significant rite of passage and something that seemed missing from my early life. It is with great irony I recall that when Pauline and I were mothers ourselves, my mother tried to forbid us from attending Auntie Doris' funeral—her sister-in-law, whom we knew very well. We were not given a reason other than my mother saying, 'Children in our family don't go to funerals!'. It was something we accepted as being forbidden. However, on this occasion Pauline challenged her and insisted on attending the funeral, causing a row between my mother and her.

Missing persons and the role people have played in our lives was the focus of conversations many years ago between Jenny and me when sharing ideas about the impact of war. One question we raised was, were people who were not parented because of the war adequately equipped to parent themselves? The imperative to have children in the face of so much death among young adults—one of the inevitable consequences of war—was powerful. Being adequately equipped emotionally might not have been high on the list of priorities at that time. Perhaps it is a more prominent feature of contemporary society, with parenting skills becoming the focus of child development studies and successful 'outcomes' being a social and public concern, rather than a private 'family' matter. What were the implications for Jenny's father of growing up in a boarding school with only his mother to parent him? When he became a parent himself, he did so in a household where his father-in-law was a major presence in the everyday life of his daughter, Jenny. My own father's parenting skills appear to echo those of James Gilmour, his father, who provided so much warmth and compassion. I know my father adored his father—less so his mother who was referred to as eccentric. Their marriage was full of bitter resentment. What this highlights is that I do not think that World War Two affected my father's ability to be a good father. His accounts of being in Europe following the D-Day landings and his delight at helping some children and his distress at not being able to help others, especially those at Belsen, must have been partly rooted in his absence as a father for his daughter, Pauline. It is interesting to remember that he was a comparatively young man in his early 20s, yet had to cope with such shocking events. More important still, this did not make him remote or unfeeling, indeed, quite the opposite. He was incredibly sensitive and compassionate, and it is even more impressive when I recall that he would have been 22 at the time.

Five years after Dad's death, in 1996, my sister Pauline died at the age of 52. Her illness, systemic lupus erythematosus (SLE, an auto-immune disease), is characterised by life-threatening crises. Pauline had SLE for 17 years, and during the later stages of her illness, she asked me to act as her advocate, a role I was happy to take on. Although she was prepared to die and often talked to me about it, her demise when it came was very sudden and shocking—giving no time for more formal goodbyes, especially to her children. While she was in end-stage renal failure and undergoing continuous abdominal peritoneal dialysis, in the end, her actual death was caused by a GP prescribing error. I found the experience of grief following Pauline's death to be quite overwhelming, especially its physical impact. I realised that I was not prepared at all for Pauline's death and was afterwards spurred on by unexplained incidents that I interpreted as her being in touch with me, to investigate more fully the circumstances of her death. Eventually, the GP responsible for a prescribing error that caused her to bleed to death apologised to me in a face-to-face meeting I arranged with him. Dying at the age of 52 made her death 'untimely', even though the quality of her life in the last few years was relatively poor.

About ten years after Dad had died, my mother moved into a residential care home. It was run by Jehovah's witnesses—a faith to which she converted after my father died. The last few years of her life involved a chaotic roller coaster ride to death, suffering dementia and severe paranoid psychosis. Many aspects of her death reminded me of the research I conducted into the care of older people at the end of their life in care homes, whose bodies were gradually 'unravelling their way to death'.[29] All of this was exacerbated by Mom's frequent hospital admissions. Although she had not really been what Melanie Klein (and my therapist) would call a 'good enough' mother, she was good to her grandchildren. Indeed, in her later years, she seemed to experience fewer of the stresses and strains that had once plagued her, although she found caring for my father when he was dying and she was in her 60s incredibly hard.

On reflection, I feel surprised that I have survived all the members of my nuclear family. I was the sickly, relatively weak child. Now, in some senses, I have been left and I am the abandoned child back in the poorhouse nursery, or the hospital isolation ward. Another small part of me is triumphant in surviving my current serious illnesses which makes me wonder if I am stronger than I thought after all. Looking outward, I wonder how it must feel for someone like Mala, a survivor of Belsen who lost most of her family in the Holocaust and who I introduced to my father when he was dying. I discuss Mala in Chap. 9 when I describe how she came to meet my father. I had wanted him to see that some people did survive and go on to have good lives and families of their own, even though many members of Mala's family and her parents were killed. I have found Mala to be very generous in acknowledging my father's death and recognising the enormity of that loss to me—while having been orphaned so young herself and in such horrific circumstances. Thinking about her reminds me that while the loss of my father remains profoundly painful, I had the benefit of being loved by him for 43 years and being taught both by his example and his love how to cope with trauma.

These reflections on missing persons and their resurrection through oral accounts, letters and photos set the scene for the accounts to come. In these we ask how, as survivors of two world wars, our parents were affected by their experiences and the impact of this on us. Now that we are orphaned and driven by the need to make sense of their loss and to leave behind a more coherent and sustained legacy, we offer an account informed by our personal experiences and self-awareness, as well as our academic knowledge. Different forms of 'data' have allowed us to produce a coherent story of family life, contextualised by what is missing as much as what is present. At the beginning of this chapter, Jenny described items that have come adrift. These require context and someone to make the connections between them, albeit speculatively. What Jenny would call joining up the dots is our interpretation of extraordinary events that happened to ordinary people and how these have rippled through the decades.

Notes

1. Light, Alison. 2014. *Common People. The History of an English Family*. London: Penguin Figtree. (P. xxvii).
2. Simic, Charles. 1992. *Dime Store Alchemy. The Art of Joseph Cornell*. New York: New York Review Books. (P. 18).
3. Corman, Catherine. Ed. 2007. *Joseph Cornell's Dreams*. Cambridge MA: Exact Exchange. (P. ix).
4. Smart, Carol. 2007. *Personal Life*. Cambridge: Polity. (P. 1).
5. Smart, Carol. 2007. *Personal Life*. Cambridge: Polity. (P. 1).
6. Simic, Charles. 1992. *Dime Store Alchemy. The Art of Joseph Cornell*. New York: New York Review Books. (P. 37).
7. Cornell, Joseph. 2007. *Navigating the Imagination*. New Haven: Yale University Press.
8. Simic, Charles. 1992. *Dime Store Alchemy. The Art of Joseph Cornell*. New York: New York Review Books. (P. 30).
9. Joseph Cornell. *Wanderlust. A guide for Friends*. The Royal Academy. 2015.
10. Reynolds, David. 2013. *The Long Shadow: the Great War and the Twentieth Century*. London: Simon and Schuster.
11. Letters home from five brothers during the World War One. http://www.familyletters.co.uk/. Accessed 11 December 2017.
12. Remarque, Eric Maria. [1929] 1996. *All Quiet on the Western Front*. London: Vintage Books. (P. 117)

13. Remarque, Eric Maria. [1929] 1996. *All Quiet on the Western Front*. London: Vintage Books. (P. 125)
14. Smart, Carol. 2007. *Personal Life*. Cambridge: Polity. (P. 86).
15. Steedman, Carolyn. 1986. *Landscape for a Good Woman. A Story of Two Lives*. London: Virago Press. (P. 29).
16. Batchen, Geoffrey. 2004. *Forget Me Not. Photography and Remembrance*. New York: Princeton Architectural Press.
17. Terdiman, Richard. 1993. Present Past. Modernity and the Memory Crisis. Cited in Batchen, Geoffrey. 2004. *Forget Me Not. Photography and Remembrance*. New York: Princeton Architectural Press. (P. 95).
18. Batchen, Geoffrey. 2004. *Forget Me Not. Photography and Remembrance*. New York: Princeton Architectural Press. (P. 95).
19. Batchen, Geoffrey. 2004. *Forget Me Not. Photography and Remembrance*. New York: Princeton Architectural Press. (P. 96).
20. Batchen, Geoffrey. 2004. *Forget Me Not. Photography and Remembrance*. New York: Princeton Architectural Press. (P. 96).
21. Shilling, Chris. 1993. *The Body and Social Theory*. London: Sage.
22. Benjamin, Walter. [1934] 2008. *Art in the Age of Mechanical Reproduction*. London: Penguin.
23. Bourke, Joanna. 1996. *Dismembering the Male. Men's Bodies, Britain and the Great War*. London: Reaktion Books, Ltd. (P. 248).
24. Davies, Douglas. 2005. *A Brief History of Death*. Oxford: Blackwell Publishing. (P. 87).
25. Morgan, David. 1996. *Family Connections*. Cambridge: Polity.
26. Joseph Cornell. *Wanderlust. A guide for Friends*. The Royal Academy. 2015.
27. Komaromy, Carol. 2000. The sight and sound of death: the management of dead bodies in residential and nursing homes for older people. *Mortality*. 5: 3, 299–316.
28. Gibson, Margaret. 2008. *Objects of the Dead. Mourning and Memory in Everyday Life*. Melbourne: The University of Melbourne. (P. 1).
29. Komaromy, Carol. 2005. *The Production of Death and Dying in Care Homes for Older People: an ethnographic account*. PhD Thesis. Milton Keynes: The Open University; Komaromy, Carol. 2010. Dying Spaces in Dying Places. In *The Matter of Death. Space, Place and Materiality*, ed. Jenny Hockey, Carol Komaromy, and Kate Woodthorpe. 52–68. Basingstoke: Palgrave Macmillan.

3

Changing Perspectives on Death, Dying and Loss

We have been talking to other people about what death means to them for decades and spent years observing what they actually do when faced with life-limiting illness or loss through bereavement. Our choice of topic can intrigue but also unnerve our families and friends. What does it say about us, that we choose this 'morbid' field of research? Are we somehow impervious to our own mortality? In this chapter we take turns to reflect on our own deaths in prospect, charting the different ways we have felt about it as the years have gone by. Both of us have lived through a time when western death-related beliefs and practices have changed in radical ways. Our biographies therefore intersect with a complex historical movement from taken-for-granted religiosity to a more pervasive secularism.

Carol When my maternal grandmother, Louisa Davis, suffered a stroke and died at home a month later, just a few months before her 84th birthday, it was the first death I had encountered (see Chap. 2). I was 15 at the time. My gran had raised eight children, four sons and four daughters, and her four daughters took it in turns to nurse her at home while she was dying. She was terrified of hospitals and at regular intervals extracted a promise from her widowed daughter, Louie, with whom she lived, that

© The Author(s) 2018
C. Komaromy, J. Hockey, *Family Life, Trauma and Loss in the Twentieth Century*,
https://doi.org/10.1007/978-3-319-76602-7_3

she would not be 'sent' there to die. This was agreed, and Louie set up a rota for her sisters, as 'volunteers', to cover either a night or a day of caring for her. My mother did not want to do the night vigil, so I went with her to provide some support. I recall clearly that waiting for Gran to die but wanting her to live stirred a mixture of emotions inside me. Partly, I was curious to witness the moment of death and see what happened, and also I was terrified and did not want to be there. Gran did not die that night, but three days later. She was alone at the moment of death, and Louie was upset that she had missed her 'departure'. My mother was relieved that she did not have to take her turn to sit with Gran that night. Despite my mom loving my gran very deeply, her fear of darkness and hauntings overshadowed her need to be with her at the end.

So my mother conveyed, and to some extent passed on to me, her two 'taboos'—being in the dark and having contact with death. When I became a nurse, I often met a combination of these two as I witnessed many deaths in hospitals. 'Having a death at night' was something most of my colleagues dreaded. Hospitals contain many ghosts,[1] and this was the time when wards were reputed to be visited by the ghosts of deceased patients. In my experience, when performing last offices or laying out a deceased patient at night, no-one wanted to be the nurse who stayed with the body, while the other fetched a forgotten item for the procedure. Echoing my mother's fear, I hated working the night shift in the semi-darkness and was in a persistent state of fear. As soon as daylight came, I felt euphoric at having endured another night. It seems, on reflection, that there was always the possibility that I might not.

In nursing—and later in midwifery—I encountered deaths at different points in the life course. Gradually, as my career progressed, I began to realise that end-of-life care was one of the most important areas in which to work. I saw it as a time when good nursing care with all of its attendant physical and emotional skills was essential. Underpinning my very powerful need to make a difference was the need to understand people. I was a 16-year-old cadet nurse working on a women's medical ward when an older patient died. I had witnessed my first death. The woman was on the bed pan and just died—a common event apparently, dying on the toilet or commode. I remember how impossible it felt to take in what had happened. The reality that someone who was alive and quite animated one moment and then suddenly dead the next was really difficult to grasp. I stared at her for a long time trying to absorb this 'fact'. What struck me most was the impossibility of seeing her completely still and not breathing. She had an old wedding photo on her locker of herself and her husband who used to visit every day, and they were clearly very close still. The photo showed a very beautiful woman looking really happy—which reminded us all of the way that ageing can transform appearances—leaving just a few traces of the younger self. It was a sad reminder that all life ends and no-one gets out of it alive.

Carol is describing her felt need to 'make a difference', an approach to life that she absorbed from her father, James Gilmore, whose full story is told later in the book. Underpinning that need is a parallel imperative to 'understand'. As Death Studies researchers, we have both worked extensively to understand how someone like the woman on the bed pan could cease to be, how she could change from a patient to be looked after to a body to be briefly cared for and then disposed of. Yet much of our work, as Chap. 1 describes, concerns the beliefs and value that *others* have lived and died by, whether at the time of their own deaths or those of someone else. Here, however, we talk about our own death histories and particularly about the ways in which our own perspectives on death, dying and loss have been shaped. To what extent have our research findings influenced or modified our personal beliefs about death? While we can only speculate on how our lives would have been outside of Death Studies, we can examine the thoughts and experiences that surrounded our professional choices, both before we embarked on our careers and in the course of our work. In addition, we can reflect on the *personal* implications of what we learned. When Carol was faced with the sudden death of a patient, she asked the question: 'what happens to somebody when they are suddenly quite evidently no longer there?' Jenny's experiences led her to reflect on the shadow side of this conundrum, the things that become visible, sometimes shockingly, when someone is dying, the stuff that remains behind once someone has gone.

Jenny Death and dying are not simply about troubling disappearances. There are also things that appear at this time—or appear in a new light.

The body of someone who is dying may change to the extent that you feel as if you are seeing it for the first time. A person's capacities may alter so radically that, perhaps in the role of carer, you now routinely see parts of their body that were always covered up with clothing. Or you may witness their body behaving in ways you were never party to before: arched in pain, stretched out in the bath, seated on a commode. After death, a person's belongings may shift from mundane taken-for-granted objects to conspicuously treasured possessions. And their body, which remains obstinately present after they have 'gone', must be disposed of, a practical but also emotional, religious and symbolic requirement.

Writing this book, for me, began with the objects that became visible to me when my father died: the photographs, letters, documents and medals that had occupied our attic when I was a child and the high cupboard in the bedroom my parents shared. My father is no longer apparent to me now, only the images of him I see recorded in photographs. But I do have the watch he was wearing when he went into hospital for the last time. Between the links of its wrist strap, there is a kind of brown residue which must contain particles of what I thought of as him. I also have my mother's engagement ring and this contains a similar dusty deposit, even now nearly 50 years after she died. It is this fuzziness that surrounds the apparent departure of individuals from the world, their hard-to-grasp cessation, which has contributed to but also unsettled the series of beliefs I once held about the meaning of death.

We were both born during the 1940s and grew up within an environment where Christianity provided an account of what happens to us when we die. Neither of us were regular churchgoers, but schools at that time offered morning assemblies and 'grace' before meals. These very regular rituals confirmed a single religious account of human life; they conferred on us a belief in an all-powerful God. He was someone who witnessed our sins from up in heaven, a place where we might hope to find both everlasting life and reunification with our dead pets.

Carol In terms of religious and spiritual beliefs, I was brought up to believe in God and Jesus—which included the notion of the resurrection and the idea that there is a place where people go when they die. I struggled with what form this might take, including the practical notions about how we would all fit in, but in my early years I was comforted by the joyful hope that any separation through death was temporary. However, I soon began to ask questions. During my nursing career, religion had never offered any explanation that fully satisfied my enquiry into why people die and what makes some deaths easier to accept than others. I yearned for some sort of justifiable explanation for the apparent randomness of suffering.

Jenny too grew up with a secure sense of life extending beyond death. This is how she described deaths in her childhood in the dissertation she submitted as part of her first degree in anthropology. She was 31 at the time.

Jenny During my childhood quite a number of great aunts and uncles, elderly friends of the family and pets died and were solemnly filed away beyond the clouds. Each death was an important event as someone left my ordered, secure world forever. But I knew they were happy behind the clouds. I could see the lights of the party when the evening sun's long, low beams escaped round the edges of a thick, dark cloud.

If Carol felt that an explanation of some kind was lacking, Jenny's beliefs were more watertight. But as we both found our way into higher education, other questions and other answers surfaced.

Carol When studying philosophy in my part-time undergraduate degree, especially the works of Sartre, I came to the conclusion that God was an invention and that Sartre's notion of existential terror, the inability to grasp ceasing to exist, was part of the explanation for the huge psychic investment in a belief in life after death. Alongside studying political ideas—particularly Karl Marx's argument that religion was the opium of the people, and various other political views (such as the more nuanced explanations of people like Stuart Hall)[2] on the afterlife as a way of getting people to behave in this life and a consolation for suffering and inequality—I began to consider notions of religion and life after death as being both arrogant and false. To me it seems that not being able to accept that we cease to exist after death is a form of individualistic extremism.

In 1975, when Jenny was 28, she too entered higher education and became open to new systems of belief.

Jenny When I chose 'the meanings of death' as a dissertation topic during my undergraduate degree in anthropology, my supervisor, David Brooks,[3] recommended that I interview myself before tackling anyone else. The piece of paper on which I wrote down my 'interviewee' responses is lost, but I do remember noting that to die 'now' would be like leaving a party early. I was 31 by this time. In the introduction to the dissertation I said that for me, by that stage, death had become a rare and 'mysteriously uneasy event with no ready place in my view of the world'. I talked about it being exiled and then laid out my plan to discover how and why this had happened.

The faith I carried from early childhood had been undermined during my teenage years. Its values and principles were at odds with my other commitment—to replace the small family I grew up in. Meeting boys and somehow transforming one of those meetings into a married life with children was a huge imperative for me. But it brought difficult encounters with a Christian injunction to maintain the purity of my body for its eventual purpose as a temple within which children might grow. This was the 1960s when many of society's values and beliefs were being questioned. While my mother worried about me giving birth to an 'unwanted' child, I dreaded being left alone in the world once the members of my very small family had all died. A straying from the paths of righteousness that seemed to go along with having a boyfriend also required surrendering my comfortable prospect of a heavenly afterlife.

To let go of this prospect leaves emotionally charged questions unanswered.

Carol It is all very well sustaining the intellectual argument that death is final and that there is no God, but emotionally it is a more difficult challenge. In psychodynamic terms, knowing something is not the same as believing and accepting it. Wearing my social science hat, I note that, ironically, psychoanalytic therapists take on an omnipotent power during the process of analysis, as they help their clients/patients to steer a difficult course through the rational and emotional terrain.

Understanding what it means to be mortal in purely intellectual or rational terms is something both of us have found challenging or indeed simply inadequate as a framework. As the anthropologist, Clifford Geertz, puts it in his work on religion, 'the events through which we live are forever outrunning the power of our ordinary, everyday moral, emotional and intellectual concepts to construe them, leaving us, as a Javanese image has it, like a water buffalo listening to an orchestra'.[4]

Jenny For many years I sought evidence that there was, indeed, something else. My undergraduate dissertation yielded many accounts of other people's beliefs about the relationship between life and death. Afterwards I went on to post-graduate study and chose a hospice as one of the field sites where I participated in an everyday life that unfolded in close proximity to death. I was struck by the ordinariness of the deaths that were going on around me. If death were some kind of grand finale, it seemed to happen too easily, too quietly, to be *The End*. This was in 1983. I was 37 and still open to the idea that there was more to the world than the here and now of everyday life.

Where has this brought me to now, in my 70s? Events that suggest some kind of afterlife continue to interest me. I grew up with the notion of 'something more' that comforted me when my pets and my relations died. It was an idea that belonged to the adults who looked after me and ensured that life itself and *my* life somehow 'made sense'. My working model that life can 'make sense', that it is a condition within which agency can be exercised and hope sustained, seems to have become entangled with an unwillingness to see it as a chance emergence upon an arbitrary planet. In the early 1990s, for example, when I was in my early 50s, I interviewed an Anglican minister who had pursued a ministry of exorcism. I had been interested in hauntings since childhood, often to my terror when needing the toilet at night. Getting out of my bed in a dark, unheated house and walking across the landing was a huge challenge, deferred for as long as possible. I wrote about the material from the minister's interview in academic articles and book chapters and interpreted it through various theoretical frameworks.[5]

Also during that period, at a time of personal stress, I had woken in the night to find a woman standing beside the bed I was sleeping in with my husband. The sense of there being three people in the room was overwhelming—and terrifying. My husband said afterwards he had never heard anyone scream like that before. The woman spiralled away into thin air, ghost-buster fashion. Then in 2015 our 20-year-old cat died while we were away from home. The night it happened I felt a cat jump up on the bed I was sleeping in. I remember its old, non-retractable claws catching on the duvet cover, felt it move diagonally across my body until it woke me up. There was no cat where I was staying. In the morning I received a text from a neighbour, telling me that the cat had died.

These experiences were disturbing rather than comforting, mainly because they jolted the view I had more or less come to accept, that a life is over when someone or something dies. Yet I retain an openness to the possibility that the world as I know it might not be the whole story—even though this position is at some remove from my clear childhood vision of the dead partying in heaven. This openness includes an interest in the world views of other religions that has its roots in my childhood. Despite my mother's suspicion of the parish church as an institution that would 'draw you in'—probably onto the flower-arranging rota—she regularly visited the Christian Science Reading Rooms in Cambridge (see also Chap. 9). She took me with her and gave me a children's book that explained that there was no room in the world for 'error' because God was all-pervasive. I remember how wonderfully shiny its floppy blue cover was. But the concept of 'error' was hard to grasp. My mother also had friends who were spiritualists. Going upstairs I would drift past their intent conversations, unnoticed. Her paintings of crosses on hillsides in flaming yellow and orange occasionally greeted me from an easel as I came in the back door after school. A change from her usual still lifes and landscapes.

So, along with ghosts, I am drawn to belief systems which offer something other than the Christian harps and angels of children's prayer book illustrations. In my early 60s, I attended a long course of Buddhist study sessions in the hope that some persuasive account of life transcending death would be provided. I also learned to meditate after reading around the practice quite extensively. I have no traditional view of a life after death now nor entertain the idea that the dead are close at hand. That said, writing such a statement about the dead makes me uncomfortable. An offended spirit might be about to put me right on that one.

Where does this leave the two of us now, engaged in a writing project that looks back over the many many deaths that occurred during the two world wars of the twentieth century? Between those wars, spiritualism flourished as families sought contact with husbands and sons who had died fighting in northern France. The historian David Cannadine refers to 'the massive proliferation of interest in spiritualism',[6] going on to argue that:

> In private séance, as in public ceremony, inter-war Britain was obsessed with death. The easy transition, so often depicted, from a death-dominated, sex-denying nineteenth century to a death-denying, sex-dominated twentieth century completely ignores this massive, all-pervasive pall of death which hung over Britain in the years between 1914 and 1939, and also the inventiveness with which the grief-stricken responded to their bereavement.[7]

While no-one in Jenny's maternal family died in World War One, her mother, Lorna, was not only drawn to spiritualism but also Christian Science, as Jenny notes. The writing of its founder, Mary Baker Eddy, featured prominently on the bookshelves in her home. While spiritualism attested to the ongoing lives of the dead and their capacity to make contact with the living, Christian Science was grounded in philosophical idealism, the belief that the material world is illusory. Sickness and evil are present only to the extent that human beings fail to adhere to 'right thinking' and lose their connection to Divine Mind. In neither case, then, were the immediacies of the everyday world seen as the whole story. With hindsight, home life, for Jenny, was an environment that foreshadowed the direction of both her subsequent academic and personal perspectives.

Jenny My current beliefs about death are perhaps not so far removed from the principles my mother was drawn to, although somehow I have worked without any obvious awareness of a continuity. Death, as I now think about it, challenges what we understand as life. Quite straightforwardly, death gives a lie to what we experience as our stable, unitary selves. It shows us to be ephemeral. But rather than seeing this as a tragic catastrophe which befalls otherwise splendid human beings, I am more inclined to question our status *as* bounded, stable entities. What I adhere to is a sense of human life as a process, rather than a thing. Our bodies might appear to remain stable—'You haven't changed a bit. I'd have known you anywhere', we tell each other after absences of many years. But we change continuously, a perception that meditation helps foster. In quietening our minds, it is possible to witness the fleeting passage of our thoughts and feelings. Repeated practice underscores the Buddhist notion that both joy and pain are transitory phenomena and it is our terror of losing our happiness, or of being stuck forever in pain, which produces suffering. The fleeting nature of our emotions, when observed, helps along a view of ourselves as fleeting entities. We are process.

The anthropologist Tim Ingold discusses similar ideas when he differentiates between 'objects [that] stand before us as a fait accompli' and 'things [which are] a place where several goings on become entwined'.[8] It is the fleeting nature of our moments that constitutes our experience of ourselves and those around us as alive. Ingold talks about 'humans, animals, plants, stones, buildings … having a continuous trajectory of becoming'.[9] If we attempt to stand still—as we do effectively when we reject or distance our deaths—then we become less alive, more 'objectified'.

This is the view I 'practise' when I feel sadness at old photographs of beautiful young people who are now bent or wrinkled—or dead. It is a kind of parallel current, running alongside the dread I experience if I count up the dwindling number of years I may live or my stomach-wobbling fear if I am waiting for the results of a scan or biopsy. One day, while meditating on the words: 'My death is certain. Only its timing is uncertain', I suddenly 'knew' a relief and joy brought about by an awareness of the fragility of being alive. I felt a sense of lightness, of scarcely being here at all, like a butterfly temporarily resting on a flower. The rest of that day flowed easily, all worry and weightiness alleviated.

But little in my immediate social environment reinforces this view, and like many epiphanies, it came and went. More readily, as handy emotional band-aid, there is the attribution of meaning, the making up of stories. Faced with a death, or its possibility, I summon up an explanation that somehow defers its implications for my own and my family's mortality. For example, if someone is diagnosed with cancer, I believe that the person will either recover completely or continue to live for some time; after someone has died, I find an explanation in their life which made their death either inevitable or highly likely—and, importantly, something that will not happen to me, my husband or my children because we are 'different'. But when a diagnosis of cancer is visited upon someone with whom I have shared a lot of my life and who in many ways is no different from me, then I am confronted with death's ragged arbitrariness, the starkness of our plight as accidental beings who live and die with the prospect of non-being.

What remains is a kind of practice, an adherence to a view of life as process—and a repeated returning to it. The meaning of memento mori—remember you will die—is perhaps not exhausted by the competing imperatives to either live a righteous life in preparation for meeting your maker or embrace every kind of pleasure while you still can. 'Remember you will die' can release me from a wearying commitment to maintaining my stolid integrity as a bounded object. It can help me recognise the vitality of life lived as process, a quickening that persists well beyond the womb.

If this is the place Jenny has arrived at—and is currently living by—Carol's intellectual questioning of any Christian framework for understanding death has led on to a lived set of understandings that derive from her personal experiences of life and death.

Carol Several events have influenced my thinking, resulting in what I believe to be the meaning of death. My father's death had the most profound impact, in that I had to face the loss of the most significant person in my life without being able to take any comfort from the promise of being reunited. My mother and my sister, by contrast, took great comfort from this notion, and I felt some envy combined with a level of pity that they were deluded in their false hopes. Indeed, because my sister was dying over a period of many years from a life-limiting illness and she deteriorated significantly in the last few years, she often talked about seeing Dad quite soon and how she knew he was waiting for her. The more pragmatic side of me considers that people need to use whatever beliefs they like to be able to manage the reality of death, what I call my 'whatever gets you through the day' philosophy.

Shortly after my dad's death, my dogs both died in old age in fairly quick succession. I felt especially broken-hearted and bereft when Percy, named after someone I had nursed and the one I was closest to, died. I really struggled to cope with this loss—of what might be called unconditional love with no recourse to language. The third event that deeply affected my thinking and feeling about mortality was when at the end of chemotherapy for breast cancer—during which I had been very ill with neutropenic sepsis and was extremely weak—I had a small stroke. I only discovered that I was paralysed on one side when I lay at the bottom of the stairs having attempted to visit the toilet in the early morning—also noting how my face was contorted and my speech badly affected. My thought was, 'I can't do this!' The experience of chemotherapy had been like running several marathons—such was the physical toll. In that moment I decided that I would rather die. Later that day, on the stroke ward, I had a second stroke that further paralysed my right hand. The struggle to recover when I was so exhausted was almost unbearable. However, I realised that I could not just give in and die—much as I wanted to in those first few days. Most significantly, at that bleak time, I worked out that some types of existence are worse than death. Since embarking on this project, I have been diagnosed with a late stage 3 melanoma. There is no systemic treatment, and I wait for the inevitable appearance of the secondaries that are in my lymphatic system and blood circulation to appear. However else this affects me, it means that my life has a new urgency because I know that everything can change in an instant.

The final recognition of what death means to me came in what felt like an epiphany while I was watching a retriever and noting that he was behaving in a very similar way to Percy. I had seen this many times before during their lives, and after their death, but I experienced an overwhelming recognition that this was immortality. That is how we continue—through genetic inheritance, not just biological but also combined with social traits. This final point connects directly to the driving force behind making sense of the experiences of my father and their impact upon me and my need for some form of continuity to sustain his legacy.

As we said at the beginning of this chapter, while both of us had written extensively on matters of life and death, those books and papers have been filtered through the intellectual requirements of academic outputs. That is what shaped the final product. Now in retirement, without deadlines to cramp our capacities for expansive thought, we have undertaken a different kind of work. It is one that has roots in our friendship, one that has entangled academic ideas with our personal challenges and the pleasures of conferences and holidays. And it is not just the outcome of digging in archives or pestering elderly relatives. Co-authorship has meant revisiting pasts we thought we knew very well—maybe too well. But as we talked and questioned one another, new connections and questions emerged, many of the latter too late to be asked. Who or what drew Jenny's mother, Lorna, to delve so deeply into questions of religion and death, for example? Our forays into higher education furnished both of us with frameworks of ideas through which to think critically about the beliefs we grew up with. But as this chapter shows, it is lived experience—whether of the uncanny and the meditative, or of bereavement and serious illness, that has allowed us each to build a relationship with our own mortality and come to some understanding of what it means to be alive.

Notes

1. Salim, Valerie. 1983. *A Ghost-Hunter's Guide to Sheffield*. Sheffield: Sheaf Publishing Ltd. (P. 50).
2. See Sartre, Jean-Paul. [1943]2003. *Being and Nothingness. An essay on phenomenological ontology*. Abingdon: Routledge Classic; Marx, Karl. 1976. A contribution to the critique of Hegel's Philosophy of Right. New York: International Publishers; Hall, Stuart. 1986. The Problem of Ideology – Marxism without Guarantees. *Journal of Communication Inquiry*, 10, 2: 28–44.

3. David Brooks' Life. https://www.dur.ac.uk/anthropology/undergraduatestudy/david_brooks_prize/brooks-life/. Accessed 13 December 2017.
4. Geertz, Clifford. 1968. Islam *Observed. Religious Development in Morocco and Indonesia.* New Haven, Conn.: Yale University Press. (P. 101).
5. Hallam, Elizabeth, Jenny Hockey, and Glennys Howarth. *Beyond the Body. Death and Social Identity.* London: Routledge. (PPs: 166–182).
6. Cannadine, David. 1981. War and Death, Grief and Mourning in Modern Britain. In *Mirrors of Mortality*, ed. Joachim Whaley, 187–241. London: Europa Publications Ltd. (P. 219).
7. Cannadine, David. 1981. War and Death, Grief and Mourning in Modern Britain. In *Mirrors of Mortality*, ed. Joachim Whaley, 187–241. London: Europa Publications Ltd. (P. 230).
8. Ingold, Tim. Bringing Things to Life: Creative Entanglements in a World of Materials. ESRC National Centre for Research Methods: *NCRM Working Paper Series* 05/10. (P. 4).
9. Ingold, Tim. Bringing Things to Life: Creative Entanglements in a World of Materials. ESRC National Centre for Research Methods: *NCRM Working Paper Series* 05/10. (P. 11).

4

World War One and its Transformations

Starting at the turn of the twentieth century, we now enter the lives of our two families and follow them through the next hundred years. This chapter takes us up to 1918 with subsequent family events or experiences to come in later chapters, each presented in chronological order. Our focus here is Jenny's paternal grandfather, Bert, and his family, from the southwest of England, along with the political, social and economic environment of Ireland at the turn of the twentieth century and into its early decades, the world into which James, Carol's father, was born in 1921.

Jenny In Chap. 2, I rooted my search for what surrounds my inherited family papers and photographs in the thoughts and feelings that have pre-occupied me since 1996 when my father died. To find out more about Bert and Arthur, his son, means venturing into the records held by a genealogy site, hunting out old maps of South Devon and Pas-de-Calais in France and navigating the proliferation of internet sites bearing information about men who fought in the two world wars. Most recently, like many people whose relatives fought in France, I also travelled to the 'foreign fields' where Bert had died. Towards the end of this chapter, there are extracts from the record of my thoughts and feelings that I made, in situ, while visiting the village where he was wounded, the hospital where he died and the military cemetery where he is buried. As I said in Chap. 1, it was only in my 20s, when anthropology introduced me to the elaborate death rituals of more traditional societies as a mature undergraduate, that I became fully aware of the absences and silences surrounding deaths such as his. The particular way my family responded to its deaths was what first drew me to Death Studies, once I had come to see their responses as culturally and historically specific. But such insights take time and education. Fortunately for me, 'making strange the familiar' is one of anthropology's primary goals.

Most of the material left to me concerns the death, rather than the life of Bert, my grandfather. He was fatally wounded near Amiens, capital of the Somme department in Hauts-de-France, at the very end of World War One. I wanted to know how and where this had happened, to access knowledge that his immediate family were largely denied. And since he fought and died in an extraordinary war, I wanted to understand the transitions he underwent—from farming to drapery to artillery, from village life in South Devon to the trenches of northern France, from peace to war. What I have pertaining to death includes his name on a military gravestone and on South Devon war memorials, his will and death certificate, his medals and the official photos of his gravestone. From his life I have a handful of photographs, one pencilled postcard and two letters he wrote to his elder son. What kind of man he was, I can only guess at. No-one I have ever known had met my grandfather. All his immediate family pre-deceased me, apart from my father who was too young to remember him. Bert's brothers and sister and their families may have had some memory, but my contact with them has been sparse, most of them based in Devon, while I grew up in Cambridge.

Digitised records help enlarge the picture. To the list above I can add his military service record, the details of where and how he died and a description of the belongings of his that were returned to his family. Recovering such information is a long-term, compelling activity. Many people make amateur genealogy a rewarding hobby, particularly in relation to war deaths and military history. I make no claim to having exhausted the available data. But scribbles of possibly relevant information now litter the backs of old academic articles that have become my printing paper As these snippets accumulate, however, as I find more 'dots', the struggle to join them gets no easier. But rather than trying to complete a dot-to-dot puzzle, perhaps it makes more sense to think of this as an attempt to 'see through' official documents and juxtapositions of dates—to the individuals whose lives they pertain to—and to imaginatively enter the spaces represented by a photograph's two dimensions. Rather than a comprehensive account, then, this is closer to a meditation on the belongings my family left behind, the stories and recollections they passed on to me (Fig. 4.1).

The items concerned have been around me for 20 years—but what have I really seen? A studio image of my grandparents with my Uncle Arthur aged about three is of beautiful quality. It is on the front cover of this book, ostensibly showing little more than a new family's status and respectability. It must have been taken in about 1913, the year before my father was born. Bert, my grandfather, is on the left of the frame in a three-piece suit, high starched collar and watch chain. His right hand is in his trouser pocket, so pushing back his jacket. Arthur stands on a chair in the middle, with Ella, his mother, to the right of the frame, her left hand on her hip. When I trace the arm that encircles Arthur's waist and the fingers between which the child has inserted his thumb, I begin to wonder which parent they belong to. I am intrigued by the juxtaposition of Bert's formal pose—indeed all three faces stare proudly towards the camera—and this half-hidden intimacy between parent and child. Just below this photo in my album are later studio images of my grandmother, alone with her two sons. Bert is not there. Is Ella now a war widow, or were these photos taken for him while he was serving in France? My grandmother's face is hard to read. She is wearing a white blouse but I know World War One brought a watershed in the wearing of black mourning clothes.[1] In this later photo it is Arthur, aged about eight, who is wearing a three-piece suit with a stiff collar. His right hand is in his trouser pocket, so pushing back his jacket.

Writing from this material is an act of resurrection. I am summoning up relatives about whom I know little, trying to put flesh on their bones. What else do I have to hand? There are photos of five moustachioed men pinned to my noticeboard. They all look strikingly like my father, David

Fig. 4.1 Jenny's grandmother, Ella, with her elder son, Arthur, on the left of the photo and David, her younger son (Jenny's father), on the right

Manning, but are clearly of a different generation. So similar are they that it is difficult to decide whether I am looking at multiple shots of just two men or five of my grandfather's seven brothers. Commemorative printouts from the Commonwealth War Graves Commission are pinned to another noticeboard. One is in memory of Gunner Herbert Manning, one in memory of Lieutenant Arthur Herbert Manning. The first has a photograph of Villers-Bretonneux Military Cemetery, 15 miles east of Amiens, showing acres of sunlit lawn; the other has a photo of the Sangro River War Cemetery in Northern Italy, equally green and sunlit. They call to mind newly chiselled marble gravestones that promise to stand forever, characterless and implacable.

But to return to the start of my grandfather's life, what can I find out about the immediate world into which his sons, my father and his brother, were born more than a century ago? What did it mean for Bert, a small-town draper from a South Devon farming family, to become a gunner, to be required to fight, die and be buried in a foreign country? How his immediate family responded to their loss is another question that preoccupies me, and I focus on that in Chap. 5.

4.1 A Farming Family

Bert was born on 11 June 1881. Given the attention we are paying to dates, Carol and I could not help but notice that he shares this birthday not only with Carol but also her father. Bert's parents were farmers, living near Ivybridge, South Devon. He arrived too late for the 1881 census but there he is in the 1891 record. By then his family were living and working at Butland, a farm near Modbury, about five miles south between the rivers Avon and Erme. His parents, William Manning and Elizabeth Ann Palk, had nine children by then—eight boys and a girl. Ten years later, in 1901, they had moved about eight miles west to Wollaton farm, near Brixton. Bert was already 20 and had left home for Bristol where he found work at Baker Baker, a large wholesale and retail drapers. It occupied premises on Wine Street and Cheese Market and was later destroyed in the Blitz on 24 November 1940.

Only five of William and Elizabeth's children were still at home in 1901: two of Bert's five older brothers, William (aged 28) and John (aged 26); two of his younger brothers, Charles (aged 15) and Sydney (aged 13); and his one sister, Emily Kate (aged 17). The neighbouring farm, Gorlofen—which is entered just below Wollaton in the census for that year—was often referred to by my father and I think belonged to the Mannings, even though it was occupied by Silas James, an agricultural labourer, and his family, at this point.

The absence of four of the family's nine children from the 1901 census makes me wonder how decisions were made about who would follow their parents into farming and who would look elsewhere for work. While Bert was in Bristol, James Palk, his 27-year-old brother, and Herman, 22-year-old brother, had set sail for Adelaide, Australia. Although James Palk is listed in the 1891 census as a 'draper's apprentice', now, ten years later, he and Herman were among 250 fellow passengers who left Southampton on 16 February 1901 on the SS Omrah. Their journey of over 13,000 miles lasted 56 days. Both the brothers appear on the passenger list as miners, and indeed the Australian economy had been thriving on the country's mineral deposits since the middle of the nineteenth century. Whether the brothers were already working as miners when they left, or whether mining was their proposed occupation, is unclear. Certainly mining was still important in West Devon at this time, whether of tin, copper, arsenic, silver or lead.

Another of Bert's older brothers, Reginald, is listed as a chemist's apprentice in 1901. He was employed by a Brighton chemist, and boarding on the premises. Ten years later he has his own business, a retail chemist at 274 Portobello Road, Kensington. In 1914 he married Bertha Greet, a young Cornish woman working as a midwife in St Marylebone workhouse in London. Their daughter, Marjorie, born in the autumn of 1915, was cousin to my father. She features in many of his schoolboy photographs. On the beach at Sidmouth, South Devon, she has her beret pulled down 20s style over a grinning face that closely resembles my father's (Fig. 4.2).

Bertha, her mother, and Ella, my grandmother, are wearing cloche hats and wielding Japanese parasols. Cousin Marjorie seems in many ways to be the younger sibling my father might have had, if my grandfather had

Fig. 4.2 Marjorie and David Manning on the beach at Sidmouth, South Devon, in about 1926

Fig. 4.3 Christopher Gould and Jenny Hockey (nee Manning) on the beach at Dawlish, South Devon, in about 1956

survived. Although Marjorie's family lived at the same London address until Reginald died in 1951, they made regular family trips to South Devon resorts. This was a holiday journey my father also made throughout my childhood when we lived in Cambridge. Later in my album I am there in photographs taken on the same beaches, with my own cousin (Fig. 4.3).

Wollaton, the farm where the Mannings lived and worked, remained in the family at least during my father's boyhood. In 1911, farming was the major occupation in South Devon, with numbers for each of the nearest two occupations—'construction' and 'defence'—being half that for farmers. Information gleaned much later from my father's cousins suggests that the family worked the adjacent farms of Wollaton and Gorlofen as one. By 1911 the agricultural labourer Silas James and his family had moved to a farm immediately to the north, Hareston. So it seems likely that the Mannings had owned both farms since 1901. Certainly their names figured in my father's boyhood memories. So his mother must have retained strong links with Bert's family after he died. One of the few labelled photos in my album shows my father as a young teenager sitting on a horse in the farmyard at Gorlofen. By 1911, however, Bert's father, William, had been dead for three years. His mother, Elizabeth Ann Palk Manning, 62 at that point, and Charles and Sydney, her younger sons, now 25 and 23, were running the farm.

In Bristol, Bert had met my grandmother, Ella, who was working as a draper's assistant at Baker Baker where he was employed. She appears in the 1901 census living in the company's accommodation on 2–6, Charlotte Street, Bristol. Sixty-three female draper's assistants are listed at this address, all single and in their 20s. Like Bert's brother, Reginald, here is another family member whose workplace is their home. My grandfather was 20 at this time and my grandmother 24. Whether they had formed a relationship by 1901 is not clear, but eight years later, on 19 April 1909, they married in St Paul's Church, Weymouth.

Together Bert and Ella set up and ran a draper's shop at 16 Fore Street in Topsham, Devon. Baker Baker, it seems, was a training ground for young men and women with this aspiration, so Bert is likely to have moved up to Bristol with a view to setting up his own business back in South Devon. In a published history of the company, a former staff member refers to her brother-in-law, Sam Wainwright Chattin, who 'joined Baker Baker after the First World War as a trainee, he is described as a Draper's Assistant on his marriage certificate. The Chattins owned draper's shops in Wolverhampton and we think he was sent to Baker Baker's to learn the trade. We suspect he left Baker Baker's around 1930 to run his own shop in Bilston ...'.[2]

Bert and Ella shared the living accommodation above their Topsham business with Ella's mother, Sarah Annie Harrison. In the 1911 census Bert is listed as a draper and furnisher, as well as an employer. I have visited the business that currently occupies that property—though the accommodation above has now been sold off as flats. Its owners have reverted to the name my grandparents chose: 'London House'. It appears in the Yellow Pages as selling fashion accessories. Adding vintage atmosphere to the main area of the shop is a draper's long wooden counter with an inlaid brass rule. It had been abandoned in the back of the shop when the premises were occupied by a cobbler who used the bench for repair work. Now refurbished and given a prominent location, it is the counter at which Bert and Ella would have measured and cut their cloth.

Years later, as a 1960s 'Saturday girl', I worked in the haberdashery department of Robert Sayle, Cambridge, a member of the John Lewis Partnership. I spent my Saturdays measuring out ribbon, bias binding or elastic, using a similar rule, also embedded in the counter. My father worked there too—in the furniture and then bedding department. He had joined the shop shortly after his release from the RAF in the autumn of 1945. It is only as I begin to connect the dots that make up my family's work history that I discover these continuities. Maybe I could have visited the site of my grandparents' shop on earlier Devon holidays but something like shyness or embarrassment stopped me announcing myself to its current owner. I felt any attempt to discover traces of my family would be futile. I had so little to go on. But at an emotional level, finding the bench, lost for so long to glue, rivets and pliers, gave me an unexpected anchor in my search for family connection.

4.2 The Arrival of Children and War

Bert and Ella's first son, Arthur, was born in 1911 after two years of marriage, and David, my father, arrived three years later on Christmas Eve, 1914. Ella was 38 by then, not having married until she was 32. Between my father's conception in March and his birth in December, events in Europe had culminated in Germany's invasion of Luxembourg and Belgium. On 4 August that year, when Germany refused Liberal Prime Minister Herbert Asquith's ultimatum to withdraw, Britain declared war on Germany. Made unpopular by his handling of the war, Asquith was replaced as prime minister in 1916 by David Lloyd George. In his subsequent war memoirs, Lloyd George says:

> Did we know that before peace would be restored to Europe we should have to wade through four years of the most concentrated slaughter, mutilation, suffering, devastation and savagery which mankind has ever

witnessed? That 12 millions of the gallant youth of the nations would be slain, that another 20 million would be mutilated?[3]

What were the implications of this carnage for my grandparents' family life? I mentioned the high-quality studio photos I have of them. Their faces have a smooth, unknowing quality, an absence of any awareness that the life they were building together was about to unravel. There they are, in the early years of World War One with the sons they dressed so well in Eton collars and sailor suits, believing the war would soon be over—and that fighting itself was a matter only for single men. About 20 such photos occupy my album, documenting these early Topsham years. Unlike contemporary family photos, where smiling is expected, these studio images reflect an earlier tradition of portraiture where seriousness was valued in what was seen as a lasting image of oneself. So although I might look for emotional transitions across these photos, it is elusive. That said, there is a formal serenity in the earlier images that is missing from later ones where my grandmother is alone. These exude just a blank sadness.

By the spring of 1915, the initial flow of voluntary recruits into the army had slowed down from the 478,893 men who joined up between the outbreak of war on 4 August and 12 September 1914. But the rapid escalation of death and injury raised problems for a military command without conscription. Between 4 August 1914 and the end of that first year, at least 90,000 British men had either died or been wounded—at the Battle of the Frontiers and at battles on the Marne, on the Aisne and, in particular, at Ypres where 58,155 British casualties were sustained. By the summer of 1915, when the cut-off date for enlistment was 38, Bert was already 33. However, by May that year, men up to the age of 40 were included, to meet the demands of the war. Two months later the National Registration Act was introduced. This required *all* men, married and single, aged between 15 and 65 to register their employment details. When the results were made available in September 1915, a residue of around 3.4 million men in unreserved occupations became apparent. Being a draper was one of them.

The following month, Lord Derby was appointed Director-General of Recruiting, and within five days, on 16 October 1915, he had established a programme later known as the Derby Scheme. Men aged between 18 and 40 could choose between either volunteering to join the army in the traditional way or enlisting with a commitment to join the forces immediately if and when they were called up. From the government's point of view, this was a half-way house towards conscription which they had so far resisted. From married men's point of view, it meant that they could enlist—and so be seen to have done their duty—but in the knowledge that they would not be called up while single men under 40 remained available for service.

This was the possibility offered by National Registration. It ended on 15 December 1915. In the days immediately beforehand, vast numbers of men came forward. Bert's military service record, form B2512, shows his Short Service Attestation, or enlistment, on 8 December in Exeter, seven days before the scheme closed. Attestation refers to the process whereby the army approves a man as fit to serve—and the man swears a legally binding oath to:

> … be faithful and bear true Allegiance to his Majesty King George the Fifth, his Heirs and Successors, and that I will, as in duty bound, honestly and faithfully defend His Majesty, His Heirs and Successors in Person, Crown and Dignity against all enemies, and will observe and obey all order of His Majesty, His Heirs and Successors, and of the Generals and Officers set over me. So help me God.

Once sworn in, Bert was sent home but as a member of the Army Reserve. For one day he had been 'in the Colours', the Colours being the embodiment of a regiment's history and reputation. He received a day's pay for that and would have received a grey armband with a red crown to show that he had come forward.

At this time 54 per cent of married men in unreserved occupations had still avoided National Registration, but there was already censure for those who did not enlist. Since tribunals were set up where married men had to make claims of business or family commitments if they wished to be absolved from military duties, a decision to come forward and attest was in many cases a safeguard *against* being called up. An official recruiting poster carried the following message: *Enlist now! You have the Prime Minister's pledge that you will not be called upon to serve until the young unmarried men have been summoned to the Colours.* Only three months later, in March 2016, married men were being called up. There was uproar from those who had trusted that they would not have to serve while single men were available. In April 1916, over 200,000 people demonstrated against conscription in Trafalgar Square.[4]

As regards the demands placed upon women in World War One, the historian, Joanna Bourke, says that in modern times the widespread enlisting of women into the armed forces has always been reserved for times of revolution or invasion.[5] However, 80,000 women did serve in the three British women's forces in World War One, as non-combatants. In response to men's arguments that women should not have the vote because they could not bear *arms*, a cartoon on the first page of *The Women's Journal* showed a suffragette woman shouting 'No! Women bear *armies*'. In other words, women bore the cost of war in many other ways: as a Land Army, for example, and through the support given to wounded men, whether as nurses, wives or mothers.

What view my grandfather held is unclear. Two 'postcard' photographs in my album show him in uniform among the ranks of what became known after 1908 as the Territorial Force (TF). Had he already joined the TF before ever enlisting? Or did he join thereafter? Its units comprised very local men training together, often with pre-existing family or work connections. The regiment Bert ultimately joined, the Royal Garrison Artillery, was among those that formed units of the Territorial Force. Hence the name of the Topsham TF: the second Devonshire Royal Garrison Artillery.

One of my photos shows him in a formal three-deep lineup. In charge is Major Henry Gould, whose son Donald was my father's best friend. To the left of Major Gould is a uniformed padre and in the back row stands Bert. Off duty, he was still proprietor of the draper's shop at 16 Fore Street, Topsham, and Henry Gould was running the Post Office next door at number 17. Hence their sons' friendship. Much later, these boys would marry sisters then growing up in Great Yarmouth on the Norfolk coast. Many of the same men are recognisable in the other photo but this time arranged more informally in a field with three bell tents behind them. Some of them are in uniform, others in shirtsleeves, one with a spade and another with a pickaxe. Major Gould still has a central position,

Fig. 4.4 The second Devonshire Royal Garrison Artillery Territorial Force camping near Topsham, South Devon. Bert Manning is fourth from the left

the only man with a seat of some kind. These images make it hard to tell whether Bert joined other Topsham men in what seems like quite an enjoyable activity, well before his last-minute enlistment under the National Registration Scheme, or whether his enlistment prompted him to join forces with them (Fig. 4.4).

How Bert's brothers were affected by the war is less clear. Figures for recruitment for Devon were well below those for other parts of the country.[6] While a six per cent recruitment rate from any given population was the goal, figures for Devon at the beginning of the war yielded around four per cent, compared with ten per cent in other parts of the country. This has been attributed to a commitment to family farms in a predominantly rural county. Particular resentment was felt when unskilled farm labourers, ploughmen and blacksmiths were conscripted. In a thesis on recruitment in Devon, Richard Batten[7] describes route marches of soldiers around the county in 1915, a strategy designed to motivate the young male population. Although a lot of food was offered to them, relatively few men came forward. Batten suggests a belief that if the country really needed them they would be conscripted. In Bridestowe, in West Devon, a man who was exhorted to volunteer said: 'We've got no time for that rummage. Let someone else do it if they like.' One young farmer said of himself and his friends: 'farmers' sons be going to stay home and look after the grub and the money'. On the one hand, the government was indeed seeking to reduce the country's reliance on imported food yet at the same time needed more men to fight. Establishing the Women's Land Army and the gradual introduction of rationing eventually resolved this tension. Recruitment figures for Cornish populations, however, were even lower. The Declaration of War in August 1914 coincided with harvest time, and many members of the agricultural population saw it as their duty to feed rather than defend the nation. In addition, the transmission of farming knowledge and expertise to the young men of the next generation was a powerful incentive for parents to discourage their sons from enlisting. Although women from agricultural families were reported to have disrupted recruitment meetings by shouting out against the costs of war, Richard Batten says that the women who came out to watch the soldiers marching through their towns and villages not only offered food but also *themselves* as recruits, in attempts to shame their men into volunteering.

Bert was not a farmer but he came from a large farming family. All but three of his brothers were listed as farm workers on census returns taken during their youth. His brother Reginald appears as a member of the London Regiment, Army Service Corps, part of the Army Reserve. Whether Reginald saw active service is difficult to ascertain. None is recorded. Meanwhile, in March 1917, Bert was called up and had to leave their business. Ella, his wife, then took up the dual role of parent and draper. For a woman to take on a business was nothing new, however.[8] In the late nineteenth century, widowed women would manage family businesses, particularly in retail and millinery, a trade in which my grandmother had been trained. Since family businesses were typical of that period, wives and daughters were often involved and might even finance a firm.

Bert announced this change to his customers via an advert in the parish magazine. Clearly he was concerned to protect their business. Using the first person, he speaks directly to his customers:

<u>London House, Topsham</u>
Dear Sir or Madam,
As I have joined his Majesty's Forces, Mrs Manning will continue the business on my behalf with a full stock of:
<u>General and Fancy Drapery and Millinery</u>
and I ask my many customers for their continued support during my absence, thanking you for your past favours and your future patronage.
I beg to remain,
Yours faithfully,
HERBERT MANNING

On 9 March 1917, then, more than two years after registering, Bert's Short Service Attestation was approved at Citadel, Plymouth. The signatory is the Hon. Lieut. Col. of the Royal Garrison Artillery, the regiment he joined. His attestation information is on his British Army Service Record, readily available on the Ancestry genealogy website. But many of its entries are difficult to make out. I realise I have more information to hand in Francis' small diary from 1909, the year she and Bert married. In it she records her height and weight and these measurements distract me. Although I know her from sepia studio photographs, when I discover that she was five feet eight inches tall and weighed nine stone one pound, that she wore size six shoes, she suddenly springs to embodied life. How tall and slim she was. Straightaway I compare my body with hers; it is another stone heavier and three inches shorter. But we could have worn each other's shoes. Ella also records her hat, glove and collar sizes but I cannot relate to these numbers now, more than a century later. Ella may have kept up her diary in the months leading up to her wedding on 19 April 1909, but these pages have been neatly cut out. Those which remain record nothing of the first eight months of her marriage—unlike the only other diary of hers that I have, for 1943, which details the weather, her small excursions and the letters she writes and receives.

What I do find in her 1909 diary are five pages of weekly accounts. They seem to record pay, in sterling and in old French francs. There are English place names alongside the figures in sterling. But none for those in francs. All the entries are dated, but the year does not seem to have been noted. I am frustrated by this potentially revealing item. I do not know which year the dates refer to, nor can I recognise the place names, apart from Aldershot. What is more, I do not know what these sums of money represent. Was it an allowance that was sent to Ella, to support herself and her sons? A soldier would have half his pay sent home to his wife. Only later do I realise that she has started the account on the right-hand page—where the year itself, 1917, is indeed recorded. She has then worked back across to the left-hand page. At this point the dates fall into sequence, joining up with the page overleaf where Bert's departure for France is noted.

But I am still misled. Fascinated by Francis' personal details at the beginning of the diary, I assumed that these were her accounts. Until something inspires me to compare the writing with that on the postcard Bert sent her while away training at this time. These are *his* accounts, and indeed they trace his journey from Topsham to the Western Front, using up an otherwise 'wasted' diary. It is possible that its record of Ella's height, weight, shoe size and so on made the book precious to him while he was away from home. It was among the possessions on his body that were returned to Ella after his death. The pre-marital pages were perhaps cut out for reasons of confidentiality, now that he was taking the book away with him. Why Ella failed to continue with this diary after her wedding is, like many questions, difficult to guess at.

I seem to have made progress but the list of place names in the diary is barely legible. These accounts, like many of the handwritten documents I have inherited, are in pencil, by now very smudged. The starting page begins fairly clearly with 'ration money' and 'Plymouth', in ink. Then in pencil it says, 'Joined up March 6th 1917', which more or less corresponds with the date that his attestation was signed in his British Army Service Record. He was at Citadel for three weeks, the name referring to the Royal Citadel in Plymouth, a seventeenth-century fortress that was built to defend the southwest coastline of Great Britain from the Dutch and still remains in military use.

During his time at Citadel, he wrote a letter to his elder son, Arthur, who would have recently turned six. It is on fairly robust, pale blue writing paper, now browned with age at the edges and lined on one side only. It has been folded into six and then 'addressed' to Master Arthur Manning, London House, Topsham, possibly as an enclosure in a letter to Ella. In inked, copperplate letters nearly two centimetres high and straddling two lines, it says:

> My dear Arthur
> I was very pleased to get your letter and I think you wrote it very nicely, you will have a nice collection of cigarette cards. I have not got one to send now will try and get some the next time I write hoping you are a good boy and a kiss x for David and yourself
> from your loving Daddy.

Returning to Bert's 'accounts', this time for 29 March 1917, I find a blurred place name that turns out to be Prees Heath. An internet search reveals that it was an army camp just outside Whitchurch in Shropshire. On a website called 'Derelict Places. Documenting Decay', I find 15 photos of abandoned buildings, broken corrugated iron roofs, smashed glass, half an upturned vehicle of some kind and concrete single-storey huts, all disappearing into young woodland and fern. The camp had been set up two years before Bert was sent there, to provide additional training resources for the growing numbers of troops. It had a capacity of 30,000 men who were housed in single-storey huts, 36 men to a hut. The website's images are atmospheric. They evoke the persistent presence of a long distant time, but I cannot imagine a peopled landscape from these relics of buildings. However, on a site called The Great War History Hub there is a project called 'Researching the history of World War 1 relating to Whitchurch, Shropshire'.[9] It carries a link to the undated testimony of Raynor Taylor, born in Oldham around 1899. Raynor describes going along with his friends to attest at the Town Hall in Oldham in 1916, soon after his 18th birthday. He was sent to Ladysmith Barracks, around four miles away in Ashton-under-Lyne, where he was kitted out with a tunic, trousers, holdall for washing and shaving equipment, towel and a kitbag. He recalls going on parade, a process that throws light on Bert's initial time at Citadel, Plymouth.

Sent to Prees Heath in 1917, Bert is likely to have shared the experiences Raynor Taylor recalls from August 1916. Raynor describes sleeping on three boards placed across some kind of support, with a palliasse mattress and pillow that men filled themselves with straw and two blankets.

They soon learned that too much straw meant an uncomfortable night. Huts were heated with a stove, and fuel was limited. Food, he says, was basic but sufficient: gunpowder tea first thing, for the bowels, a cold breakfast, a cooked lunch, sandwich tea and a supper of 'stew', made of leftovers. Washing and toilet facilities comprised a night bucket at the hut door and a covered line of taps for washing. He describes a complete lack of privacy as men lived, ate and slept together. Here I see the beginning of Bert's transition from being a draper. It was an occupation that Edward VII described as 'a dignified calling … essential to the nation's welfare and to the advancement of civilization' in his speech at the annual dinner of the Incorporated Association of Retail Distributors. Getting used to a life without privacy is something Eric Maria Remarque portrays in *All Quiet on the Western Front*, his account of soldiering in World War One. The use of communal toilets meant that for hours at a time a circle of men would sit out in the field on 'thunderboxes', playing cards on the lid of an old margarine tub. 'It has become so natural to us', the narrator says, 'that the convivial performance of this particular activity is … highly valued'.[10]

Training, Raynor says, began with basic drill, learning to keep in step; equipment such as a rifle was issued only when the rudiments had been assimilated. Once equipped though, he remembers a new awareness that '[w]e looked like soldiers'. The aim of the training, he says, was to learn to do everything automatically, as part of a group. Being taught to dig trenches was also important. In addition, Prees Heath acted as a store for supplies, with its own railway depot feed. Later, as the number of casualties grew, it became a military hospital—almost certainly by the time Bert was sent there for training.

Three weeks after arriving at Prees Heath, my grandfather was on the move again. In the largely unpunctuated postcard below, he describes marching from Prees Heath to Whitchurch and getting caught in a shower on the way. He and the men he trained with had clearly absorbed the rudiments of drill by this time and were able to keep in step for the five-mile journey. His pencilled card is postmarked 'Reading, 7.30 pm, 14 April 1917'. He would have changed trains there for Aldershot, and he addressed the card to Mrs. Bert Manning, London House, Topsham, Devon.

My dear Ella
We are in the train now standing in Warwick Station they say the next is Leamington I am very disappointed in the country around here so flat and poor looking we are going on to Reading then change for Aldershot I am having a very pleasant journey, and its a nice day only one shower when we were marching to Whitchurch have just run into Banbury now we are at Heyford next stop Reading Just going to have half a Meat P. and 2 jams [?] very nice too will write tomorrow Goodbye
With love Bert

When I read this, I realise for the first time that they were known to each other as Bert and Ella and not Herbert and Frances as their birth certificates suggest. Its message implies that Bert was unfamiliar with landscapes beyond the West Country. When I travel now in the opposite direction, from Sheffield to Exeter, I am invariably struck by the increasing lushness of the Somerset and Devon countryside, its more dramatic landscape. In the 1950s, my childhood family holidays began with a day's journey by Morris Minor from the East Anglian fens, ticking off the counties until we reached my father's much-loved 'high hills' and red earth of South Devon. Bert's journey took him east out of that landscape and into unfamiliar towns. His childhood was spent in an agricultural world which stretched about ten miles in all directions. Though he had worked in Bristol and married my grandmother in Weymouth, there is no evidence of him travelling any further into England until that journey to Aldershot.

Bert returned home on leave for three days on 23 April 1917 but remained at Aldershot until 18 May. Then, from 24 May, his accounts show him stationed in Lydd on Romney Marsh in Kent, a key training camp for artillery, somewhere that gave its name to the explosive, lyddite, invented on nearby shingle wastes. These records suggest he had leave after his time at Lydd and before moving to Codford, ready for embarkation to northern France. On 29 June, he made a will. As someone with property, who owned and ran a small business, deferring making a will for so long might suggest he still hoped to avoid active service, that perhaps he believed the conflict would end before he was needed. Equally, he may have been prompted by the forces' requirement that all men on

Fig. 4.5 Bert Manning in the uniform of the Royal Garrison Artillery, taken in about 1917

active service carried a pay-book that included a form that acted as a will. Bert may have wanted a more formal and elaborate recording of his wishes (Fig. 4.5).

By 4 July he was at Codford on Salisbury Plain, where large training and transfer camps accommodated tens of thousands of troops waiting to leave for France. Finally, on July 17 1917, he set sail from Southampton for Le Havre in France, arriving the following day. From then on, Bert records only his weekly payments of 10 and then 20 francs. No place names are noted. Only later do I notice that in a different colour pencil he has added 9 Siege beside the words 'Paid France' written in his usual purplish indelible pencil. On the opposite page, against 'Jan 12. 1918 20 (francs)', he writes '203 SB', by now using the army acronym for Siege Battery.

From here on I am reliant on archival information and the World War One forums, particularly the military diary of the 86th Brigade of the Royal Garrison Artillery. No letters from Bert survive, other than the one below, again written to his elder son, Arthur, this time on 20 February 1918. It was for Arthur's seventh birthday on 27 February 1918. There is no address, other than BEF [British Expeditionary Forces], France, and it is written in pencil on cheap notepaper. The envelope simply says: 'Master Arthur Manning, London House, Topsham, Devon, England'. A red stamp indicates that it has been passed by the censor. It is franked but bears no postage stamp. In handwriting that more closely resembles that used on his postcard to Ella the previous year, he says:

> My dear Arthur
> I am writing just a short letter to wish you Many Happy Returns of your birthday, and hope you will a pleasant day. I am enclosing a £1 note 10/- each for David and yourself. You will let dear David have half as I did not send him anything for his birthday, being so near Xmas. Mother will put it in the bank for you both. I am very glad to hear you like your new school. I shall want to see some of your work when I come home, am also glad you are so pleased to go to Sunday School. Give my love to love Mother and Granny, and a big kiss each XX for dear little David and yourself and with best love
> From your loving
> Daddy
> (Gunner H Manning)

Other than the records Bert kept in my grandmother's unused 1909 diary, there is no personal material among the items I have inherited. Finding out where Bert was and what he was doing is complicated by the fact that many of the units, or batteries, of the Royal Garrison Artillery left no record of their movements in the form of a military diary. This was because they had no continuity of higher command, instead being assigned to Army Corps or sometimes divisions, as and when they were needed. Indeed, men themselves might be switched between batteries, as was the case with Bert.

Certainly the development of more powerful artillery was key to the way warfare was being conducted at this time. The military historian, John Terraine, said that '[t]he war of 1914–18 was an artillery war: artillery was the battle-winner, artillery was what caused the greatest loss of life, the most dreadful wounds, and the deepest fear'.[11] In 1914, however, the army had had little by way of heavy artillery (large military weapons capable of firing munitions beyond the line of an enemy's infantry which used small arms).

The 203rd Siege Battery of the Royal Garrison Artillery, of which Bert eventually became a member in January 1918, had first gone to France in December 2016. Siege batteries were made up of about 180 men, of whom 5 would be officers. Over a hundred horses could be used to pull ammunition and other supplies, a battery's primary role being to destroy enemy artillery, as well as their supply routes, railways and stores. Imperial War Museum image Q1374 shows 20 or 30 men of the 156th Siege Battery hauling an eight-inch howitzer into position at Longueval, during the Battle of the Somme in September 1916.[12] Under the direction of their officers they are bunched together, leaning backwards away from the barrel as if in some village green tug of war. Towards the end of the war a siege battery was likely to be equipped with the largest guns the army possessed, 9.2-inch howitzers. They were about 8 feet high and 12 feet long, capable of firing 290 lb. shells over a range of 10,000 yards. In front there was a dirt box—camouflaged and filled with soil—to keep the gun stable.

Bert's 1918 recordings of his pay are for 20 francs on the 4 and 15 July. Throughout he appears to have been paid fortnightly, if erratically. Then his record ceases. What were his experiences between setting sail on 17 July 1917 and this final entry in his records almost a year to the day later? When I examine the larger military landscape of World War One in 1917, I find that it was only during this period that the role of British troops extended beyond supporting the French offensive. This was partly as a result of the Battle of Arras, fought between April and June in 1917, about 40 miles north of Amiens. Its cost in both French and British men's lives was enormous. However, it left the British Expeditionary Force with a larger body of troops than the French.

Was Bert sent to participate in the subsequent Battle of Ypres? Also known as the Third Battle of Ypres or Passchendaele, it took place between 31 July and 10 November 1917 and formed part of the Flanders offensive. Although fighting as a whole was taking place along a front that stretched 440 miles from Swiss border to the North Sea, for Great Britain the area between the northern coast of France and the Dutch border was crucial in that it ran right along the enemy-occupied Belgian coast. This put mainland Britain in serious danger, a particularly urgent matter once Germany resumed unrestricted submarine warfare on 1 February 1917. Previously, then, in 1916, at a meeting in London of the Admiralty and the General Staff, it was seen as imperative that the Flanders operation be undertaken in 1917. Joseph Joffre, the French commander-in-chief signalled his agreement to this on 8 December 1916. When Joffre was replaced by Robert Nivelle, however, there were delays until on 7 May 1917 a final decision was made to divide the Flanders offensive into two parts, the first being the preliminary attack on Messines Ridge, south of Ypres, on 7 June. The Battle of Ypres then commenced on 31 July but continued until November, by which time Bert had been in France for four months.

Up until March that year, Bert's days had been spent selling fabric, furnishings and haberdashery. Then from July 1917 onwards he found himself fighting within a small siege battery that was constantly being moved from one corps or division to another. Whether or not Bert actually fought in the Third Battle of Ypres is unclear. Certainly the 'diary' where he recorded his pay carries a list of place names located in that part of the Western Front: Ypres, Bemmett, Cambrai, Henin, St Leger, Blainville. What I can say with more confidence is that he fought against the five German spring offensives that took place to the east of Amiens between 21 March and 17 July 1918. Amiens became a focus for the German Army because of its importance as a vital rail hub supplying the front line. Fighting by British and Australian troops at Villers-Bretonneux, 15 miles southeast of Amiens, had blocked the German offensive on 4 April 1918, and although the German Army advanced 28 miles, their supply lines had become overstretched. Then in July 1918, under the command of General Sir Henry Rawlinson, 350,000 Allied men were marshalled along a 17-mile front to the east of Amiens. In a letter to my grandmother, detailing the circumstances of Bert's subsequent death, George Bale, a corporal in 203rd Siege Battery, says: 'There is a sap [supply trench] just outside of Amiens towards Villers-Bretonneux where we spent a few days before we started the bombardment, there is a lot of chalk work on the surface. I mentioned this so if you did happen to see or visit it you may be consoled with the thought that you had been where your beloved husband had spent some of his last days'. I have more to say about this letter later in the chapter.

On 8 August, a week before Bert died, the British Fourth Army, together with Australian and Canadian forces, fought back hard against the 2070 German guns assembled for a decisive attack on Amiens. 8 August 1918 was known as 'The black day of the German army' and saw the Allies advance up to eight miles into the German front and take 12,000 prisoners and 450 guns. This was the beginning of the end for Germany. On a map included in Prior and Wilson's *Command on the Western Front*,[13] I can see that on 8 August the British front line ran through four tiny villages to the east of Amiens—Harbonnieres, Caix, le Quesnel and Rouvroy-en-Santerre. It was in Rouvroy-en-Santerre that Bert received his fatal wound when shrapnel penetrated his skull.

Nearly 100 years later, in August 2017, I visited Rouvroy-en-Santerre while cycling round the area with Bob, my husband, and made a record, on the spot, of what I saw and felt. Although, for practical reasons, we had gone first by car to the hospital where Bert died, then to his grave and finally by bike to the village where he was wounded, extracts from my notes are presented here according to the chronology of Bert's last days. The comments and references I subsequently added to them are not italicised:

It is 99 years to the day that Bert died at Dury Asylum (the site of the Clearing Station to which he was taken), a coincidence we hadn't planned – except that it's his great grandson's birthday tomorrow and we're going home for it. It's a hot, sunny day and the sky is huge and blue over this flat countryside. My tiredness fell away as soon as we set off on bikes from Rosieres-en-Santerre, my legs completely tuned to the pedals, easy riding along flat field roads. I kept examining the ploughed fields for evidence of warfare but all I could see were plastic bottles and drinks cans here and there, the only intruders now. But since we were the tallest items in the landscape, perched up on our bikes, it was possible to imagine the sense of vulnerability felt by men who knew to keep their heads down.

We're in Rouvroy-en-Santerre now, eating sandwiches and a peach on a very hot bench outside the church. This is where Bert was wounded and I wish there was something here to connect me with him. But there's nothing. Just a small gun – a Howitzer? – set up on a plinth under the trees near the church – in the shade we'd like to be sitting in. It has no inscription whatsoever. This breezy warmth and the church spire, topped with a cockerel, inspire a welcome sense of transience, of stepping off lightly. At the field edges there are poppies which can't just be poppies. A large crater by the side of the road as we explore the whole village is surrounded by modern fencing and a notice that says 'Acces Interdit. Danger'. There is water at the bottom. No-one is around to ask if it's a shell hole. In Warvilliers [a nearby village] *there is another huge crater hole and the churchyard has an extension with the graves of Canadian war dead and a plaque with information which suggests that Bert may have been wounded between 8 and 9 August when the Allies moved further east. What was happening to him in those four or five days before he died, if that is the date of his wounding? Where was the wound exactly?*

At the very end of *All Quiet on the Western Front*, the character Kat dies from a tiny unobserved shrapnel wound to the back of his head inflicted while the narrator is carrying him to safety after a previous wound to his shin. Kat is his best mate. It gives me some image to go on. 'Without my noticing it, Kat got a splinter of shrapnel in the head on the way. It's only a little hole. It must have been a tiny, stray fragment. But it was enough. Kat is dead … … … I look about me. And then I turn right round, and then I stop. Everything is just the same as usual. It's only that Private Stanislaus Katczinsky is dead.'[14]

What else? We asked two youngish women about the big holes in the ground (we found a third one in Le Quesnel) and both women assured us that they were wells or ponds. I don't believe them. But I forget how distant World War One is for them. They've been invaded again since then. And the landscape – not flat like Holland, flat like the sea, with undulations – it's all the valley of the Somme. There are lots of small cemetery extensions where different countries buried their dead soldiers – in the place where they died, it seems. Maybe the same kind of burial site would have been Bert's if the shrapnel had killed him outright.

If the date when Bert was wounded can only be guessed at, the *place* of his death on 14 August 1918 is recorded, 47th Casualty Clearing Station (C.C.S.), and then located in the mental asylum at Dury, just south of Amiens (now the Philippe Pinel Health Centre). It is about 25 miles from Rouvroy-en-Santerre. On Sunday 13 August 2017, we went to the Philippe Pinel Health Centre by car, and I made these notes:

This is where Bert was brought with shrapnel in his head. Finding the place, we were endlessly confused since there is a Philippe Pinel hospital in Amiens itself. But this is the one – red brick, formal architecture – not unlike my father's school. Laid out around a central grassy area with trees, mature as well as newly planted. We headed south out of Amiens and soon found it – imposing gates and a tree-lined avenue beyond, no-one about and a security gate in place. But I went to the control box and a man was there. I was enormously relieved when he understood exactly why I'd come. It strikes me that there's something very intimate about coming here first and I find myself thinking repeatedly, 'I hope they were kind to him here'. Reflecting back, once he had left England it is unlikely that anyone treated him with the kind of tenderness his wife and children may have offered – until, just possibly, here where he was dying. Unless he had visited brothels in the intervening period. All the accounts of World War One make much of them. I find it hard to imagine. But then he is my grandfather.

Casualty Clearing Stations like the one at Dury were sited behind the lines, further back than the Aid Posts and Field Ambulances. They were staffed by men from the Royal Army Medical Corps, along with Royal Engineers and men of the Army Service Corps. From 1914, trained nurses who were particularly experienced might also be posted to Casualty Clearing Stations. Initially four nurses, in addition to the Royal Army Medical Corps staff, were considered sufficient, but by 1916 there could be as many as 25 nurses at one Clearing Station. The scale of Clearing Stations also increased over time, many providing beds for 500 to 1000 wounded men, all requiring urgent medical attention, often surgery.

They were likely to be located near rail links to speed the passage of wounded men from the front—and, if possible, back to it—but are known to have moved frequently as the front shifted back and forth.

In what follows, surgeon John A. Hayward, Medical Officer at Queen Alexandra Hospital, Roehampton, describes volunteering for service as a temporary captain in the Royal Army Medical Corps in April 1918. His diary contains an account of his time at Casualty Clearing Station 47 where Bert died.[15] After referring to the overwhelming nature of the work in general and the intense fatigue it brought, Hayward says:

> It was not long before I was again put to the test. Our C.C.S. was ordered to take up quarters with two others in a huge deserted asylum close to Amiens, in expectation of the grand attack of the IV Army around Villers-Bretonneux ... the attack began on the day after our arrival ...
> On that evening our barrage opened – a continuous roar of heavy guns which shook the ground, and trembled the walls of our building, and the sky and fields were lit up with the flashes and explosions of dumps and star shells. In the early hours of the morning came the ambulances in a continuous stream ...
> The stretchers filled the numberless rooms, and then flowed out into the corridors ... many had to lie for hours without help, or die unattended ... Through the night, with dimmed lanterns, doctors and orderlies went down the rows doing what they could, but we were snowed under – and we could neither operate on nor evacuate cases fast enough to make much impression on the heaps.....
> It took nearly a week before we had cleared up and evacuated the cases, and everyone was exhausted. It was clear that insufficient time had been given to the medical side to organize for the number of casualties that might be expected in a battle of this magnitude, and the exigencies of the fighting must have the first call on transport. It was probably unavoidable, but, the pity of it; and, after all, as old Caspar said, 'It was a famous victory.'

I had read Hayward's account before visiting the former asylum at Dury, and while I was there, I wrote:

> *I thought a lot about the eye witness account written by the English medic and what he said (and I left out of my description) about the buildings at the back of the hospital where the bodies just piled up. It's very odd to be walking round a*

deserted psychiatric hospital on a Sunday – we could be anyone. One or two patients are about. It's hot and sunny. A peaceful place. I'm glad Bert died here, away from the violence and the din of the Front. I know it wasn't at all peaceful then – but it is now. And death did release him from it all. I feel a sort of letting go. I've seen where his death happened – maybe I've done that for my grandmother – completed her vigil for her. But now we're going to his grave, and maybe the man at the security gate was another hand meeting mine as it reaches back into the past and finds the past is there, available to me. Connection and anchorage.

As was often the case, those who died in a Clearing Station were likely to be buried in a nearby military cemetery. The letter sent to Ella by the Imperial War Graves Commission on 25 May 1920 does indeed inform her that Bert's remains were buried [temporarily] in the Dury Hospital Military Cemetery. I was surprised and pleased to find that the cemetery was virtually part of the hospital:

We found the adjacent cemetery where he was first buried – but the key to the wrought iron gates was missing. The cemetery was set in a lawned area at the back, where the hospital petered out into scruffier, modern buildings. I have no record of when news of Bert's death reached Ella. The form used for 'men of other ranks' simply states: 'It is my painful duty to inform you that a report has this day been received from the War Office notifying the death of … (followed by blank spaces for the number, rank and name of the deceased). I am to express to you the sympathy and regret of the Army Council at your loss. The cause of death was … (followed by a blank space which is likely to have been filled in with the words 'Killed in Action')'. If Ella did receive this form – bearing in mind that telegrams were reserved for officers, it has not been kept. Now with digitised access to many of the documents associated with men's recruitment to the military, it is easy to discover what killed him. I find it strange and almost unseemly though, that I should have this information when neither she nor her sons did. On the Ancestry website there is also a form that details the bureaucratic tasks completed after Bert's death, initialled by whomever informed her. Below the initials it says 'Note of sympathy, 21.8.18'.

The form she received is likely to have ended by saying that the deceased's effects would be forwarded in due course. From the Ancestry genealogy website, I know she did indeed receive Bert's letters, photos, pipe, diary, purse, matchbox cover, tobacco pouch, pair of scissors, wristwatch and strap, postcards, photo wallet and penknife. Though the list was dated and signed, it is difficult to read. The number 25 can be made out, and perhaps the items were collected together for dispatch on 25 August, about ten days after Bert died. While the diary is very likely to be Ella's, the one I now possess, I cannot identify any other items. It is possible that the photos and the scissors have always been there among my family's belongings, unnoticed by me. In the boxes and cases of material brought down from my father's attic, there were two leather photo wallets, one burgundy and one dark blue. Both showed signs of wear, the leather hardened and scuffed at the corners. Both still contain a photo of my mother, the second including me as a small baby. They are identical in design, opening like a book to reveal a single photo under plastic with a leather strap to keep the wallet closed. Given their worn appearance—and my family's habit of not throwing things away—I imagine that Bert was carrying one of these two wallets when he died.

From the letters Ella received and kept, it is evident that she planned to visit Bert's grave at Dury Hospital Military Cemetery. One of them, from the Imperial War Graves Commission, refers to an enquiry she made on 18 May 1920, asking for information and advice. It is a discouraging reply, written on behalf of the Principal Assistant Secretary and dated 25 May 1920:

Madam,
In reply to your letter of the 18th instant, I am directed to inform you that the particulars of the grave of Gunner H. Manning, in Hospital Military Cemetery, Dury, are Row 'G', Grave 13. This cemetery (formerly called British Military Cemetery) is situated North of Dury and just South of Amiens.
In order to visit the grave, it will be necessary for you to obtain a passport at the Passport Office, Lake Buildings, St James Square, S.W.1., and within fourteen days of your departure, a visa at the French Consulate.
I am also to state that you may experience serious difficulties in finding accommodation and in travelling, and it is regretted that this office is unable to grant you any assistance in this respect.
I am,
Madam,
Your Obedient Servant

Nowadays, the return of service people's bodies to the UK is expected. For example, during the 13 years of the UK's military involvement in Afghanistan, from 2001 to 2014, the sight of bodies being repatriated through Wiltshire country towns became commonplace. The cherishing of these bodies, given in the service of their country, is now taken for granted. Yet in 1920, when Ella simply wants to visit the place where her husband's remains are buried, she receives a formal, discouraging response. I do not know if she ever went, and the Commonwealth War Graves Commission visitors' books are not available. As the historian, Thomas Laqueur, notes, after the many battles that make up European history, bodies would be hastily buried at or near the place where soldiers had died, with very little by way of grave markers. In January 1915, however, according to Laqueur: '[f]or the first time in British military history scattered bodies were to be gathered together, reinterred, and individually marked'. Importantly, he goes on: 'by March … the policy of complete state control over the bodies of the dead and their final resting place had been laid down'. What policy-makers wanted was 'to prevent the public from putting up unsuitable effigies in [military] cemeteries' and so to make all graves uniform.[16] In response, as historian Joanna Bourke notes, '[f]amily and friends struggled with the War Office for the bones of their loved ones … [h]owever, during the war, the claims of military authorities over the bodies of men prevailed'.[17]

Ella, it seems, was not deterred by her letter from the War Office and wrote to George Edward Bale, mentioned above, to get more information. He was a Leicestershire shoemaker who served in the Royal Garrison Artillery alongside Bert. George was nine years younger and had been in France since June 1916, a year ahead of Bert. Originally a private, George is listed as a gunner in May 2016 and towards the end of the war promoted to the rank of corporal. It may be that he was in charge of the gun detachment Bert was serving in when he was wounded. From George's reply on 22 June 1920, it is evident that Ella was also considering taking her elder son, Arthur, with her on the hoped-for visit to Bert's grave. In a very different tone to that of the Imperial War Graves Commission, George combines information about what he refers to as Bert's 'accident' and place of burial with a eulogy to Bert and words of condolence for Ella:

Dear Mrs Manning

Please excuse the delay in replying to your letter, you will notice the alteration in the address hence the cause. Any information I can give you I shall be pleased to do so at any time. As far as I can gather Dury is a suburb of Amiens & only a car ride. I did not have the chance to visit Berts grave; although I searched everywhere I thought I may find it, it was not until after we had moved from that district that I got to know where your Dear Husband was laid to rest. One of the men had to go into hospital and whilst out for a stroll he visited Dury cemetery and got the particulars for me. I was pleased to hear you were taking Arthur with you as Bert was so fond & proud of his boys. Tell him from me that if he only follows in his fathers footsteps he will be a joy & blessing to all around. His father was a noble gentleman & a real good pal. The place where Bert met with his accident was Rouvroy & is about ten miles[18] from Amiens as near as I can guess. I have been trying to get a map so I could point the spot out. There is a sap [supply trench] just outside of Amiens towards Villers-Bretonneux where we spent a few days before we started the bombardment, there is a lot of chalk work on the surface. I mentioned this so if you did happen to see or visit it you may be consoled with the thought that you had been where your beloved husband had spent some of his last days. Please excuse the wording of this letter as I find it very difficult and painful. I will now close with every good wish, may you receive consolation and rich blessing.

I remain

Your Dear Husbands Chum

G.E.Bale

Seven years later, the Imperial War Graves Commission wrote to Ella again, from 82 Baker Street, London. Dated 12 December 1927, their letter says:

Madam

As you are aware, the late *Gunner H. Manning* was buried in Dury Military Cemetery.

This Cemetery was in close proximity to a French Asylum, and in order to reach the graves it was necessary for relatives and other visitors to go through fields which were part of the asylum property and in which there were lunatics and shell-shock cases at work.

We discussed the matter very fully with the French Authorities who met us with their usual warm sympathy, but they urged us to consider the annoyance that might be caused to visitors to the cemetery owing to the presence of these patients, and fully persuaded us that the risk could not be prevented. We were therefore, forced to the decision that, in the interest of the relatives, it was necessary to remove the graves and to re-bury the bodies in the nearest British Cemetery, where they would rest undisturbed in perpetuity and where no difficulty of access would arise.

Owing to the conditions obtaining the time the casualties occurred, it was necessary for the burials to take place on this site which, under normal conditions, would not have been selected as a permanent Cemetery.

I may add that, for the reasons outlined above, the French Authorities have removed the bodies buried in the French Military Hospital at Dury Hospital and I feel sure that you appreciate the necessity for the removal of the British graves.

The remains of *Gunner Manning* now rest in Villers-Bretonneux Military Cemetery, the number being Plot *6* Row *AA* Grave *9* and the permanent headstone will be erected over this grave in due course.

I am
Your Obedient Servant,
(signature)
For PRINCIPAL ASSISTANT SECRETARY

Whether the War Graves Commission was attempting to claim part of the asylum's land as an access route and were refused by 'the French Authorities' is not clear. But the letter is a carefully phrased account of what must have been a difficult undertaking both for those who exhumed the bodies and for relatives discovering that a son or husband's body had undergone further disturbance, beyond their fatal wounding. When I visited the former asylum, other factors emerged:

> *I realise that I never expected a cemetery to be in existence at the hospital, simply that there was space nearby where a surplus of dead could be interred. As we left the hospital I asked the security man for the hospital archivist's number, hoping to find out whether my grandmother did make a visit to Bert's grave in Dury. When I explained that my grandfather's body had been moved to Villers-Bretonneux in 1927 he said that all bodies are moved after ten years' burial – as I know – in France. What period was Bert's body in Dury? About nine years.*

What was the real reason for its removal – would they tell British families that the French are not buried in perpetuity?

Two years later another letter from the Imperial War Graves Commission to my grandmother 'begs to inform you that the permanent headstones have now been erected in Villers-Bretonneux Military Cemetery'.

The Commonwealth War Grave Commission states that in response to relatives' distress about the decision not to repatriate men's bodies, bereaved people were encouraged to personalise the headstone with words they could choose from a prescribed list (with a limit of 66 characters and a charge of threepence halfpenny per letter, subsequently dropped in favour of a voluntary donation). Lines from a biblical text or a prayer were encouraged, but the Imperial War Graves Commission retained the right of veto if words they deemed unsuitable were chosen. In the page of the 'Comprehensive Report B Headstone Personal Inscriptions' that includes the inscription Ella chose for Bert's headstone, there are seven others, all different, with the number of letters recorded in the final column. Only three of them make a clear religious reference, including my grandmother's, another two citing 'glory' as the outcome of a death.

The text Ella chose, 'Until the day break/and the shadows flee away', is from the Song of Solomon, part of a passage that reads: 'O my dove, *that art* in the clefts of the rock, in the secret *places* of the stairs, let me see thy countenance, let me hear thy voice; for sweet *is* thy voice, and thy countenance *is* comely. Take us the foxes, the little foxes that spoil the vines: for our vines *have* tender grapes. My beloved *is* mine, and I *am* his: he feedeth among the lilies. Until the day break, and the shadows flee away, turn, my beloved, and be thou like a roe or a young hart upon the mountains of Bether.[19] Was Ella aware of the passionate language surrounding her words when she chose them? Do they tell me something about their feelings for one another?

After visiting the Philippe Pinel Health Centre, we drove east to Villers-Bretonneux Military Cemetery to which Bert's remains were eventually removed. This was my second visit as I had taken some of my father's ashes to scatter on Bert's grave in the late 1990s:

Sitting on the shady side of the Great Cross at the Australian Cemetery where a little girl has moved to make space for me. She has a tiny handbag decorated with poppies. Her grandfather was already here but didn't move up to make space. Now they've all left. Bert is buried a few yards away, to my left, on the hot side of the Great Cross. 'Here he is', I said to myself as we worked our way up the rows of graves. And I felt it was good to find him – good for me – good for him – a sense of family connection with someone who'd gone ahead, whose remains are lying on this wide expanse of gently sloping hillside, an important site of successful fighting for the Australian troops. A huge and beautiful vista of quiet countryside and of the churches of small towns and villages. A white and grey snail shell was lying near Bert's headstone. I considered taking it away – but then set it on top of the stone, by way of decoration. A little gift. Flowers I had considered, like last time. But no. Why let them die among the dead? The empty shell was far more fitting. I looked at Ella's choice of words on Bert's grave. Until the day break and the shadows flee away ..... It's clouding over now – greyer. But mostly the sky is very blue. We climbed 150 steps to the top of the Lutyens Memorial that overlooks the cemetery, making me feel very unsafe at the top, but hoping to get a view of the villages where fighting happened for my grandfather. There was certainly a sense of the open expanse, how quiet it is now. There are scraps of informal memorialisation on a very few of the graves – and reading a booklet that reproduced a widow's letter to her dead husband made me fill up, as did reading out one or two others. In all though, there was a sense of letting go lightly. Something rests in peace, but I'm not sure what. The graves, so numerous when we're among them, look like a mere sprinkling from the top of the tower, like delicate lines of pearls laid out on the green. The insignificant dead. Not such a big thing. But it's the personal memorialisation that humanises it all. Bob gave Bert an informal salute as we left.

How did my grandparents' family actually experience so dramatic a change in their everyday lives from 1916 onwards? The sparseness of my papery legacy yields only the few clues set out here. Whether or not Bert returned on leave between February and August 1918, I do not know. What other letters he wrote to his family I cannot say. Only the two sent to Arthur survive, apart from the postcard pencilled to Ella on the train on 14 April 1917.

It was when I had spent time exploring Arthur's subsequent life and his death in action that I wrote the following in the diary of my progress: 'Only at the end does another penny drop. Why were so few letters saved?

Maybe that is the wrong question. Why were Bert's letters to the young Arthur *kept*? Because Ella wanted Arthur to have something of his father when he was older, a trace of the relationship he was bereaved of. Arthur should have had them. Not me.'

4.3 Living with the Legacy of Conflict in Ireland

Carol's parents and her grandparents had experiences of or legacies from World War One, but these were very different to those of Jenny's family.

Carol Ireland has had a long and bloody history of conflict and division dating back many centuries. It was divided mainly along Catholic and Protestant sectarian lines. The six counties that now comprise Northern Ireland were dominated by Protestant and other non-Catholic religions, while the South was mainly Catholic. A brief overview of its history highlights how—since the twelfth century—there have been various forms of English control of Ireland and attempts to unite Ireland with Britain alongside varying degrees of resistance to that control. Several centuries later, in 1541, Henry VIII was recognised as the King of Ireland, but this was soon followed by the rebellion of Irish Catholics. Further attempts in the seventeenth century to impose Protestantism throughout Ireland also met with Catholic resistance. The eighteenth century saw radical reform with the Act of Union, a further attempt to quell rebellion and unite Ireland with Britain. However, it was not until the early twentieth century that a compromise in the form of Home Rule for Ireland was agreed with the British Government. Even so, its enactment was suspended when the outbreak of World War One intervened. It is significant to note that the division in Ireland that is so deeply rooted in its past persists still in many forms and was part of our family legacy.

While the division between religious and geographical groups made it more likely that Unionists, mainly concentrated in the north of Ireland and committed to remaining part of Britain, would have enlisted during

World War One, in reality, just as many Irishmen from either side of the Unionist and 'Republican' divide enlisted. In part, this was because, as mentioned, the Home Rule Bill that was passed despite fierce opposition from Unionists was suspended with the onset of World War One. As a result, despite deeply entrenched divisions, many Irishmen from both sides of the divide served side by side in World War One, 210,000 in all, of whom an estimated 35,000 died. In the absence of conscription for either World War, those men who joined up had volunteered to do so.

As far as I know, none of my father's family were involved in fighting in World War One, something my Uncle George has confirmed. My paternal grandfather, James Gilmour, introduced in Chap. 2, was born in 1881 and would have been 33 at the time of the war. It seems that for him, family life and work would have been his priority. His wife, Margaret (nee Kairns), my grandmother, born in 1887, was a full-time mother of six children, all of whom survived into adult life. At busy times, however, she would have had to help on the land as well and so would have had no involvement in the war effort.

Economically, agriculture in Ireland benefitted from World War One insofar as the difficulties associated with importing food into Britain during the war meant that Ireland could profit from what was called a boom in the market, producing agricultural crops and exporting them to the mainland.

The immediate post-World War One period, however, was a time of internal civil unrest with conflict between the IRA (Irish Republican Army) and the Ulster Unionist Party and other pro-British Protestant groups. Therefore, while men from both sides of this divide fought and died together in the trenches of Europe and elsewhere, the war was followed by fighting *between* them (mainly men) over the imposition of Home Rule. The guerrilla war mounted by the voluntary IRA against the British Government forces in Ireland was an attempt to establish an independent Republican State by force, seen by some as the only way to achieve an independent Ireland. In 1918, Sinn Fein, the left-wing Irish Republican political party, had established an independent Irish Republic in Dublin, but they seemed to have little power. After several years of violence and recrimination, peace negotiations began in the 1920s, although violence continued for several decades with serious eruptions in

1921 and in the 1960s. Given this historical context, being born in 1921 into a Protestant family that was deeply entrenched in the Protestant faith, my father grew up among people who would have been opposed to Home Rule—seeing it as *Catholic* rule: Home Rule was 'Rome rule'.

In the north of Ireland, then, where James, my father, and his ancestors were born, two-thirds of the population were Protestant and one-third Catholic. His family lived in County Derry (Londonderry) in the northeast, one of the six counties that now comprise Northern Ireland. The 1921 census shows a population of 1,264,000 people in these six counties. In World War One, 1356 men out of Londonderry's population of just under 160,000 people were reported to have been killed.

My paternal grandparents lived just outside Kilrea, a small town in County Derry. Historian, John Bradley, highlights how between 1850 and 1921, the year my father was born, most of Ulster (Northern Ireland) remained predominantly rural in contrast to Belfast which was rapidly industrialising.[20] Potatoes were the staple crop in the whole of Ireland, and the loss of the crop due to potato blight over a century before in 1845 and on several successive years had led to starvation and disease with many hundreds of thousands of people dying every year and many emigrating to England, America and Australia. The south and southwest of Ireland were the worst affected. A poor response from the British Government in terms of relief fanned the flames of unrest, especially in the south of Ireland adding to the deep resentment and bitterness against Britain.

As children growing up a century later, we were familiar with knowledge of the potato famine which was a significant part of 'our' history. However, despite the wounds from the famine, the major occupation in rural Ireland continued to be farming, with 70 per cent of the workforce typically made up of family members and less than two-thirds of paid workers permanently employed. This was the life that my dad was born into. His father, James, a gardener by trade, was predominantly employed as a farm labourer. Their daily life at the time of World War One would have involved basic, probably subsistence, living. In correspondence with the Coleraine Historical Society, I was told that many farm labourers moved around from job to job without security of tenure until the district council was persuaded to build cottages for people working on the farms. Each came with an acre of land so that tenants could grow potatoes and vegetables, keep hens or a pig and be relatively self-sufficient. It seems likely that my paternal grandfather might have been one of these tenants, moving from his first marital cottage. Further, during that time and for many years, school leaving age was no later than 14, with most schoolchildren expected to become part of the workforce at busy times such as the harvest.

My grandparents' first family cottage, the ruins of which I visited as a child, comprised a large living room where cooking, eating and any relaxation took place and small attached, bedrooms. My memory is that it was made of stone, whitewashed and called Rose Cottage—which might be a fictional memory—but it certainly still had beautiful, highly scented roses growing around the door. One half of the cottage accommodated farm animals, in their case pigs. Everything was on one level. Certainly with six children, this first cottage would have been very cramped. Later James and Margaret, my grandparents, moved further down the lane, called Cool Hill, to a larger cottage which had some land attached and which was most likely provided to them as tenants by the council. They continued to live there until after my grandfather died in 1959. There was nothing to make life easy insofar as there was no electricity, domestic telephones, running water or sewage. Water would have been collected in buckets, called pails, from a freshwater well with a standpipe, and light provided by oil lamps. I describe visits to this cottage in Chap. 9 and how the lack of running water and electricity persisted.

The sights and smells of their rural life have stayed with me, the oil lamps and the peat fires. I also remember vividly how the water in the white buckets was a pale yellow colour. All cooking was done on an open range in a large fireplace, over a peat fire. People owned part of a peat bog from which they would cut peat, called turf, with a special two-sided spade called a sean. (Currently this use of peat has been banned because of its effects on peat bogs and subsequent damage to the environment.) Laundry would have been done in a sink in the scullery or for people with more outbuildings, a washhouse in one of the outbuildings, with water being boiled on the open fire. Homeworking for women with children was hard, heavy work. More than that, women were expected to help in farmwork with such things as feeding animals, milking cows and rearing chickens. Despite this harsh existence, it seems that people in rural Ireland were better nourished than those in the urban parts, being able to provide food for themselves. Owning a plot of land made a significant difference to their ability to grow food and, subsequently, their nutrition.

The latter would have been very important since this was the pre-NHS era and so any medical needs would have to be paid for and home remedies would have been tried prior to seeing a doctor. Therefore, it was in everyone's interest to keep well, and certainly adequate nourishment would have made a significant contribution to better health. However, despite the introduction of qualified midwives, with the Midwives Act being passed in 1918, for Margaret, my paternal grandmother, her children would have been delivered at home by a local 'unqualified' midwife, called a handy woman. As Chap. 5 highlights, this situation of hard domestic labour for the working classes persisted well beyond the first half of the twentieth century. In Britain, during World War One, public health measures were proposed in order to promote better health, especially welfare drives to reduce infant mortality by such interventions as housing subsidies, the introduction of professional midwifery and free milk in schools. This included Northern Ireland but not the south. Even so it was the 1940s before such welfare reforms were instigated.

4.4   Life in the Industrialised West Midlands

Meanwhile, in 1914 my mother's family led a very different kind of life in a small town in the industrialised West Midlands. Her family history shows that women in previous generations, her maternal and paternal grandmothers, had worked mostly in service, although her mother, Louisa Harriet Appleby, was a barmaid and the daughter of the owners of the public house they lived in. Chapter 2 describes how my maternal grandfather, Frederick William Davis, lived next door and married Louisa in December 1901 when they were both 22. Perhaps, typical of that time for many people, they met, married and lived their lives, locally. Grandad worked as a bootmaker, and, at some point after they started a family, he became self-employed and owned a shoemaking and shoe repair shop.

Grandad's mother, Harriet Davis, born in 1854, was unmarried and, as described, when she was pregnant with Frederick at 25, reputedly the child of her employer, returned from service to live with her parents. Indeed, her own paternal grandmother, Mary Davis, gave birth out of wedlock to a son, her father Edward Davis. This meant that the family name, Davis, was passed down the female line for four generations. Even though Harriet's father was married to her mother, because he was illegitimate, he carried the name Davis. The census shows that he died in the poorhouse at the age of 65 in 1890.

Harriet, my great-grandmother, lived with her son Frederick, my grandad, and her daughter-in-law, Louisa, my grandmother, until she died in 1929. My mother remembered Harriet well, even though she was only six when she died. Grandad Frederick and Grandma Louisa went on to have nine children, one of whom died at birth. Their first-born child, named after his father, was born just over seven months after they were married. So it appears that they too 'had to' get married, as my cousin Barrie has pointed out. My mother, Nellie Davis, their youngest child, was born in 1923, 21 years after her eldest brother, Frederick, and five years after the end of World War One. Louisa, my grandmother, would have been 41 or 42 when she had my mother, by all accounts menopausal. As Chap. 2 describes, Frederick, my grandad, had a reputation for being a traditional Victorian father who ruled the house and dictated what his wife and children could and could not do. Religion was also a feature of their life, and my mother was brought up in the Methodist faith.

Like the Gilmour family, there are no accounts of Davis family members serving in the armed forces in World War One—although at that time in industrialised areas of Britain, women were expected to contribute to the general war effort through factory or land work. My attempts to find out why my maternal grandfather, Frederick, was not called up have yielded no solid information. He was 35 when war broke out but, as we know from the experience of Bert, Jenny's grandfather, older married men were called up as the war progressed. Perhaps, as a bootmaker, he might have been involved in essential war work. His mother, Harriet, remained single and had no further children, so there were no siblings who might have been involved in World War One. Louisa, his wife, had one sister and no brothers. She would have been too tied to the house raising her children and helping in the shop to do factory work. Indeed, married women with children were not expected to do war service.

My mother's family account shows how, like my father's family, they were relatively self-sufficient people, growing their own vegetables in their large garden and rearing rabbits to eat. While rationing was introduced in 1918, it seems that my grandparents, being more self-sufficient despite the family size, might not have been so badly affected. However, there were other dangers to civilians at that time particularly in urban areas. The West Midlands was at risk of being bombed during World War One and in 1916, 70 people were killed in that area by Zeppelin raids—thought to have been aiming for Liverpool. Indeed, in the vicinity of Walsall, close to where my grandparents lived, 35 people were killed.

What both sides of my family shared was a commitment to a self-sufficient lifestyle, with religious faith as an intrinsic part of their upbringing. Although they had suffered little direct harm as a result of World War One, they nonetheless grew up knowing that the world could change dramatically and that a sense of uncertainty had become the norm. Neither my father nor my mother's family appeared to see education as very important, and both expected their children to make a useful contribution to the household as soon as compulsory education ended—for them at the age of 14.

The difference is that the Davis family did not see themselves as working class. Grandad Davis was a business man in that he owned a small shop and his own house. The only photograph I have of him shows him to be very short in stature, quite stocky in build and extremely well dressed, wearing a hat and with a spray of flowers in his lapel. He has a broad grin on his face. I suspect he has no teeth—as he looks rather 'gummy'. He appears in the wedding photo of his daughter Florence, one of my mother's sisters. On the back of the photo the date 1938 is written. My mother, who would have been 15, has her head turned and is laughing and looking at her sister Louie in the background who is also laughing. They must have been sharing a joke. The photograph conveys great joy and happiness. Of relevance here is that it shows they were relatively well off—in that there are two bridesmaids and several bouquets of flowers. It is not the photo of a society wedding, but neither does it show poverty. If I just saw the photo and knew nothing of the people in it, I would say they looked middle class.

This chapter's accounts set the scene for what happened between the two world wars which is what we consider next. It is worth highlighting the similarities and differences in our grandparents' situation and how they impacted upon the fortunes of our parents. For Jenny's ancestors, life was tragically altered by her grandfather's death. For Carol's parents, there were no direct experiences of the consequences of war—other than the way that its more distant ripples affected their consciousness and made them aware of the loss of so many young lives. The Zeppelin raids brought death close at hand to the Davis family, while for the Gilmours, centuries of conflict and fighting in Ireland were an everyday part of life. It is not at all clear if there were more material consequences, other than the impact of rationing and access to food. The absence of young men from the labour market would have been minimal in Ireland—and because Grandad Davis was self-employed, it seems unlikely he would have been affected. The Davis sons seem to have been spared the danger of having to enlist; their eldest son Frederick, being born in 1902, would have been 12 at the outbreak of war. The story now continues in Chap. 5 as we explore family events between the wars.

Notes

1. Taylor, Lou. *Mourning Dress. A Costume and Social History*. London: George Allen and Unwin. (P. 267).
2. Smith, Jenny. 2015. *A Family Affair: The History of the Baker, Baker Department Store in Bristol*. Self-published, unpaginated.
3. Lloyd George. David. 1933–1938. *War Memoirs of David Lloyd George*. London: Nicholson and Watson. Cited in First World War Day One. The Road to War. London: The Guardian and The Observer. (P. 28).
4. www.parliament.uk. Accessed 5 October 2017.
5. Bourke, Joanna. 2014. Women and the Military in World War One. http://www.bbc.co.uk/history/british/britain_wwone/women_combatants_01.shtml. Accessed 13 December 2017.

6. White, Bonnie. *2008. War and the Home Front: Devon in the First World War, 1914–1918.* https://macsphere.mcmaster.ca/handle/11375/16691. Accessed 13 December 2017.
7. Batten, Richard. 2013. *Devon and the First World War.* https://ore.exeter.ac.uk/repository/bitstream/handle/10871/14600/BattenR.pdf?sequence=1. Accessed 13 December 2017.
8. Hudson, Pat. 2011. *Women's Work.* http://www.bbc.co.uk/history/british/victorians/womens_work_01.shtml. Accessed 13 December 2017.
9. Raynor Taylor – Life at Prees Heath Army Camp. http://thegreatwar.whitchurch-shropshire.co.uk/raynor-taylor-life-prees-heath-army-camp/. Accessed 14 December 2017.
10. Remarque, Eric Maria. [1929] 1996. *All Quiet on the Western Front.* London: Vintage. (P. 6).
11. Terraine, John. 1982. *White Heat. The New Warfare, 1914–18.* http://www.longlongtrail.co.uk/how-the-british-artillery-developed-and-became-a-war-winning-factor-in-1914-1918/. Accessed 14.12.17.
12. Photograph of 8-inch Howitzer. Imperial War Museum. http://www.iwm.org.uk/collections/search?query=Q1374&items_per_page=10. Accessed 14.12.17.
13. Prior, Robin and Trevor Wilson. 2004. *Command on the Western Front: the career of Sir Henry Rawlinson 1914–1918.* Barnsley: Pen and Sword.
14. Remarque, Eric Maria. [1929] 1996. *All Quiet on the Western Front.* London: Vintage. (P. 198).
15. Hayward, John. 1930. Memoirs and Diaries – a Casualty Clearing Station. http://www.firstworldwar.com/diaries/casualtyclearingstation.htm. Accessed 14.12.17.
16. Laqueur, Thomas W. 1994. Memory and Naming in the Great War. In *Commemorations. The Politics of National Identity*, ed. John R. Gillis, 150–167. Princeton: Princeton University Press.
17. Bourke, Joanna. 1996. *Dismembering the Male. Men's Bodies, Britain and the Great War.* London: Reaktion Books Ltd. (P. 211).
18. Though Rouvroy-en-Santerre is actually about 27 miles from Amiens, the corroborating evidence suggests that George Bale's guess is simply not very accurate.
19. Song of Solomon, 2: 14.
20. Bradley, John. 1991. The History of Economic Development in Ireland, North and South. *Proceedings of the British Academy*, 98, 35–68, The British Academy, 1991.

5

Family Life Between the Wars: 1918–1931

At this point in our story of war and family life in the twentieth century, Bert, Jenny's grandfather, is dead. Three years later, in 1921, James Gilmore, Carol's father, was born. More than 20 years of peace-time separated the two world wars, yet the intersection of generations lends a continuity to this exploration of our death histories. In addition, of course, World War Two is in many ways an outcome of World War One. Jenny begins now with an account of how her grandmother and two sons responded to their losses—of a husband and father, as well as a business partner and provider.

Jenny I still do not know whether Ella, my grandmother, visited Bert's first grave in Dury or indeed his second one at Villers-Bretonneux where his remains were reburied in 1927. The Philippe Pinel Health Centre at Dury has no records of the people who came to the temporary graves of servicemen who died in their hospital while it was used as a Clearing Station. Nor is there a complete record of visitors to military cemeteries such as the Villers-Bretonneux Military Cemetery. Whatever she did or did not do, I am unlikely ever to know. What I can record—because I stumbled upon it—is that she paid for a Roll of Honour in

St Margaret's Church in Topsham, 'in proud and loving memory of Bert Manning from his wife and sons'. Echoing the words she chose for his second gravestone, the Roll of Honour is headed with a biblical text: 'Greater love hath no man than that he lay down his life for his friends'. Bert's name also appears on the war memorial in St Margaret's churchyard—as well as on the war memorial in the churchyard of St Mary's Church, Brixton, South Devon, where he grew up.

Along with memorialising her husband, Ella had a business to run. In his will, Bert said of his 'business of Draper' that 'she (Ella) shall be at liberty to carry on during such a period as she shall think fit … with power to employ at such salary as she shall think fit any manager of the said business'. This is what she did, while Sarah Annie Harrison, her mother, continued to live with the family and is entered in the 1911 census as a 59-year-old widow of 'private means'. I would dearly love to know more about Ella's early life and understand how her mother came to be living with them in Topsham. I have tried repeatedly to find out why Ella appears to be living apart from her mother when she was four; in the 1881 census, she is listed alongside her grandmother and uncle, both of them teachers, at a school in Harefield, a village on the northwest boundary of London. Yet clearly she was not orphaned since Sarah Annie, her mother, reappears in the census for Topsham in her 50s. Whether Ella's father had died is another matter—but her parents' names, 'Thomas Harrison' and 'Sarah Annie Robinson', pervade the genealogical records, making it very hard to differentiate them without additional information.

To imagine Ella's situation once she was widowed means recognising the care her mother might have provided for Arthur and David, aged seven and four, respectively. Photos of Sarah Annie Harrison show a very elegantly dressed woman in long, heavily embellished clothing with a matching parasol. I realise she is wearing some of what I now think of as 'my jewellery'. I also notice that she is absent from the informal photographs of her daughter, son-in-law and grandsons. Hers are all studio portraits. I believe my father told me that they had domestic help in the house. But no-one outside the family is listed in the 1911 census. In my father's diary entry for 23 March 1930, when he was away at boarding school, it says: 'I wrote two letters, one to Mother and one to Granny.' His use of 'Granny' rather than 'Grandma' hints at a more intimate relationship than her grand photos suggest. But she is not someone he ever spoke about to me.

An advert Ella placed in the Topsham parish magazine in April 1919 indicated her immediate concerns about her livelihood and that of her immediate family. Referring to herself in the third person, she addressed her customers directly, thanking them for their 'support' and, despite having been widowed for only eight months, promises to 'do her utmost to give the very best value and satisfaction'.

The following year, another advert appeared, with 'Mrs F.E. Manning' in large bolded letter, immediately below 'London House'. She was by now, unquestionably, the sole proprietor of the business, selling 'Horrockses Calicoes and Flannelettes, C.B. Corsets[1] and a good assortment of Rugs, Matting, Mats, Curtains and Curtain Nets'.

An oral history from the 1980s, provided by the Topsham Museum, gives a customer's view of her shop. One interviewee said:

> Next door where Underhill's shop is now was Manning's the drapers. This was quite a high class shop, the Mannings looked after it and you could buy almost anything there in the clothing line.

Another one remembered:

> There was Mannings up in the town where Underhills are now, they were the rather posh sort of outfitters shop – ladies outfitters and so on – and this (another drapers in Fore Street, run by Pansie Medley) was more the working class thing. Now, I would go there (to Medleys) and buy something because it was a little bit cheaper than up there, but they were very good.

In my father's 1932 diary, after he had left school and moved away from Topsham, he describes visiting 'Mrs Medley' on occasional visit to the town. So the Mannings and the Medleys were friendly, perhaps each with their own niche in the local market.

5.1 The Armistice and its Aftermath

David was approaching his fourth birthday when the Armistice between Great Britain, Germany and France was signed on 11 November 1918. In September, the German Supreme Army Command had informed Kaiser Wilhelm II that they could no longer sustain the fighting and that the Western Front was about to fall to the Allies. Rather than the surrender of Germany, the Armistice was an agreement that Germany would retreat from all the territories that it had occupied and that it would renounce all its weapons, return all prisoners of war and make reparations at a cost of about £22 billion in today's money, a debt only paid off in 2010. Failure to agree to these terms would result in fresh military action by the Allies. It was six months later, after extensive negotiations, that the Treaty of Versailles was agreed.

Looking ahead to World War Two, as we do in Chap. 6, it is noteworthy that German resentment at the conditions imposed upon the country through the World War One peace negotiations ultimately found its outlet in the invasion of France in 1940. This sense of anger and humiliation is evident in in the potency of the Armistice Carriage that became a symbol of both triumph and humiliation. In 1918, in the hidden location of a private train belonging to Marshal Ferdinand Foch, Supreme Allied Commander, the German delegation had no choice but to sign up to conditions imposed by their enemies. Twenty-two years later, when Adolf Hitler forced France to surrender to Germany, he chose the same railway carriage in which to exact their agreement, a vehicle taken to Berlin during the Occupation of France and displayed as a proud trophy in the Lustgarten, a park in the heart of the city.

International machinations such as these spawn the extraordinary times we are exploring here, chains of events in which thousands of ordinary lives are lost and ordinary people are traumatised. For four-year-old David Manning, the death of his father, aged 37, was nothing out of the ordinary. The memorial Roll of Honour in St Margaret's Church, Topsham, records 69 names from a town barely larger than a village. Yet nearly a hundred years later, in 2014, only 1.3 men per thousand in the UK died around the age of 37. These figures show the vast scale of loss undergone by small boys like my father, especially when compared with what today's children might expect. David and Arthur grew up without the continuities they might have assumed in the everyday world of a small-town draper and his young family.

While Ella was pivotal to his life until she died in 1943, he rarely spoke about his father and, like many men of his generation, tended to be emotionally withdrawn. As I said in Chap. 1, when he visited my young family it was difficult to find much common ground. Historian, Martin Bashforth, links the 'absent father' to '[t]he wider history of family dislocation and dysfunction', adding that 'however that absence might have occurred, [it] is not something affecting isolated individuals. It forms part of the social history of the twentieth century and has profound contemporary resonance'.[2] When he grew up, David took up walking and cycling, like many young people in the 1930s. As hobbies, they were a source of companionship for him almost until his death in 1996. Accounts of his walks were a staple of his interactions with family and friends, rather than any more personal or intimate subject matter. Yet it was during a walk with him towards the end of his life that he said to me, 'You know I do think about my father sometimes and wonder what he was like', a question he may have carried for 70 years and perhaps returned to more frequently as he grew older.

What is there beyond the details of international military relations, genealogical sites and my family's diaries, wills, adverts to take me into the landscape of my father's early childhood? There are books such as Richard van Emden's *The Quick and the Dead: Fallen Soldiers and their Families in the Great War*, which tells me that:

> More than 350, 000 children lost their fathers during the Great War, and the vast majority have themselves since died. … After 1918, the mood was to honour the dead but also to forget the war, to move on and be grateful to those whose noble sacrifice had guaranteed everyone else's life, liberty and freedom. Loss was so general, so communal, that survival was reward enough.[3]

My father and his brother were among that 350,000. van Emden says that the lives of those children were forged 'not only without the guiding influence of a father but all too frequently in the teeth of unremitting and abject poverty'.[4] Yet Bert had left £2008 7 s 5 d [now £128,000 approximately] to my grandmother in his will. This astonishes me, that the family had this kind of wealth. That said, they owned and lived in the large property in the centre of Topsham that housed their shop. Bert also belonged to a profession that took pride in providing for its members' orphaned children. As a result, both his sons were sent to the Warehousemen, Clerks and Drapers' School in Purley, near London, Arthur within a year of his father's death.

This meant that the rupture of Bert's family had happened within a wider context of strong professional continuities. To be a draper, to be a member of the textile trade, was an identity with implications I was unaware of when I began to explore my family's past. The Warehousemen, Clerks and Drapers' School came about in the 1850s when a group of textile warehousemen and clerks met after the death of a colleague to try and save his children from the workhouse. These men, to achieve their jobs and a measure of 'respectability', had all received a 'fair education'. They swiftly resolved that 'a school be founded for the children of deceased and necessitous warehousemen and commercial clerks'. Within the prevailing spirit of Victorian philanthropy, they soon secured voluntary donations from fellow employees, their success then attracting support from the owners of wholesale firms, as well as from Charles Dickens and eventually Lord John Russell. Even the 20 acres in Purley which became the school's first site was provided by the clothing family, Beddington, and in 1863 its foundation stone was laid by Edward VII. As part of his 1898 speech at the annual dinner of the Incorporated Association of Retail Distributors, he described being a draper as 'a dignified calling … essential to the nation's welfare and to the advancement of civilization' (see also Chap. 4). The school's current website makes a connection with Kate Middleton, Duchess of Cambridge, picturing her in the arms of her husband, the future king. When Olive Lupton, Kate's great-grandmother, inherited the textile company William Lupton and Co, Whitehall Mills, Leeds, funds were provided for the school so that 'any orphaned or needy children of Lupton employees would be accepted into Russell School Croydon or Russell Hill Purley'.

Although the school still exists, it has moved from its original premises and operates independently under the name of Royal Russell School. So I cannot visit the rooms my father snapped in sepia with his Box Brownie camera as a schoolboy—photographs that depict him or his brother in school uniform, with Eton collars. But the school archivist is welcoming and there is scope for finding out more. She sends me the date when David became a boarder, aged nine, in June 1924, remaining there for the next seven years. His brother, Arthur, started school in October 1919, aged eight, 14 months after their father died. Arthur left in 1927, after eight years.

These dates might seem stark and impersonal, but they provoke questions. While Arthur was away at school, what did it mean for David to have his mother and possibly grandmother's exclusive attention for five years, from four to nine years old? Certainly, in the studio photo of the family, taken in about 1919 (see Chap. 4), Arthur squares up to the camera while his mother's attention is directed towards David who has his hands in her lap. Or did David feel lonely, as the only child in the house while his bereaved mother was occupied with a business? And what did it mean for Arthur to be away from home so soon after his father's death?

I do know that my father went to Underhills school in Topsham as a small boy. He often told the story of being taught to knit, sitting beside a boy who always dropped his stitches while David 'made' them, ending up with too many. Or was it the other way round? Then there was the story was about the box of 'treasure' he and Donald Gould from the Post Office next door had lowered into the cavity wall of David's house. They would draw it up periodically—until one day the string broke. I think of it lying there, or what remains of it, somewhere in the fabric of 16 Fore Street, Topsham. In the Drapers' School magazine, there is an account of boys lifting a piece of turf from the playing field and burying 'treasure' under it, returning later to unearth it—if another boy had not found it meanwhile. I have a postcard photo from Topsham, taken outside a hotel or pub by an Exmouth photographer. It shows a crowd gathered round a charabanc (an early form of bus, used mainly for pleasure), ready for some kind of outing. There is bright sunshine and a man in a panama hat who seems to be in charge. My father is the small boy, perhaps seven years old, standing at the front of a group of children clustered alongside the vehicle, closest to the camera. Many of the boys are in sweaters or ill-fitting jackets, wearing big 'newsboy' caps. My father stands out in his white shirt, buttoned to the collar, with a tie tucked in behind the S-belt that holds up his shorts. His hair is cut in a fringe, neatly combed, and unlike the two little boys grinning behind him, he eyes the photographer seriously. Another boy, head and shoulders taller, has his hand on David's arm, as if holding him back.

5.2 The School Magazine and the Diaries

Photos like this, along with my memories of my father's small collection of boyhood stories, are a limited resource for recreating his early years after his father had been killed. However, the Drapers' School archivist gives me access to the school magazine since the 1900s. I also have two diaries my father kept. The first is for 1929, a Letts pocket diary with just a line or two for each day. He did fill in the entire year, though his pencilled entries are sometimes too smudged to read. He was 14 at the time. The second diary is a notebook—or the residue of a notebook, without a front cover and only the stubs of its first 20 or so pages. The remaining 34 pages are a diary he kept for March 1930. It measures 12 centimetres by eight and at the beginning he fills two pages per day with neat fountain-pen writing. The last page says THE END and I suspect he went home the next day. After THE END I find more stubs of missing pages and a cardboard cover with a list of numbers added up in pencil. Blank pages, it seems, were never wasted in the Manning family. They remind me that, as a child, discarded envelopes were my drawing paper with a Christmas bonanza of all the envelopes the cards had arrived in.

My imaginings about my father's long journey from Topsham to Purley are fuelled by what I find in these diaries. In the 1929 pocket diary, when he was 14, he notes in the memo space for the week beginning Sunday 13 January, 'I take a 36 bus from Padd[ington] to Victoria and <u>vice versa</u>'. (This was the time he went back to school late after an illness). So his diary does the job that a smart phone might now, by giving him ready access to route. His brother had left school two years earlier and no-one, it seems, accompanies David across London.

From the school magazine I learn more about the status of the textile trade in nineteenth- and early twentieth-century Britain. I begin to get a more nuanced sense of who my father was. Part of his identity resides in my grandfather's turn-of-the-century training in 'the dignified calling' of being a draper at Baker Baker in Bristol. When my father left the Drapers' School and its associations with both royalty and eminent members of the textile and clothing industry—Selfridge, Austin Reed—he followed his parents' path into Baker Baker and from there to the furniture and bedding departments of Robert Sayle, a drapers' store that opened in Cambridge in 1840 and became part of the John Lewis Partnership in 1939. The Partnership's philanthropic orientation towards its staff—its societies, social events and cheap holiday accommodation—was a mainstay of my father's leisure time activities and later his retirement.

The Drapers' School had other influences on the man my father became. In its very early days, pupils had undergone a harsh regime of early morning prayers in their nightwear and punishments that are brutal by today's standards. In a 1924 issue of the magazine, a former pupil wrote of his experiences in 1889: 'My mind went back thirty-five years when, as a boy at Russell Hill, I was one of those trailing up the hill returning to the Schools after the holidays, each with our black bags and sundry parcels, accompanied by our friends ... I recall again the first night in the dormitories, when, I am not ashamed to own, more than one of us sobbed ourselves to sleep under the bedclothes.'

Looking back to my father's own schooldays in the 1920s and 1930s, he would recall a very simple diet with jam on the boys' bread and margarine as a weekend treat. His notebook diary, kept when he was 15, sheds light on his priorities at the time. Certainly his weekends were marred by the prospect of finding out his weekly position in class and being 'reprimanded' or of receiving a 'tanning' on Monday morning if it was poor. Only one tanning—which I presume is slippering or caning—was actually administered during the month he kept his notebook diary, but his pocket diary says 'had a tanning from Pan (teacher's nickname) for drawing in form'. Drawing, it transpires (below), was the one subject for which he received a school prize. He was in detention very regularly, though often as part of a larger group of boys. In his pocket diary, aged 14, he notes on Monday 25 February, 'Another week of detention'. By

Thursday he says, 'In detention from 2 to 3.45. It is getting monotonous'. In later life he spoke of the demands of his school life with a kind of relish. 'It didn't do me any harm', he would say.

But other elements of his adult identity were becoming visible in his brief diary record of schooldays in 1929 and 1930. An acute time awareness, for example, is evident in repeated entries, such as 'Mr Holloway gave an organ recital in the evening from 6.30 to 7.20' and 'I skated from 3.30 to 4.10. I was in detention for Mr Baldwin from 4.20 to 5.0'. On Saturday 16 March 1929, he was in detention again—the precise time is hard to decipher—and says, 'because I looked at my watch I got quarter of an hour extra'. Many of these references seem to be to ad hoc events, yet he records their timing with precision. Much later, when he would visit me and Bob in the early, disorganised days of our marriage, he grew restless if meals or indeed morning coffee and afternoon tea did not appear on time. I can still hear the change jingling in his pocket as he prowled about, waiting. Carol speculates that at a psychodynamic level, it was perhaps an unconscious act insofar as he was recording apparently trivial details in place of what was lost to him, a father and schooling closer to home. Continually noting when activities and events began and ended might have been a form of control that helped stave off potential chaos. Even though his mother appears to have kept the drapery business running smoothly, with the resources of her mother's presence and boarding school for her sons, the emotional impact of widowhood in the flowering of her adult life cannot be underestimated (Fig. 5.1).

Along with the timing of school events, my father also marked off the days before he could go home. His 1929 pocket diary shows that he went back to school late after the Christmas holidays, on Tuesday 15 January, because he was suffering from a hand infection. Two weeks later he prefaces his Tuesday entry with 'Only eight weeks'—and continues counting down the weeks with a similar entry for every Tuesday until he goes home for Easter. When he returns to school on 17 April, he writes the number 104 in the top right-hand corner of the four-line space allocated for that day. From then on, until the summer holiday, he writes the number of days remaining in the same corner of every diary entry. Since the numbers are in pencil, whereas the entries are in ink, he probably pencilled in all the numbers ahead of time, counting out the days before he could go

Family Life Between the Wars: 1918–1931   115

Fig. 5.1 Ella, Jenny's grandmother, with her son David (Jenny's father) on the steps of the Drapers' School

home. What does this tell me about him, living apart from his home and family? What impact did the loss of his father, and its consequences, really have upon his emotional life and sense of self? Few of his feelings or reflections are recorded within either diary's catalogue of events and activities. My attempts to scroll back from the man I grew up with are hampered by the way he kept his emotional life largely private.

His relationship with his older brother is one area that intrigues me. I remember him saying that he had little to do with him because of a four-year age gap. But whether he felt upstaged by him is something I also wonder about. Certainly his brother shone in ways he did not. In the school magazine for 1927, Arthur is recorded as the new sergeant of No. 3 Platoon of the cadet corps (see also Chap. 7). My father never features in the magazine. As mentioned, he reveals worries about achieving a poor position in class in his diary, and the fly leaves of books that the brothers were awarded at Prize Day highlight discrepancies between them: Scripture, Mathematics, Reading and General Proficiency are inscribed on Arthur's books, only drawing for David's. All told, Arthur was awarded 11, compared with David's 5.

The seven years my father spent travelling back and forth from Topsham to Purley did not exclude a home life entirely though. Nor was his life without pleasure. His pocket diary refers to Topsham friends and family with whom he 'had some fun'. Inside the front cover of that diary, there is a pin-up girl of the period, cut out of the newspaper and seen from behind in frilly shorts and a bra. In its personal memoranda section—where I might hope to glean information—he playfully records his weight as one stone two pounds and his height as nine feet ten inches. On 11 August 1929, he records a visit with his mother to Launceston on the border between Devon and Cornwall, also to Yellowmead, his uncle's farm on Dartmoor, and to Gorlofen, another uncle's farm near Brixton. He seems to have stayed on one of his father's family's farms while his mother went home a week later, going to market, to the races, helping a neighbouring farmer with the corn, driving bullocks, cleaning the car, cutting the hedge and weeding the front garden. On 15 August he travels to Plymouth with his cousin, Winnie, and 'brought back a couple of young turkeys'. He also visits Tintagel, Polzeath, Ilfracombe and Clovelly. So it was a holiday and he was taken to a whole range of Devon resorts, presumably in the car he cleaned. I recall their place names from our own family visits to Devon in the 1950s.

By now I can recognise the roots of my father's future life, his hobbies, his sense of identity and belonging. I find him playing ping-pong at school (described in a 1920s issue of the school magazine as 'the latest craze') in a notebook diary entry. Along with Robert Sayle's amateur dramatic society, competitive table tennis featured strongly in his later social life. My mother resented the time it took up, but it was important to him. When Bob, my husband, and I got engaged, my father was recently widowed. We three would socialise—and table tennis was something we could share. His notebook diary also shows him enjoying Gilbert and Sullivan operas while at school, later a feature of my childhood. The family trips he initiated gave me a lasting taste for their lyrics and music. When I look at a map of the area of Croydon and Purley that surrounds his school, I find the place names that feature in his school walks in crocodile pairs: Shirley, Croham Hurst, Featherbed Lane, Selsdon. This careful recording of everywhere he walked recurs in his later walking diaries and, as already mentioned, later still in his distancing conversational style that so often focused on walks he had done.

5.3   The Pathe News Film

Alongside the diaries is a silent 1920s British Pathe News film that records the school's historical connection with the textile trade. Its opening caption reads: 'How the Textile Trade of Great Britain cares for its orphans and war orphans'. The film is grainy grey and I watch it in the knowledge that my father and his brother could be among the boys depicted: in whites applauding on the steps of a cricket pavilion, diving in the school's swimming pool, receiving books as prizes, drilling in strict formation or carrying out exercises, such as co-ordinated leapfrogging, and tending their own garden patches. In his notebook diary my father says on Monday 24 March 1930, 'We drew lots for our gardens and we shall start digging them soon'. On the Wednesday: 'After games I dug my garden'; on the Thursday, 'Dug my garden after a jolly decent cinema in evening'; and on the Friday, 'I dug my garden in the afternoon'. The silent news film puts my father's childhood at a vast distance from my here and now. But his personal record of digging his garden, day after day, helps close the gap.

I also achieve a degree of proximity via the school prizes, already mentioned. These are the 16 leather-bound editions of books such as *Westward Ho!*, *Twenty Thousand Leagues Under the Sea*, *The Three Musketeers* and *The Swiss Family Robinson* that sit, in alphabetical order of author, among the novels on my bookshelves. The school motto is embossed in gold on the front cover: 'Non Sibi Sed Omnibus'. Translated as 'Not for oneself but for all', it fits the silent images of synchronised bodies. As noted, my father received his five books as a prize for drawing on 12 July 1930, a year before he left the school. Among what is now *my* collection, boys' adventure stories are prominent: Sir Walter Scott, Captain Marryat.

As a child these books seemed too grown-up for me. They lacked appeal with their tales of men and boys' derring-do. What I did read avidly were my father's *Just William* books, stories full of fun characters I could get to know. I recall trying to pace my reading, rather than hungrily going onto the next chapter. Trying to make the Christmas book last was what my father had done, he said, when he received a new book every year. Only two of them bear an inscription though: 'D.G.Manning, Christmas 1926' and 'To David, Christmas 1928, From Mother'. He would have been 12, and then 14.

The school-prize books lined the walls of my parents' home and now mine, the backdrop of my life. I have read none of them, though I relished the drama and savagery of George Cruickshank's illustrations in Arthur's copy of *The Pilgrim's Progress*. I wonder if my father and his brother pored over the tissue-thin pages and the tiny fonts. Or whether the books' purpose was otherwise served, the bookplates glued to marbled endpapers demonstrating to parents the school's prestigious patrons, the draper luminaries who handed out the books in person: Lady Lloyd George, Lady Skinner, Austin Reed Esq.

To sum up then, I am surprised to find so many continuities in my father's life, to discover what it meant to be part of the draper's trade and how enduring and all-encompassing this had been for my father. I am also taken aback to find the activities and practices that shaped and coloured my childhood have roots in my father's life as a war orphan.

Maybe my recognition of them derives from a certain tone or atmosphere that pervaded my childhood, one spent among the belongings of several generations of my paternal family. Something indefinable hangs about the leather-bound school prizes, the photo albums and diaries, the weight of a past that intrigued me, yet to which I could not belong. From the hindsight of later life—and years of academic research and writing in Death Studies—I am aware that the continuities of my father's life had their costs. The practice of intimacy was largely withheld from my schoolboy father. When his brother and mother later died on the same day in November 1943, it is hard to imagine how he felt. The sequences of losses he experienced and their interpersonal consequences diminished all our lives. They were extraordinary events yet somehow absorbed or muffled by my paternal family's professional situation, their membership of the textile trade. The particularity of all this needs to be recognised in any attempt to understand the large-scale muting of anger and grief during the last century. Broader-brush representations of 'that generation of men' or 'the brave new world' of the 1940s Welfare State are a place to begin, but it is the specificities of family life that show an emotional regime coming into being and lived out.

5.4 Family Life in the Gilmore Household

While Arthur and David Manning were regularly setting off from home for boarding school between 1919 and 1924, James Gilmore was born—on 11 June 1921 near to Kilrea in County Derry, Northern Ireland. As the young Mannings moved away from their grandparents' agricultural environment, travelling from South Devon to Purley each term, James remained very much part of his family's life in his early years. In Chap. 4, Carol provided the context of life in Northern Ireland and her father's birth into sectarianism. She continues here.

Carol When we were growing up, we were aware of the divide between the north and the south of Ireland—and the deeply entrenched prejudice within my father's family against 'the Catholics'. I am sure I had no understanding of this and certainly no way of judging for myself the rights and wrongs of the situation, so just took it for granted that this was how it was.

Looking at the history of Ireland in Chap. 4, it is clear that my father was born at a time of partition and civil war—in 1921/1922—although it was not until 1948 that the Irish Free State was granted full independence from Britain. It coincided with my parents leaving Ireland to live in England after the war.

Though Belfast had urbanised rapidly, Ulster remained predominantly rural with farming as the major occupation for as many as two-thirds of the population. Yet there was little secure employment and after World War One few had formal educational qualifications and therefore were left dependent on farm labouring.

During World War One there was no rationing, and food was in plentiful supply because the system that allowed tenant farmers land—as was the case for Dad's parents—meant they could grow enough food to feed themselves as well as working the land for their landowning employers. So for Dad, growing up in Northern Ireland meant being part of a family that mainly lived off the land. Chickens ran freely and James Gilmour, my paternal grandfather, grew all their vegetables. They ate well and lived within a strong local community, where neighbours called in freely, without even knocking at the door. Granddad James was a gardener, but his main income was from farm labouring. My uncle, George, told me recently that their parents were very strict and they had to do as they were told. However, Dad had also told me once, when sympathising with my reluctance to return to school after a break, that he hated school and played truant much of the time. In 2017, I visited his old home and the school he attended. Called Cullycapple School, its setting is entirely rural, in Aghadowey, Coleraine, just over seven miles from Dad's home. I recall him telling me about having to walk there but that he mostly just climbed trees and played in the fields.

The tradition of the local community contributing to the harvest labour continued for many years and was still the case when we went on holiday and the dates coincided with the harvest. Indeed, I found it very different from home life and exciting. Much of the work was carried out by hand and many years later, when I lived in a cottage in England with my first husband, Stuart Komaromy, Dad came and scythed the very large overgrown garden with what seemed consummate ease. My dad and his family also attended church every Sunday and paid a fee for their pew, an accepted part of being a member of the church. His whole childhood would have been steeped in religion and an unquestioning belief in the Protestant faith—but he was also indoctrinated into the ills of Catholicism, a prejudice that stayed with him all of his life and emerged as what I interpreted later to be irrational bias. The Gilmour family also belonged to the Orange Order, established in 1798, which is a Masonic-style order. It is fundamentally a sworn allegiance to the Protestant faith, named after the Dutch William of Orange who was victorious in the Battle of the Boyne, fought in 1690 against James II. It secured the Protestant ascendancy in Ireland. This battle continues to be celebrated on 12 July each year, and attendance at Orange Day parades often dictated the date of our holidays for many years so that we could attend the big parade in Londonderry and wave small Union Jack flags. As I look back, I am shocked by the unquestioned dimensions of all this. It is not surprising though, given the quality of education that my father would have received when he did attend school. I cannot imagine that values like balance and an ability to critically evaluate situations and events would have been part of his education.

The differences between the upbringing of our two fathers, James and David, are very stark. Growing up in rural Ireland with very little hope of a future that would take my dad out of subsistence living, and with no educational qualifications, contrasts sharply with the higher value placed on education by David and Arthur's parents, mainly their widowed mother and grandmother after their father died. In terms of parenting skills, I am aware that my father adored his father and had a close relationship with him. My memories from childhood holidays are that Dad and his siblings believed George to be their mother's favourite. I have shreds of fragile memories that it was because he was believed to be the most pious in terms of his faith. However, this was always considered to be a misreading of George by their mother, since his siblings thought that he was not as solidly devout as he appeared to her. The sibling rivalry for their mother's approval continued well into their adult lives. On reflection, it seems that my father might have modelled himself on his father's parenting—and he was an incredibly kind and gentle man. Here I am speculating on the basis of how they were together; they seemed to have an implicit understanding often shared in talks about Grandad's garden. Perhaps unlike Jenny's father, my Dad was shown a great deal of warmth and affection by his father. It may even be the case that because his parents seemed to be estranged from one another, Grandad James and my father had an even closer bond.

5.5   The Route to Brighton

If Jenny's father and uncle grew up in very different circumstances from those Carol describes for James, all three of these men nonetheless underwent a profound rupture in the otherwise predictable patterning of their lives as a result of World War Two. David and James had set up new families by the end of that war, but the losses and the trauma that it, and the previous war, had inflicted became woven into the ways of life that were played out within those new families. As Chap. 1 explained, these were the backgrounds we each of us brought to our meeting in Brighton in 1995. In what follows Jenny goes on to describe the years leading up to 1939 and what this meant for her father and late uncle.

Notes

1. C.B. corsets were manufactured by Charles Bayer.
2. Bashforth, Martin. 2012. Absent Fathers, Present Histories. In *People and their Pasts. Public History Today*, ed. Paul Ashton and Hilda Kean, 203–222. Basingstoke: Palgrave Macmillan. (P. 217).
3. Van Emden, Richard. 2011. *The Quick and the Dead. Fallen Soldiers and their Families in the Great War*. London: Bloomsbury. (P. 4).
4. Van Emden, Richard. 2011. *The Quick and the Dead. Fallen Soldiers and their Families in the Great War*. London: Bloomsbury. (P. 4).

6

War in Prospect, 1930–1939

By the end of the last chapter we saw the lives of the three men later caught up in World War Two beginning to diverge. As a young man, James Gilmore remained within a rural economy that largely replicated the worlds of his parents and predecessors. Arthur and David Manning, though, had left behind the agricultural environments of their paternal grandparents and uncles. Sent away from their mother, the boys acquired a middle-class education as war orphans. World War One had cost the life of their father and left their mother in sole charge of the family draper's business. Through the experiences of Arthur and David in the brief period before another world war impinged, we now explore the opportunities that opened up for them and the choices they made.

6.1 The Great Outdoors

The employment Arthur and David found after leaving school removed them entirely from the land. But outside working hours they became part of a growing trend towards walking and cycling in the countryside. In Germany, from the mid-1890s, a whole movement had encouraged young people to shake off urban social constraints through *Wandervogel* (transl. wandering bird) or rambling in nature. Freedom, independence and a spirit of adventure were seen as its positive outcomes, underpinned by a view of nature that derived from nineteenth-century Romanticism. In 1909, Richard Schirrmann (1874–1961), a school teacher, also founded the Youth Hostels Association (YHA), an organisation that afforded young people cheap, mainly rural accommodation that let them to wander from place to place. In parallel Robert Baden-Powell (1857–1941) had set up the Boy Scouts Movement in Britain, following the 1908 publication of *Scouting for Boys*.

By the mid-1930s, however, when Arthur and David's lives were mirroring this trend, *Wandervogel* was outlawed in Germany as bourgeois, elitist and selfish. In its place the National Socialists, under Adolf Hitler, formed the overtly militaristic Hitler Youth programme. The desire for a healthy body remained, but as an icon of the Hitler Youth and a Nazi belief in the genetic supremacy of the German peoples. Drill, discipline and hardness were its characteristics, rather than an individual sense of freedom and adventure.

In England, by the time Arthur and David left school (in 1927 and 1931, respectively), the Youth Hostels Association was firmly established with 75 hostels already open by the early 1930s. Yet as Chap. 7 describes, youth movements of this kind became radically divided, leading to very different outcomes and a military conflict that was to subsume the entire world. Compared with James Gilmore, Arthur and David's work was overwhelmingly sedentary—banking and drapery. Yet their weekend horizons stretched beyond the confines of the office and shop in a form of leisure that for David reinforced a lifetime's commitment to rambling. Jenny takes up the story.

6.2 Leaving School, Leaving Topsham

Jenny Aged 16, my father left the Drapers' School on 31 March 1931. The previous year, on 4 November, my grandmother paid a premium of £300 for a year's insurance with the Sun Insurance Office, Century House, Lockyer Street, Plymouth. It was for the storage of 'Household

Goods and Personal Effects' in Messrs. Brock's Furniture Storing Warehouse, 43 Preston Street, Exeter. She was packing up the contents of 16 Fore Street, Topsham, the address my father still hoped he was going home to in 1996 when he was ill, confused and soon to die. But already by 1930, the 20 or so years the Manning family had spent at this address were coming to an end.

In a photo album I believe my grandmother compiled, two photos are glued either side of the words 'David in the Sitting room', written in white ink on the black page. Underneath she has written, 'Taken during Xmas holidays 1931'. My father looks about 17, studiedly serious. Reading a book, he poses below a deep wallpaper frieze of foliage garlands, beside him, a mantelpiece with a pair of decorative vases, one of which survives on a window sill in my house. In the second photo, his book is laid out on an occasional table I remember from my parents' home and which I kept for a while. We sawed off the lower half of its barleycorn legs in the 1960s, to make a coffee table.

I have another photo of that sitting room in my own album. I assumed it was taken in their Topsham home. Scrutiny of the dates in my grandmother's album, along with her insurance policy, suggests I was wrong. This is the sitting room in the new house she has bought in Hampden Road, Bristol. The suite is covered in a jazzy 'modernist' fabric and there are satin cushions on the chairs. Another of her albums has a photo of the frontage of 27 Hampden Road at the bottom of the very last page, which is also the inside of the cover. Frustratingly the thick black paper is badly worn away. I am sure, though, that she has written 'Dream House' underneath it, in her white ink copperplate. (She has given slightly whimsical captions to other photos in this album, for example, 'Feeding time at Newquay' under a picture of Uncle Jim, her brother-in-law, with a Cornish pasty in his hands). Maybe my grandmother never felt her accommodation above the Topsham business was a proper home. It had no garden. But I had never considered this possibility. Her Fore Street house looks so grand— or 'flamboyant', as the 1971 Topsham survey describes it. Even before this, though, during the eight years prior to her marriage in 1909, she was living in a hostel in Charlotte Street, Bristol, along with 63 other female draper's assistants from Baker Baker. For most of her adult life, then, up until her mid-50s, she had never had what might be called a 'proper' home, with gardens at the back and front. A home not associated with business.

When my father left school at Easter 1931, it seems he came back to a different city and a new house. My grandmother's insurance premium was reduced to 6 s per annum on 24 April 1931, a month after his schooling finished. All his family's household goods and personal effects were now in the Hampden Road house, and in a diary for 1932, he gives this as his address. It may be that up till then my grandmother had a considerable body of family papers, the letters she received from Bert while he was in France, for example. This move felt like a fresh start perhaps and she chose to keep only certain items.

From my father's first diary entry, on New Year's Day 1932, I see he is now employed by Baker Baker, the wholesale and retail drapers where his parents first met. I can only speculate on how the family's decision to move back to Bristol came about. It may be that my grandmother was ready to give up her business at this point—she was nearly 55—and perhaps longed to go back to where she has spent her early adulthood. Equally an apprenticeship at Baker Baker was probably an almost taken-for-granted employment opportunity for my father. It is hard to know whether these were the factors in play and, if so, which of them was foremost. I do remember an observation of hers that my father often repeated, that once you turn 60 your health troubles begin.

This chapter describes the inroads I managed to make into the eight years of my father's life between 1931 and 1939, years about which I knew little. I do not recall us ever going to Bristol as a family, unlike Exeter where my mother's sister and her husband, my father's old friend Donald, lived with their two sons. As I began, most of what was available to me were 23 postcards of youth hostels, along with a pile of small snapshots of men in thick socks and plus fours. They clustered in smiling groups, mainly in the West Country and the Lake District. Sometimes there are women too, in argyle socks and jackets with lapels or high-neck sweaters. These are stylish women who would not look out of place today on an upmarket knitting pattern. I have not stuck these images into my family album because I recognise no-one in the groups, apart from my father and sometimes his brother, Arthur. I also have my father's membership card for the Youth Hostels Association, dated 1939. The wardens of the hostels where my father stayed have stamped their hostel's name into a grid printed inside the card. The list begins on 11 February that year with 24 entries across the next six months—ending in August 1939. Somerset hostels, Minehead, Batheaston and Wookey Hole, appear more than once.

My father was an enthusiastic youth hosteller and there would have been previous cards, I am sure. Maybe he kept this one because it has eight blank spaces where more hostel names could be entered. But a month after the last stamp, war was declared on Germany by Britain and France. There is a second YHA card, but not issued until nearly 20 years later, in June 1958. I remember him persuading my mother that we could go youth hostelling as a family, in Derbyshire. I was 12 at the time. It was a mixed success, raining most of the time and my mother not enjoying it, though whether that was about more than the rain I am not sure.

On 1 December 1939, aged 24, my father was also issued with a green pass card by the Air Raid Precautions (ARP) service, set up in 1937 to monitor the black-out in homes and commercial premises, to direct people to air raid shelters and to help rescue people caught in bombing raids. Though wardens were meant to be at least 30, many younger people, such as my father, were taken on. At its peak there were 131,000 air raid wardens, 20,000 of them women. As Chap. 7 explains, just over six months later on 21 June 1940, my father was conscripted into the RAF. This meant leaving home for another six years of institutional life. By the time he was 31, he had spent 13 years mainly outside his family home as a result of war, close to half his life at that point. Though he was not actively involved in World War One and spent World War Two teaching aircraft recognition in Bedfordshire and Lincolnshire RAF camps, his childhood and early adult years reveal the less obvious impacts of war on family life and relationships. Here, though, I begin with his early days of grown-up life in Bristol.

6.3 Reading Between the Lines

Adolescence is often seen as a time of betwixt and between when someone like my father has left boyhood behind and yet is barely an adult. He was also betwixt seven years of institutional life, seeing his mother only on holidays, and a subsequent domestic life shared very closely with her. I find myself feeling protective towards him as he undertakes 'grown-up' employment yet seems still to be completing his childhood. It is as though I am attributing him with the vulnerability of a liminal participant in a rite of passage, someone who only in due course can emerge as a full-blown member of a society.[1]

As he began his apprenticeship at Baker Baker in 1931, World War One was more than a decade behind him. Yet by the end of the 1930s, the direction of his life was again shaped profoundly by war. What is apparent from his schooldays though are the continuities as well as the ruptures that formed his early years. Being a draper was an identity his father had claimed for himself when he left the family farm. It informed my own father's sense of self as he became a pupil at the Drapers' School, going on to work in Baker Baker, the Bristol wholesale draper.

As I have said, there is little information about my father's adolescent years, apart from anonymous walking photos, two photo albums his mother made and a diary and a walking journal he kept. My response to these materials reflects my own adolescence in the 1960s. As the only child of parents with troubled pasts—my father's loss of his entire family of birth, my mother's artist father who failed to generate a secure family income—I grew up in a very protective environment. I also, perhaps, took on my parents' wariness of what the world might throw up. What I now read out of my father's challengingly detailed accounts of the minutiae of his everyday working and leisure life are parallels of my own fear of never finding my way out of the humdrum of homework, girl guides and church—and into the full excitement of Cambridge life in the 1960s.

My father's eye for detail, his recording of the times when things begin and end, suggests a concern about exercising control in a world he did not feel at home in, particularly at school. His mother's diary for 1943 also notes the time whenever air raid alerts sounded. They were small business people, accustomed to keeping careful account, but were they business people shadowed by a sense of loss that perhaps had to be overcome for the sake of that business? In what follows, I give a flavour of the fine grain of my father's recordings of his life, as well as the constrained nature of his working and social worlds.

6.4 The Mannings at Home

27 Hampden Road, Knowle, Bristol, is another of my family's homes I have visited, albeit remotely, with the help of Google's Street View. I look at the property on screen, caught in the sunshine of the early twenty-first century, and then compare that image with the 1930s photo in my album. The latter shows the front of a late nineteenth-century, three-bedroom terraced house with wrought iron railings and a gate. The gate is gone now, and only knee-high brick walls separate its strip of front garden from the road and the adjacent house. Its elegant railings will have been removed for munitions in the intervening war. Probably, like nearly three-quarters of the iron railings and gates taken away, they were reputedly never used, just dumped out of sight of the public. The original sash windows are also missing, along with the moulding around them. When I look on the A–Z, I see that Hampden Road is just one street away from Arnos Vale Cemetery, an historic site that featured in my much later life as a Death Studies academic. Estate agents' photos for properties on Hampden Road reveal expansive views towards the wooded cemetery landscape from the back of these houses.

In my 1930s photo, the front of the house is almost unpeopled. Just the tiny figure of my father, standing inside the front gate, looking at the strip of garden in front of their house. Behind him a striped canvas curtain appears to screen the hall. Presumably the front door has been left open. A similar curtain is visible in the doorway of the adjoining property. Deep shadows suggest it is summer.

David and Arthur were entering adulthood at this point. Again, I turn to photos. Two in particular show each of the young men standing alone in Broomhill Lane in Clutton, a village eight miles south of their Bristol home. They are wearing improbably large trilby hats, suits, collars and ties. They even have walking canes. Arthur carries off the outfit—he has a larger face, more prominent bone structure. But David looks like a woman in drag, with his round, boyish face. Another photo is labelled, 'Taken at Bridgewater during Staff Outing'. David is there at the far end of a lineup of men in front of a large coach. He is a head shorter than most of them. But still wearing that big trilby hat, though most of the men are bare-headed.

Arthur by now is 20 and employed by the Westminster Bank in Wellington (now the NatWest Bank), over 50 miles southwest of Bristol, not far from Taunton. He began there in 1928, a year after leaving school. Established in 1836, the Westminster Bank was expanding fast at this time, mainly by acquiring other banks. Its paid-up capital—the amount of money received from shareholders in return for shares—had risen from £9 million in 1923 to £40.5 million in 1935. These dates encompass the period when Arthur worked for them, moving between different branches in Somerset every few years: in 1933 he left the Wellington branch for the bank in Bridgewater; then from 1935 to 1937, he was in the Exeter branch; and finally, between 1937 and 1939, he was in the bank in Langport. He had lodgings in Drayton at this point, about three miles from Langport—and around 50 miles from Bristol. But more of this to come.

The NatWest Bank's archivist has no information about the positions he held, but he must have been making his way up the banking hierarchy. As my father's diary shows, Arthur would come home from Wellington to Bristol on the same train every last Saturday of the month, returning to his lodgings on Sunday. Regularly, my father and/or grandmother met Arthur from the train and saw him off afterwards. He turned 21 that year and fortuitously his birthday fell on the last Saturday of the month. The two brothers and their mother sat up late that night, until 12 midnight. They were playing *Sorry*, a board game not unlike *Monopoly* that came onto the market in the early 1930s. It seems a very low-key celebration, reminiscent of those of my childhood. Equally, being together with their mother was obviously important for these two young men.

6.5   Out to Work

I have information about my father's job in the wholesale department of Baker Baker Department Store in Bristol from two sources: his Collins Gentleman's Diary for 1932—which he filled in fairly consistently until 14 August that year—and a short history of Baker Baker compiled by local historian, Jenny Smith, in 2015. My father's diary finally peters out on the 14th anniversary of Bert's death. There is no mention of his father, neither here nor in any other of his diaries. His mother too makes no reference to Bert in the one diary of hers that I have—for 1943.

My father would have been employed in Baker Baker's premises in the High Street and Wine Street area of the city, long associated with the drapery business in Bristol. The trade evolved there first as a by-product of the local woollen industry. In 1872 the company was known as Baker, Baker & Co. Warehousemen and Drapers. Already it had two branches in Bristol, one wholesaling to drapery and department stores throughout the southwest of England—known as the warehouse—and one retailing. Retailing seems to have been carried out in buildings in Wine Street and Bridge Street, the Wine Street frontage being modernised in 1909 with continuous windows behind free-standing pillars. The company also had a building in Mary-le-Port Street, and this may be where my father worked most of the time.

None of these buildings are standing today, after the Luftwaffe's bombing raid destroyed all the company's premises in the Blitz of 14 November 1940. Only the hostel for its female staff in Charlotte Street—where my grandmother lodged before marrying Bert—remained intact. The wholesale business operated from there until the 1950s. Taken over subsequently by companies such as Courtaulds, which later shifted their business outside Europe, Baker Baker eventually went into receivership and closed in 1991. Online, I access street-level photos of Wine Street in the 1920s and 1930s. Less than a hundred years have passed, yet Wine Street has an almost Dickensian quality, heaving with activity, pedestrians all in hats and long coats spilling out over the road, little traffic visible. It is all busyness, the complex shop frontages crowded with signage. I picture what my father refers to in his diary as 'an Unemployment

Demonstration' taking place there on 12 April 1932. Eight years later all this had gone. Photos of Wine Street after the Blitz show nothing but a wreckage of heaped rubble and tottering buildings, a whole world of commerce obliterated. The images are a reminder that family life during two World Wars was shaped not just by the death or emotional wounding of parents. Even the everyday need to go out and buy a piece of elastic, or the occasional pleasure of choosing new corsets, brought the risk of violent destruction.

Among the online images of Wine Street is an advert for The Cadena café at number 14. The Cadena Company had grown up in the southwest of England after 1895. In May 1924 the *Western Daily Press* reported that the cafe had expanded their Wine Street premises to include a 'grill room' for gentlemen only. In his 1932 diary, my father says 'Had dinner in City with Mother at Cadena' on 7 June. He had also been there for tea on 29 April and previously on 29 March, the same day he went to the King's Cinema, Old Market Street, in the afternoon, to see *Friends and Lovers* and *Waiting for the Bride.* Just as he constantly notes the time in his schooldays' diaries, so he systematically records the time he finishes work and the time he goes to bed. Leaving work later than 5:30 pm appears to be resented, particularly if it is caused by the arrival of late customers. On 17 June he says: 'Hot day. We were behind with orders. They were not sent off until 4.30. Left work 6.50. My holidays begin.' The next day he and his mother were on the train to Launceston, to visit the rest of his father's family and for David to help harvest hay. I find a sense of release in these words, an echo of my own exhilaration as I left school and Cambridge behind for the prospect of the red hills and sandy beaches of South Devon.

But what was my father's working day like? In some ways, mysterious. His diary entry for New Year's Day 1932 says: 'We have been dressing out the squad after stock taking. Sold a fair amount of job stuff in the afternoon, so were entering sales all afternoon. ... Left work at 5.30.' It is hard to picture what he was doing, but Paul Baulch, who worked at Baker Baker in the 1950s, tells me: 'Dressing out seems to mean displaying the samples on stands or dummies. We used to call stuff bought in cheap (end of lines etc) and stock that wasn't selling Job stuff.' Another term that is unfamiliar to me, but mentioned a number of times, is 'town travelling'. I assume it refers to taking samples out to retail drapers in the city. Not something my father was doing himself. Certainly Baker Baker produced an enormous catalogue of their wares that was widely distributed. As Jenny Smith describes: 'the BB Spring Catalogue of 1912 ... 640 pages long, it was sent out to retail drapers and haberdashers'.

To set the scene for my father's working day, I try to imagine the interior of a wholesale drapers in the 1930s. He mentions Baker Baker's millinery and hosiery departments in his diary, but according to Jenny Smith, a wholesale store was 'the mirror image of a department store ... except that everything was sold in dozens or by the gross'. Other departments, she says, included 'grey calicos, china, cocoa mats, belts and trimmings, corsets and baby linens, tapestries and floorcloths, waterproof cloaks and electro-plated cutlery, toys, hats, and linoleum'. A veritable emporium materialises as I read this list.

On 8 March 1932, my father is paid and promised a rise in April. His entries make it clear that he has an apprenticeship, for he says: 'Most of the apprentices were moved. I was moved to Y dept.' But what was Y department? Though he never says specifically that he is working in wholesale, his tasks suggest days spent behind the scenes, rather than as a member of customer-facing retail staff who, Jenny Smith says, observed a strict dress code: black dresses and stockings for women and no jewellery; black jackets and pinstripe trousers for floorwalkers (supervisory staff). My father, however, seems to spend his time grappling with large quantities of wholesale stock: 'A lot of curtain net came in in the morning so we were kept busy unloading' (2 January). Two days later: 'A lot more curtain net came in', and the following day, 'more Spring stuff came in'. Then, 'marked a lot of laces which took me all the afternoon' (11 January); 'Had a job of sorting corsets all the afternoon' (15 March); 'I have been sewing tickets on corsets nearly all day' (4 April); 'Continued to sew on tickets for travellers samples' (7 April). This is not to say that there were no customers—but these would have been owners and buyers from smaller retail business. If they came in near the end of the working day, they were unpopular, as mentioned. But mostly my father describes his days as 'very quiet', a term he used throughout his working life to refer to the amount of business done.

His record reminds me of Saturdays and school holidays in the 1960s that I spent in the stockrooms of a Cambridge food store, aged about 14 or 15. Boxes and boxes of washing powder, tins of soup and beans, all needed marking with their price, using a rubber stamp on the end of a black plastic wand I pressed repeatedly into an ink pad. Bar codes lay in the future and even self-service was only just coming in. I would sit alone among the vast cardboard boxes piled up in stockrooms above the store, wondering if my (social) life would ever begin. Outside in Cambridge market place, young women in duffle coats, black stockings and winkle pickers inhabited an exotic beatnik era, backcombing their hair into extravagant French pleats. Only occasionally did I get to weigh, bag and price loose glace cherries and sultanas on a shared stockroom counter, much more interesting work and a chance to escape my solitude.

Perhaps my father had more company. He usually says '*we* were kept busy …'. But not always. I am pleased when someone's name is mentioned occasionally, particularly if it is linked with a social activity: 'I walked home with Silvey in the evening' (19 January); 'Parfrey was moved to Hosiery (temporarily) (11 March)'; 'Helped Parfrey with Bathing Suits. Also went to tea with him at Cadena' (29 April); 'Parfrey in K' (6 May). But mainly his entries evoke the boredom of my teenage days, of work made up entirely of repetitive tasks and little by way of a social life to look forward to. For a very junior and therefore deployable member of staff, the chance of company leading to friendship can depend entirely upon where you happen to be needed at any point in time.

6.6 Mother and Son

What was my father's scope for an adult social life when he 'got out' of work (as he normally put it), around 5:30 pm? I sense that he enjoyed his evenings and weekends, but in ways that still left him hovering between boyhood and adult independence. His mother—for so long a holidays-only presence—appears to be his main companion. Working on the house and garden he shares with her is mainly what he documents. I see 27 Hampden Road slowly taking shape through his 1932 diary entries: 'After tea Mother and I put up a new clothes post in the garden. Finished about 9.30 pm' (19 January); 'Put up shelves in the bathroom in evening which took us until about 11 o'clock' (22 March); 'Put up curtain rods in kitchen also cleaned out small kettle. We put up one of the curtains' (4 April); 'Cut paper and frieze for kitchen in evening' (12 April); 'Papered kitchen. Started 2 o'clock, finished 11 o'clock. Altered the clock' (16 April). On 18 April he is hanging pictures in the kitchen and two days later making a boot cupboard. Then on 22 April, he is painting the scullery until 11:30 pm. He also refers to fitting a ventilator in 'my' shed plus a padlock; and he is buying seeds, cutting the lawn and painting the railings.

So he and his mother seem to operate as a team, though the dynamic between them is not obvious. On the one hand, he undertakes the tasks of a head of household; on the other, Ella seems to be in charge, with David as her obliging handyman. When they are not busy fixing up the house, they are playing games together ('Played crib[bage] and faro [Victorian card game] in evening. Mother won both'). Sometimes she meets him after work, and they go shopping or take tea at the Cadena; sometimes she meets him during his breaks. These details remind me of trips into Cambridge with my mother when something like an item of school uniform had to be bought. She found them challenging, and many visits to the toilet preceded our walk from home to the bus stop. Once in town though, my father met us in the tea shop near Robert Sayle, the John Lewis shop where he worked. To me the tea-shop environment seemed luxurious. My father seemed under no pressure to get back to work, as might now be the case. I would be given half a meringue, always wanting a whole one. Too rich, they said.

On Sundays in Bristol, my father invariably went for a country walk, and again, these seem to involve his mother: 'Took a bus to Avonmouth and walked along toward Henbury then down through Coombe Dingle where we had tea and on to Westbury to church' (7 February 1932). Arthur walks with them on his monthly visits. In the late 1930s though, when my father would go off on bike rides and, I suspect, his mother's arthritis was worsening, Arthur and she would go out together in his car.

In the early 1930s, though, my grandmother not only shared and indeed provided a lot of my father's leisure; she also took charge of his health. On 2 January 1932, he says, 'I have got a cold coming, but Mother is giving me Owbridges [lung tonic] so hope it will cure it.' Detailed recording of his health characterises the diary, along with the time when work or an evening activity finishes. On 10 February he says, 'I am not feeling quite O.K.' and after work the next day, 'Went to the Doc in evening to get some medicine for my cold. Had to wait an awful [long] time'. The next day, a Friday, he stays off work and just sits by the fire, but by Saturday, he is in bed and being visited by the doctor who diagnoses flu ('Mother slept in a chair in my bedroom', 13 February). The doctor is back on Monday and says he can get out of bed the following day—which he only manages by tea time. He stays in his bedroom all of Wednesday, but on Thursday he comes downstairs, albeit walking with a stick. He has a doctor's appointment on Friday, but his mother goes on his behalf because the weather is so cold. He is back at the doctor's on Monday for a prescription—plus, 'Mother went out in the afternoon. She bought "SORRY" which we played in evening. Also Ivory Castle [a 1930s version of Snakes and Ladders brought out by Gibbs, the toothpaste company, to advertise their products].' Finally, after two weeks of illness, he goes back to the doctor on Friday 26 February and is signed off as fit for work. Whether they had health insurance, available since Lloyd George introduced it in 1911, is not recorded. But if not, the concern my father records about his bout of illness must partly reflect its costliness in medical fees.

Illnesses do feature in all my father's diaries. As a child I recall my father suffering from catarrh, sitting over a bowl of steaming Friar's Balsam [an inhalant] with a towel over his head. Yet as I grew older, I do no recall him being ill a great deal, and these references to poor health from his childhood into his adult years are at odds with how I think of him.

6.7 Transitions to Adulthood (1): Sketching

As I observed, David often takes responsibility for home maintenance and DIY, yet he comes across as quite childlike, depending on his mother for health care—with her sleeping in a chair in his room when he has 'flu and going out to buy him games as entertainment. How did he make the transition to independence? And what took him beyond days spent labelling corsets at Baker Baker and nights playing cards and fixing up 27 Hampden Road? He notes the films he sees—and his 1937 walking journal refers to 'a cinema show' while staying at a youth hostel. He also often reads, adventure stories. But what I had not recognised was his serious interest in drawing. This and his commitment to youth hostelling were core to the person he was becoming. Already he had school prizes for drawing and he writes about it in his 1932 Bristol diary. Later, in 1937 and 1938—when he was about 24—in a journal that records his bike rides and youth hostelling trips, he often refers to sketching. On Sunday 1 May 1937, he says: 'As the weather was warm and sunny, I decided to do some sketching in the afternoon for my drawing course.' I had no idea he had taken a drawing course. I assumed that when he met my mother, he compliantly went sketching with her. She was living with her father, Meredith Watling, a professional landscape artist. Their house was full of paintings and art paraphernalia. Eventually it became David's home for the rest of his life. Somehow my father's paintings were never rated as highly as his wife and father-in-law's, leading me to see him as willing novice. When he first showed Meredith one of his watercolours, he was complimented on the quality of paper, but nothing was said about the work. This was repeated as a good-humoured joke for years. Now I see that drawing was something my parents shared from the beginning. I am also reminded of a sketch book dated 1863 that contains his grandmother Sarah Annie Robinson's expert pencil drawings of scenes in Warwickshire where she came from. By way of frontispiece, she has inscribed her name and wreathed it in carefully painted flowers and foliage. These materials might suggest an inherited skill on my father's as well as my mother's side of the family. After all, I went to Art College myself, albeit for less than a year. Conversely, perhaps I am just seeing a nineteenth-century hobby that was still popular between the two World Wars—one that infused my Cambridge upbringing.

Back in 1937, sketching was a recurrent feature of my father's record of his time off work. On Sunday 30 May, his journal says: 'Cycled out to the Round House to do some sketching, and took my tea. Arrived home about 5.16 pm' [I can see that he has carefully altered his original record from 5:15 pm to 5:16 pm]. The Round House turns out to be a toll house in Stanton Drew, about six miles from Hampden Road. The following Sunday, there he is again, this time with his mother who travelled by bus, while he cycled. Later in the journal, there is a two-page sketch of Eskdale from Hardknott Pass in the Lake District, made on a June day when he stayed put with a knee injury, while Gordon Baggs, his friend, walked onto the next hostel. (The previous Sunday he had written: 'My right knee is playing the very deuce with me', an expression that sounds theatrically 'public school' to me. It stands out in this journal where many of his less theatrical but still distinctive ways of speaking are already in place: 'all this palaver delayed me nearly an hour and a half', when he tries to get a puncture mended; 'we retired to bed'; 'a marvellous dinner'; 'a crowd of us went for a walk'.)

6.8 Transitions to Adulthood (2): Walking

The record of my father's commitment to walking begins with his school diary, described in Chap. 5. So detailed are his accounts that I can easily retrace them on maps of the Croydon area. Once he leaves school and walks every Sunday, usually with his mother, his 1932 diary describes their routes through the countryside around Bristol in considerable detail. It is now very clear to me that walking, cycling and sketching had become mainstays of his social life before he was called up in 1940. As well as the YHA, the Ramblers Association was also set up in 1931, to provide public access to the countryside and keep long-standing footpaths open. My father espoused its principles to the end of his life. For all that he was a cautious man, I have walked behind him across large fields where a footpath has been ploughed up by a local farmer. I may have been nervously looking over my shoulder, like a character from the *Dad's Army* credits. But my father, approaching 80, strode on, head down, claiming his right of way without a qualm.

Four years older, his brother Arthur appeared to pave the way by going on walking holidays, while David had barely left school. Arthur's walking journal for 1931 has a different tone, written more confidently and fluently. A flourish in the way he addresses his mother on postcards sent from the various destinations—'My dear Mother'—contrasts with my father's plainer 'Dear Mother'. That said, some of Arthur's language strikes me as arrogantly elitist: 'we looked around for a drink and an obliging rustic showed us the way to the pub. It went under the name of the Caradon Hotel but it was, to my mind, the worst kind of country pub … and the beer was rotten'. Arthur is 20 at this time, working at the bank in Wellington, Somerset. He is walking on the Cornish coast with someone called Gee, but they lose their way all the time: 'We wandered through some fields absolutely lost until we came to a sort of lane which we went along until we came to some few houses and a farmyard. Here we asked where we were and were told Lizzen. We weren't very much the wiser then. But they directed us to Lansallos and from here we cut across some fields … '. They proceed, but 'it was still raining like the devil and foggy. On getting over a hedge I cut my finger'. Clearly Arthur and Gee were not keeping to the beaten track. Googling the place names he lists, I realise they were trying to walk the South West Coast Path, not formally established until the 1990s.

Unlike my father who would book accommodation and send letters ahead enquiring about train times and facilities for storing tandems, Arthur and Gee seem to make little preparation. I found no mention of a map. Yet among the very many maps I retrieved from my father's house after he died, there were two beautiful Ordnance Survey Tourist maps—for Dartmoor and Exmoor—with the artist Arthur Palmer's Edwardian-style painting and lettering. Both are signed and dated 'A.H.Manning June 1937' and 'October 1938'. By this time Arthur was in his late 20s and possibly more organised. But in 1931 I find that 'when we [Arthur and Gee] actually got into the village there was not a soul about anywhere, so we eventually decided to see if the pub could put us up. We called at the White Hart and the door was opened by an old fellow with a beard who reminded me of Kaiser Bill'. They were refused a bed and sent off to Mrs. Richards—who was away—and they go to the wrong house anyway. The 'old soul' whose door they do knock on offers to put them up, leaving them 'in sole possession' while she goes to chapel with 'her old man'. This 'shows how honest we look'. Two other people call by, neither of them surprised to find the young men, 'which only goes to show that Cornish people are rather philosophic', writes Arthur.

I have quoted him at some length. Although my father's writing is telling in its own way, it is comparatively formulaic. When he shares a trip with someone else, his journal carefully documents their expenditure, the items bought jointly and independently. Arthur expresses his opinions and his feelings. Whether his views are to my liking or not, they bring a sense of relief. It feels like direct personal contact, something I had little experience of with my father.

When David expanded his Sunday walks, though, he also expanded his social life. His journal refers to regular outings with Gordon who I assume is a friend. Sometimes Gordon meets him after 'biz', as my father now calls Baker Baker after seven years of working there. He also meets up with Arthur at various destinations, the two of them travelling in Arthur's car to friends and relatives in South Devon, often with a walk involved. But the mainstay of his activities involves friends from the Bristol YHA. In March 1939 this group feature in a full-page spread in the *Bristol Evening Post* (see also Chap. 7). The accompanying text sums up the ethos of 'hiking' and cycling between the wars, referring to 'young people who are enjoying life to the full, free from worries and cares of the modern world – breathing the fresh air – enjoying their recreation surrounded by the glories of nature – members of the Youth Hostels Association. Latest figures published show the amazing increase in this movement, the present total membership being close on 80,000'.

My father is pictured there, among a group of men and women who look anything but young to me. But these are pre-1960s 'teenager' days, so the hostellers' clothing and hairstyles look decidedly middle-aged. Despite the references to freedom from worries and cares, to fresh air and the glories of nature, it is 1939, and war is not only imminent but expected. On the back of the yellowing page that my father faithfully filed away are descriptions of a display of the work of the 902 RAF Balloon Barrage Squadron. The piece finishes by saying: 'With a nucleus of 200 Regular Royal Air Force men, the three Bristol Balloon Barrage Squadrons need hundreds of men, but the vacancies are being filled up very rapidly and prospective recruits are advised to apply promptly.' Immediately below is a headline: 'Goering's Newspaper attacks Poland', referring to the *Essen National-Zeitung* which Field-Marshal Goering was connected with. The piece describes German families living in Poland being 'systematically attacked', referring to a report about 'the plight of German workmen in Upper Silesia and the Olsa area, alleging that they can get neither work nor bread'. Immediately below is a photograph of Mr. and Mrs. H. Chapman erecting one of the first air raid shelters to be distributed in Bristol in their garden in Knowle, the area where David and his mother were living. Made of galvanised corrugated steel, it looks improbably flimsy at this stage of its construction. Meanwhile, another item appeals for Bristolians to support the Lord Baldwin Fund's efforts to rescue and support 1000 refugee children (500 Christian, 500 Jews).

In July 1938, my father had joined the Bristol YHA Group on a two-week walking holiday in the Bavarian Alps. I remember him saying how anxious his mother had been about him going there at a time of political and military turbulence. But his journals suggest a pervading optimism and what now seem like innocent pleasures enjoyed by the walkers of that era. Of an earlier YHA weekend at Wookey Hole hostel on 20 March 1937, he said: 'there were thirteen of us altogether, so the Beetle drive [a dice game in which parts of a beetle are drawn] which I had arranged was quite a success'. In November that year, at Batheaston hostel, he says: 'After supper Lionel Menefy gave a cinema show, having brought the projector over on the tandem. We had a whip round to cover the cost of the films and the surplus which amounted to 4/3d was put in the hostel box [a significant amount, since the average hourly wage for men at that time was 1 shilling and 6 pence]. Following this came a Beetle Drive, which in turn was followed by dancing and games until midnight when we retired.' The page devoted to the local YHA group in the *Bristol Evening Post* describes the hostel common room, a place where 'acquaintances thrive and experience broadens in conversation and sing-song'. Sure enough, on 28 March 1937, my father writes, 'After supper we had a sing song before retiring' and, on 25 June 1938, at Malvern hostel (where female members of the group are mentioned): 'We eventually arrived at about 8 o'clock to find the girls already there. After supper, we went up to the top of a nearby hill, and had a bit of a sing song.'

6.9 At Home in a Group

As mentioned, my father spent many of his early years in institutional settings. In later life he seemed most at home in clubs and societies, usually work-related, and later as a member of Cambridge Rambling Society. Christmas he often spent walking at Holiday Fellowship centres, having tired of our disorganised festive routines. Had he not been introduced to my mother while stationed at RAF Cranfield in Bedfordshire—a blind date of sorts—it is hard to imagine him entering an intimate relationship with one other person.

When I read descriptions of the group fun of Beetle Drives and singsongs I find myself wanting him to just get a girlfriend and break out of his rigid, distancing language where, for example, going to bed is always 'retiring for the night'. Perhaps this is another echo of my own years spent longing for a first boyfriend. In his walking journal entry for 18 April 1937— after a page and a half's description of his route—he says 'I arrived at Chris's lodging at 11.5 am.' Who is Chris? A man or a woman? The two of them go for a short walk to a reservoir, but Chris has to get the 5:25 train to Gloucester. He 'sees *her* off' and I am excited. His writing livens up for that journal entry. When he describes the punctures he gets on the way home, he says: 'What I had to say about that is not fit to be written down. Well, there was only one thing to do, and that was to walk into Cross and try and get it repaired.' But Chris never reappears. In June 1937, on his Lake District cycling and walking holiday with Gordon, they meet 'two Leicester girls' and seem to walk together to the same hostels. This sounds more promising. David and Mary, one of the girls, go for 'a bathe' at 7 am, and two days later, he and Gordon take the girls to the pictures. Like Chris, however, Mary never reappears in the journal. Gordon and David just see the girls off in Windermere and cycle on for another 72 miles.

My father met my mother in Cambridge on 26 September 1940—if the surrounding of that date with starburst lines beside her address in his notebook means what I think it does. This is only a few years after his peace-time days of cycling and walking in the countryside and his evenings of wholesome pastimes. There is no diary or journal for the period between 10 September 1938 and 1 January 1941 (when he made a start on his next 45 years of diary-keeping, albeit in the tiny spaces of the five-year diaries my mother introduced him to. Clearly she knew her man). To me it seems likely that he may never have had a girlfriend before meeting my mother. What women meant to him as he grew up is difficult to guess at. His thoughts and feelings on this matter have not made it into his brief diary entries, and his walking journal is mostly a record of where he went, how much he spent and what the weather was like.

6.10 Brother and Mother

As mentioned, Arthur's walking journal makes for different reading. It includes opinion and comment: 'it was a beastly foggy morning'; '[Pensilva] … it wasn't very interesting, just the usual run of Cornish villages'. Arthur attracts me as a character, good-looking, thoughtful, a man who would hold my interest. But it is difficult to get much purchase on his life. There are no schoolboy or adolescent diaries dutifully recording his days. As noted in Chap. 5, my father said he had little to do with Arthur because of their four-year age gap, one I imagine was exacerbated by age-segregated year groups at boarding school. I sense that my father was overshadowed by Arthur, but apart from the disparity in the number of school prizes they were awarded, it is an intuition I cannot easily evidence.

Arthur's military record shows that on 26 April 1939 he enlisted in the Territorial Army in Taunton, about five months before war was declared. This meant that he became a full-time soldier with the outbreak of war on 2 September. His pay-book has an address at the time of his conscription—Brick House, Drayton, Somerset. I found Brick House on an estate agent's site and contacted Margot Lock, one of the owners, along with her husband, Jeff. Margot's mother-in-law had been Arthur's landlady while he worked in the nearby Langport branch of the Westminster Bank. Brick House is a large detached Georgian house in a rural setting and had been the premises of a tomato growing business when Arthur lived there. His landlady was a matriarchal figure, said Margot Lock. She kept pigs and chickens and would have looked after her lodgers well, making them part of the family. There was only ever one lodger at a time, and they were accommodated on the third floor of the house with wonderful views over the surrounding countryside. Letters Arthur wrote to Mrs. Lock while serving abroad had been lying in her daughter-in-law's box of family memorabilia for nearly 70 years, along with a letter sent by my father, after Arthur had been killed.

I remember my father telling me, possibly several times, that Arthur was engaged. The plain, bottle-green rugs that lay on the floorboards in my parents' bedroom in Cambridge had supposedly been made by Arthur and his fiancée in preparation for their future home. But engagements have no official status, and since everyone who knew Arthur is dispersed and almost certainly dead, there seems no way of finding out if he had a wife-to-be. I have no photos of Arthur as part of a couple, no references in his letters—and when I asked Mrs. Lock's daughter-in-law whether she knew of a fiancée she said she had no evidence at all that she could pass on.

Arthur's 1931 walking journal for 15 May does say, 'We staggered into Padstow where we sent a couple of cards and I collected a letter from Joan.' Like Chris in my father's diary, Joan remains a mystery. Perhaps Arthur was engaged at this point. Perhaps they had broken it off by the time he was living at Brick House.

The life of Ella, their mother, is equally difficult to trace during the late 1930s and early 1940s. 27 Hampden Road remained in the family until my father sold it in December 1950. I assume a tenant lived there, at least during the seven years after Ella's death. Ella is recorded as Arthur's next of kin in his army pay-book, but living at 1 Alexandra Terrace, Exmouth. My father's cousins, Winnie and Elsie Tothill, considerably older than him, also lived in Exmouth, and there are many diary and journal references to visiting them over the years. So my grandmother may have moved down there to be near them. On Arthur's Territorial Army attestation form though, she still has the Hampden Road address. The diary she kept for 1943, the year she died, was for a guest house in Tolcarne Road, Newquay. Photographs in an album that belonged to Arthur have the heading 'Mother's Holiday, 1934' and show views of Newquay, a resort she knew well and may have chosen as a home when her arthritis worsened. On 12 January 1935, in an envelope bearing the words 'For Arthur and David in the event of my death', she wrote a letter that begins:

> My heart has been troubling me for some time, so if I should die suddenly without making a proper will I want you to divide everything I leave equally between you two. I only wish I could leave more.

She describes the whereabouts of her receipt for the 'business papers' she has lodged in the Westminster Bank, and then details which of her sons are to receive key pieces of jewellery and wristlet watches. My father is promised the kitchen clock which makes me smile after reading so many many recordings of the time in his diaries.

Notes

1. Van Gennep, Arnold. [1908] 1960. *The Rites of Passage*. Chicago: The University of Chicago Press.

7

At Home and Abroad

On 1 September 1939, Britain and France declared war on Germany. By 1942 three of the young men who feature in this book—David, Jenny's father; Arthur, her uncle; and James, Carol's father—had left their young civilian lives behind. When the war ended six years later, on 2 September 1945, none of them went back to the jobs they had in 1939. Indeed for James, as was the case for many other service people, the war had a ragged conclusion, and he was not demobbed until 1946. By the time military conflict was finally over, both David and James were married and had moved away from their former family homes—in Bristol and Kilrea, respectively. Arthur was dead. For all three of them, their transition to young adulthood was profoundly shaped by the events set in train on 1 September 1939.

Arthur was conscripted into the army and David into the RAF in the course of 1940. James, however, barely 18 when war was declared, numbered among the 38,000 men and women in Northern Ireland who volunteered for the armed services. This was after long political wrangling as to whether or not to extend conscription to include Northern Ireland. The question was finally resolved on 27 May 1941 when the British Government declared that men and women from Northern Ireland would be exempt. In this chapter we trace these three men's responses to the war and consider the very different outcomes of their military experiences. James Gilmore's very specific exposure to what had gone on in Bergen-Belsen concentration camp is then the focus of Chap. 8.

But first an extract from a letter sent to Jenny's parents in 1945 by her uncle Donald (Gould), the boyhood friend of her father's who later married Dorothy, her mother's younger sister. At the time of writing, Dorothy was pregnant, possibly with twins. Donald was stationed in India and facing the possibility of three more years away from home. He says:

Every time I come into our tent, I look at Dorothy's photo on the box beside my 'charpoy' (bed) and think what wasted years of our youth this is. We are only young once after all, and no matter what happens afterwards we shall never be able to recapture this period in our life, shall we? Particularly I did want to be home to help in the initial bringing up of our baby – but still it's no good grumbling about it, is it.

In what follows we consider the extent to which Donald is speaking for Arthur, David and James as well.

7.1 War in Prospect

From their diaries and other materials, there is little evidence of Arthur and David Manning consciously living in the shadow of war during the 1930s. Even so the page on youth hostelling that David saved from a March 1939 *Bristol Evening Post* provides a different story. On its reverse, as described in Chap. 6, almost every news item refers to the imminence of war: recruitment for Balloon Squadrons, the distribution of domestic air raid shelters, claims to oppression among German workers in parts of Poland. Only from Arthur's military record, secured by Jenny from the Ministry of Defence, did she find out that Arthur had already joined the Territorial Army, in Taunton on 26 April 1939. He was then called up on 2 September when war was declared. The Military Training Act, passed on 27 April 1939, was the first example of conscription being used during peace-time and came as a direct response to growing international tension. It required all fit British men aged 20 and 21 to take six months' military training. It was on the day before the Act was passed that Arthur, then 28, joined the Territorial Army, suggesting that he thought a more widespread mobilisation was likely. David meanwhile became an ARP warden in Bristol in December 1939.

What had been happening in Europe and beyond while Arthur, David and James were beginning to make their way in the world? The war that was later to take over their lives—and in Arthur's case take away his life—resulted in the deaths of between 50 and 85 million people, including civilian casualties. Although its dates seem clear-cut—1939–1945—World War Two was preceded by a period of considerable military activity and territorial expansionism on a number of fronts. This was partly fuelled by the 1917 Bolshevik Revolution in Russia and the fear roused among European powers that revolution might spread. One response to this threat was the rise of fascism—a right-wing, authoritarian form of nationalism that took hold in Italy, Spain and Germany. When Adolf Hitler came to power in 1933, he pursued expansionist nationalism, breaking many of the terms of the Treaty of Versailles drawn up in July 1919 by the Allied powers, involving little negotiation with Germany.

This was also a period of economic depression, initiated by the collapse of the Wall Street Stock Market in October 1929. As a result, sectors of western populations were at odds with governments over their conditions—and even in Wine Street, Bristol, David had witnessed an unemployment demonstration in April 1932. Between 1935 and 1939, then, when he and his brother were walking West Country moorlands and cliff-tops, Hitler was introducing military conscription, remilitarising the Rhineland and making Austria and then the Sudetenland (the north and west of Czechoslovakia) part of Germany. What claims was he pursuing through these measures? That the German people should be united and exercise their right to self-determination, that as a nation they required more territory, or living space (*Lebensraum*), with more scope for developing agriculture to feed themselves, particularly in Slavic territories to the east. A belief in racial hierarchies underpinned Hitler's expansionist plans. The German peoples—as Aryans—needed to fully reclaim their ancient territories in northern parts of Europe. Hitler's vision of the future was therefore of creating a Third Reich, a Germany that would reign supreme. It drew on the resonant image of the First Reich, the

Roman Empire, and the Second Reich—which usually refers to the single state of unified German territories between 1817 and 1918.

In 1936 Hitler made alliances with Japan and Italy, both of them seeking to expand their own control over neighbouring territories. Since the beginning of the twentieth century, Japan had competed with Russia for control of Manchuria in the northeast of China, an area rich in the resources needed for Japanese expansionism. In 1931 Japan set up a puppet state in Manchuria and was moving into the rest of China. Faced with the spread of communism, Italy, under Benito Mussolini, was actively trying to create a new Roman Empire in Mediterranean Europe, invading Ethiopia in 1935, then Greece, and finally Albania in 1939.

The Soviet Union, meanwhile, had maintained neutrality until August 1939. However it had lost considerable territory in the Baltic States and Eastern Europe and in principle was ready to ally itself with Britain and France in order to defend Poland from German invasion once that eventuality became imminent. On 23 August 1939, however, the Soviet Union made the Molotov–Ribbentrop non-aggression pact with Hitler, anticipating that German military aid was their best chance of claiming territory in Eastern Europe. When Poland was invaded in September 1939, then, it was by Soviet and German forces. Relations between them remained friendly until Hitler invaded the Soviet Union in June 1941, largely in response to independent Soviet expansionism in the Baltic States and Eastern Europe. It was after this that the Soviet Union, under Joseph Stalin, joined forces with Britain and the USA with the aim of defeating Germany and its allies.

What was Britain's response to the events leading up to World War Two? And how did that affect Arthur, David and James? The evidence of a build-up of military power in Germany was not seen by other European powers as entirely a threat. In light of the spectre of communism, a stronger Germany could have advantages in deflecting its growth within Europe. In addition, there were politicians in France and Britain, including Prime Minister Neville Chamberlain, who believed that the conditions of the Treaty of Versailles were unfairly punitive, a view that predisposed them to accede to reasonable amendments.

In addition, with World War One coming to an end only twenty years earlier, diplomatic *negotiation* was prioritised in a determined attempt by

Britain and France to avoid another war. Recognising this concern, Hitler's diplomatic tactics were to make apparently justifiable demands, always with the threat of war if they were not granted. Once granted, another request would be made. When he sought to unify Austria and Germany (the Anschluss), the leader of Austria asked Britain and France to help prevent this who did nothing, believing Hitler's promise that his expansionism would stop with the Anschluss. Within six months, though, he demanded that the Sudetenland area of Czechoslovakia become German. In the Munich Agreement of September 1938, signed by the leaders of Germany, Britain, France and Italy, this demand was agreed, on condition that no further expansion took place. But in March 1939, Hitler invaded the rest of Czechoslovakia. The likelihood that Poland was his next target, with its corridor to the Baltic Sea through previously Prussian territory, led Britain finally to threaten war if invasion took place. Chamberlain believed this was something Hitler would not risk. When he did indeed invade Poland on 1 September 1939, his action inevitably precipitated what was to become World War Two. Jenny now takes up this account from the local point of view of Arthur, David and their relatives.

7.2   Living with War

Jenny The declaration of war on 1 September 1939 brought no immediate threat to families like my father's. The period that followed came to be known as the 'phony war', even though the Soviet Union and Germany were on the offensive in Poland, closely followed by Hitler's invasion of Finland. Preparation in the form of gas masks had however been distributed to the British population and in January 1940, rationing was introduced. In the Scandinavian countries though, Hitler's military offensive continued with the invasion of Norway and Denmark. By May 1940 the German Armed Forces (the Wehrmacht) and the Nazi air force (the Luftwaffe) had invaded Belgium, France and Holland in what was called the 'lightning war' (Blitzkrieg), and by the end of the month, Belgium and Holland, as well as Paris, were occupied by German forces.

The next step for the German forces was to drive back the British Expeditionary Forces who were fighting alongside their French allies in northern France. Only through the combined efforts of the Royal Navy and volunteers with sea-going vessels were British and French troops rescued from the Port of Dunkirk between 27 May and 4 June 1940. Hitler, however, was planning Operation Sealion, an invasion of Britain by land, targeted towards a 40-mile stretch of the southeast coast. While coastal shipping convoys and shipping centres were the focus for German air attack in July that year, Hitler feared that an invading German Army would be vulnerable to attack by the RAF, a concern that led him also to target British air fields and air craft factories. Only after that were British towns and cities attacked by air. Radar, however, proved key to Britain's narrow victory in what became known as the Battle of Britain, a military conflict that ended in September 1940. It was the first defeat of German forces in World War Two and the first military campaign fought by air. As such it firmly established the superiority of the RAF. How did my father, his mother and brother carry on family life while these and subsequent military events were taking place?

Throughout the war, the 'Blitz' or bombing of British cities continued with heavy civilian losses. Baker Baker, for example, the Bristol draper where my grandparents and father worked, fell entirely victim to such a raid on 14 November 1940, as Chap. 6 describes. In my grandmother Ella's diary for 1943 while living in Newquay, she notes an air raid 'alert' 65 times in the first 11 months of the year, sometimes up to 4 times in a single night. What she did when there was an alert—apart from recording the precise time that she heard it—is unclear. The last one she mentions was on 3 November 1943. The following week, she was bedridden, her arthritis and lumbago now compounded by pneumonia. The doctor was visiting regularly. A month later she was dead.

Arthur, my uncle, had joined the army, as I go on to describe. He sent letters to my grandmother throughout 1943, first from Iraq and then from Northern Italy. It was their only means of communication. Between 1 January and 24 November 1943, she received 36, some of them subject to considerable delay if military lines of support were threatened. To find out about his experiences in more detail, I obtained his service file from the Army Personnel Centre in Glasgow. By reading across from the details it contains—often cryptic and heavily abbreviated—to broader brush accounts of the events of World War Two, especially in the Middle East and Italy, I began to understand what was happening. Until then I had been baffled by the many tiny snapshots I had inherited of smiling young men in swimming trunks somewhere in a desert. These images were mixed up with postcards of Cape Town, Cairo, the Valley of the Kings in Egypt, the Garden of Gethsemane, Mosul. They challenged my knowledge of the geography as well as the military history of a war that took hold of the world immediately before I was born. Like the 1930s photos of walking groups that I omitted from my album, having no idea who I was looking at, I had to retrieve the snapshots of deserts and cities in Africa from my daughter, Jo, who saved what I would have discarded.

7.3 Arthur on Active Service

Arthur's full-time service (known as embodiment or becoming part of a body of active service people) began with the outbreak of war on 2 September 1939 when he joined the 5th Battalion of the Somerset Light Infantry as a private. Between 22 January and 6 July 1940, he spent time training in Warminster and then Trowbridge, Weston-super-Mare, Crowborough, Rye and Lydd (where Bert, his father, had been immediately before embarking for France in 1917, as Chap. 4 described). In November 1940 he was posted to the Special Service Brigade then being organised by Brigadier J.C. Haydon. By that time, on 11 May, he had been made lance corporal (the next rank up from private)—and on 6 July became an acting corporal, a position he held until being sent to Egypt the following year.

The Special Service Brigade was made up of five battalions, and from Arthur's service record I can see that he was in Battalion No. 4 which subsequently became No. 8 Commando. Commandos were small units of about 450 men, each one then dividing into troops and further into 15-man sections. Their intended role was as assault infantry who would spearhead future Allied landing operations. My father's address book has an entry for No. 7 Troop, No. 8 Commando, at Inveraray, Argyllshire. In a letter to my mother on 31 October 1940, he describes Arthur's situation in a more personal light:

> I had a letter from Arthur a couple of days ago apparently he is still in Scotland, but is expecting to be shifted at any moment now. He still does not know when he will get his leave, poor chap. When the letter reached me it had been opened by the Censor, so I imagine that he must be engaged upon some very secret work. Of course he did not mention what he was doing, which was a good thing, as he may have got into a row for giving away official secrets.

With this information about where Arthur was between July 1940 and February 1941, I then find a second clue in my father's address book, another shipwrecked fragment left behind by my family. It is an entry that reads: 'No7 Troop, "B" Batt., Lay Forces, Middle East Forces'. This address is not headed with Arthur's name but appears under the Inveraray address (now crossed out), where Arthur had been for training. So he had been part of Layforce which I discover was indeed a formation made up of Commandos sent to the Middle East. It was formed by Colonel Robert Laycock in February 1941 and comprised about 2000 men. Its role was to carry out raids that would sever enemy lines of communication in the Mediterranean. By August 1941, however, Layforce itself had been disbanded since the Allies were doing badly in that theatre of war. The Commandos then took on a supporting role vis-a-vis other troops throughout this area.

Another source of information is the two letters Arthur sent his landlady, Mrs. Lock, in Drayton, Somerset (see Chap. 6). His first, dated June 1941, refers to the last time he saw her on his leave in January that year. He describes leaving England by ship on 1 February 1941, the point at which Layforce was being formed. The troops went via Cape Town, to avoid danger from military attack in the Mediterranean Sea. Their destination also offered scope for training in safe areas where the terrain and climate mimicked that of the military zones they were headed for. Nearly three years later, Tony Benn's diaries and letters[1] describe similar experiences in the RAF, travelling by ship from Glasgow to Durban, leaving on 14 January and arriving on 19 February 1944. On reaching South Africa,

Tony Benn and his fellow troops went by train to Bulawayo in Zimbabwe where he learned to fly.

Arthur, in his June 1941 letter to Mrs. Lock, says:

> We've seen quite a bit of this country since we arrived in March [that year] though I'm afraid we haven't a very good opinion of it. We're lined up in tents out on the sand the whole time and have been plagued continually by flies and at other times with fleas, sand storms and terribly hot winds. When the hot wind blows and brings the dust with it life becomes almost unbearable.

But where is he exactly? He continues:

> The only thing to the credit of this country is the swimming. We've been lucky enough to get plenty of it. The sun shines all the time and the sea is the most lovely blue and warm. The beaches are all of almost white sand … (Fig. 7.1)

From his service record, it seems that he was in Egypt which was occupied by British forces and had been since 1882. It remained under British control until 1952. The Suez Canal was crucial in terms of supplies reaching key front lines. Once Arthur arrived there in March 1941, I can see from his service record that he attended the Middle East Officer Cadet Training Unit and in July that year was in Cairo. He remained in Egypt until 15 November 1941 when he was 'granted an emergency commission in the Indian Army', as his record puts it. The record shows him being posted to the 1/5 Essex Regiment on 6 January 1942. What happened after that—both to Arthur and the events he was caught up in—is not easy to piece together. What is clear though, from a letter he sent my mother two years later, is that he never returned to England.

In that letter, Arthur tries to reassure my mother that her relative silence when she was among the family seeing him off in February 1941 was not a problem. He says:

> I don't think you need reproach yourself for not speaking more when you saw me on Exeter station. There was very little opportunity for conversation anyway and it was probably my fault. I hate seeing people off by train and also hate being seen off, stations are dreadful places to say goodbye.

Fig. 7.1 Arthur Manning in Egypt

Reproducing his words here, I am mindful of the many goodbyes he must have endured as a boy when leaving Exeter by train for another term at the Drapers' School in Croydon. He finishes by saying, 'Let's hope it won't be too long before someone can meet me off a train in England. It's two years since I left now and it seems a long time'. Reading his letter alongside the photos of his smiling, whimsical face, his look of eagerness for the next adventure, I so wish he had made that longed-for return and become part of my life.

Instead I trace his movements from the residual photographs, letters and address books—a poor substitute—and work out that he went from

Egypt to Iraq in November 1941. It was a country where considerable fighting had been going on. Seven months before Arthur arrived, British interests in Iraq—centred on the oil supply—had been threatened by a military coup d'etat on 3 April that year. This saw the installation of a pro-German Government that sought diplomatic alliances with Italy. Its leader, Prime Minister Rashid Ali, ordered the withdrawal of British forces from the country. Previously, in 1920, Britain had been granted a League of Nations mandate giving them administrative powers over Iraq after the defeat of the Ottoman Empire in World War One. Iraq then remained a semi-independent kingdom, still administered by Britain, until it was officially granted independence in 1932.

In response to the coup d'etat, G.H.Q. India Command were instructed by the British Government to send an expeditionary force to Basra where British troops were still officially stationed under the conditions of Iraq's independence in 1932. Having secured control of Basra, the Indian brigades made their way north to Baghdad where they joined forces with 'Habforce' (Habbaniya Force, made up of troops from Palestine, also under British administration from 1920 until 1948). The final outcome of the fighting in Iraq was the defeat of the pro-German Government on 31 May 1941 when British troops entered Baghdad and an armistice was signed. This episode is known as the Anglo-Iraqi War, and Iraq subsequently became a base for Allied attacks on Syria and Iran. On 18 June 1941, Lieutenant General Edward Quinan was placed in command of all the ground forces in Iraq, and these included Indian and British troops. Initially known as Iraqforce, it was renamed Persia[2] and Iraq Force or PAI Force on 1 September 1941. It was after this, on 15 November 1941, that Arthur received an 'emergency commission' in the Indian Army, becoming a second lieutenant and then lieutenant in PAI Force, a role he held until 27 April 1943.

Meanwhile, David, my father, was a corporal in the RAF. I wonder whether Arthur was viewed as officer material in a way that my father was not. In the Drapers' School Magazine for 1927, for example, Arthur is recorded as the new sergeant of No. 3 Platoon of the cadet corps (see Chap. 5). This inclines me to see him as ready or even eager to make an ambitious and possibly dangerous contribution to the war. I find this choice hard to empathise with. My father secured a relatively safe role, training men in aircraft recognition on Lincolnshire and Bedfordshire air bases. To avoid conscription, in place for women from December 1941 onwards, my mother gave up her job as a window dresser. It was a role I imagine she must have loved, but instead she found a reserved occupation in the Post Office drawing office. So neither of my parents put their lives on the line, it would seem. In his photographs Arthur appears as a strong, handsome, confident and *happy* young man with everything to lose by putting himself at so much risk.

I am able to locate him two years later, on 21 March 1943, when he wrote a second letter to Mrs. Lock. PAI Force is part of his address—but it seems he saw little action during the nearly 18 months he spent in Iraq: 'We've been having a pretty dull time over here for a long time now', he says, 'and we are all sick to death of this country'. He has been on training courses and indeed had leave in Palestine and Syria, hence all my tiny photos of sites in the Holy Land. He remarks that the local people are 'living in precisely the same way as they did in Biblical days. They still plough their land with a wooden plough, pulled by any animal that they've got; camel, mule, donkey or a cow. I haven't seen any women pulling a plough yet but they do practically everything else!' Christmas 1942 he reports as a good time 'with plenty of the usual Xmas fare. Turkey and pudding and all that goes with it, also plenty of beer'. They had had 'a lot of fun' bargaining for the turkeys in local villages and then fattening them up on 'cookhouse scraps'. 'Believe me they were delicious', he says. What is happening in a military sense? He was not, of course, allowed to write down any information about what was happening, nor about where he was. In rural Somerset, Mrs. Lock and her husband were running a tomato growing business in the greenhouses behind Brick House, as Chap. 6 describes. So Arthur's account of farming methods and livestock in Iraq might have seemed an appropriate way of filling the three pages of his air mail letter.

For the Allies, Iraq and Persia were important as part of the supply route to Russia in support of the Soviet forces. Since German troops were advancing through southern Russia in 1942, British forces were built up in this area. It therefore seems likely that Arthur's emergency commission in the Indian Army (still the British Indian Army at this point) was prompted by the need to increase the size of this defensive force. When the threat of a German invasion by this route subsided in early 1943, British presence in this area was reduced. From my grandmother's diary for 1943, I can see that Arthur left Iraq on 17 May 1943: 'Letter from Arthur, he has left Iraq'. Immediately before this, he had been stationed at addresses in both Baghdad and Basra, according to my father's address book.

There are no subsequent addresses for Arthur, either in my grandmother's diary or my father's address book. But on 8 September she wrote: 'Alert 8.10 am, 6.30 pm. Italy surrendered. Sent magazines to Arthur. Wrote to him'. Where was he at this point, and how did events in Italy bring about his death two months later in the vicinity of the Sangro River? Along with 2500 British and Commonwealth troops who died defending the nearby Adriatic shoreline from the retreating German Army, he too is buried in the Sangro River War Cemetery, information that is easy to recover from the Commonwealth War Graves Commission website. Yet his body had lain there for over 70 years without my knowing or reflecting on its whereabouts. It is unlikely that my father ever visited his brother's grave.

7.4 The Italian Campaign

Italy under Mussolini had been a firm ally of Germany, yet when both the Italian and German Armies were defeated in North Africa in May 1943—with Germany already defeated at Stalingrad three months earlier—Mussolini's popularity and power in Italy were seriously undermined. By July 1943 the Allies had carried out their first air raid on Italy's mainland, at which point King Victor Emmanuel of Italy dismissed Mussolini from office. Marshal Badoglio, who was key to the ousting of Mussolini, then formed a new government and sought an armistice with the Allies. This took six weeks to arrange, and in that time Hitler mounted a fierce defence of Italy, determined to block the Allies' passage to southern Europe. On 9 September 1943, the Allies invaded Italy by land at Salerno on the west coast, about 30 miles south of Naples. This precipitated the surrender of the Italian Army, as my grandmother notes in her diary. German forces, however, continued to fight in order to block the Allies' access to Europe via the north of Italy. Within a month, the Allies had control of the whole of southern Italy. Hitler's response was to create a series of defensive lines across the country as a way of slowing down their advance, buying him time to invest most of his resources in the Winter Line south of Rome.

Arthur's service record shows that he became part of the British North Africa Force (BNAF) from 3 October 1943. On this date, a battalion of the British Eighth Army's Infantry Division had moved north to the German Volturno-Viktor line, crossing the Biferno River. From the sea, two commando battalions had landed north of the Biferno. The German forces then retreated to behind the Trigno River. It was here, on 2 November, that fierce fighting drove them back further north to the important Winter Line on the ridges behind the Sangro River. And it is here, to the best of my knowledge, that Arthur died.

When the Army Personnel Centre sent me a copy of Arthur's service record, his original 'soldier's service and pay book' was included, in its own envelope. On page one, under 'Instructions to Soldier', it says: 'You will always carry this book on your person.' So it must have been retrieved from his body and archived for over 70 years. What followed his death was another 18 months of the most bitter and costly fighting of the entire war, much of it hand-to-hand, including the famous battles of Anzio and Monte Cassino. It was only on 2 May 1945 that defeat was admitted by the German forces in Italy.

7.5 The Aftermath

What were the implications of Arthur's death for his family, friends and work colleagues? I find it immensely sad to realise that Arthur and his mother died within weeks of each other. Turning to her 1943 diary, I see that her very last entry is for 24 November 1943 ('Wrote to Arthur and Lorna [my mother]'). Arthur had been dead for 22 days by this time. She made no entries on the next 15 days and died on 9 December.

It is hard to imaginatively reconstruct how poorly she was or how rapid her final decline at the age of 67. She records her two visits to the doctor and his two home visits to her in the hotel, making only two direct references to health problems—lumbago and arthritis—noting the 'herbs' she sent for. Certainly the length of her diary entries diminishes towards the end, and at times the writing suggests she had restricted use of her hands. Throughout the entire diary she refers only twice to how she is feeling. Once, on 28 January, when there is no fire in the hotel until the evening, she writes, 'nearly dead with cold', and once, on 6 February, after a delay of around 20 days, she says 'Letter from Arthur [dated] 11 January. So pleased to have it'.

My father's diary for that year has an entry for 27 November, three days after his mother's diary falters to a close. It notes a telegram from her, asking him to come down to Newquay from RAF Ingham, just north of Lincoln. He arrives there the following day, having taken a sleeper from Paddington. In his diary he writes: 'Told that Arthur is missing, believed killed on Nov 2'. Although he does not say who 'told' him, I suspect that it might be his mother since she is listed as next of kin in every section of Arthur's service record, the last date being 26 June 1943. It therefore seems likely that she knew Arthur was missing, that her physical suffering during the last fortnight of her life was exacerbated by the fear that her elder son was dead. My father's diary entry for 9 December refers to 'another telegram', this one confirming Arthur's death.

When my father first arrived in Newquay, he spent the day with 'Mother' in her bedroom at the hotel. Presumably it was then that she showed him the first telegram. Where he was staying is unclear—maybe in the same hotel. Two days later he developed flu, was seen by his mother's doctor and was visited by the RAF MO who ordered him into sick bay. He was collected by ambulance at 4:30 pm. Three days later Lorna, my mother, arrived in Newquay, and my father was discharged from sick bay four days after that, at which point he noted in his diary: 'Mother is much weaker than when I went into Sick Bay. Lorna and I went to see about getting a nurse for her in afternoon.' Nurse Oats turned up for duty the following morning, 8 November. Then on 9 December my father wrote: 'Mild and sunny. Mother passed away peacefully at 4 pm. Received another telegram from the War Office confirming that Arthur was killed in action on Nov 2.' It seems likely that the telegram was sent to Ella but he opened it. Ella's death certificate, another succinct document, records her cause of death as (a) bronchopneumonia, (b) hypostatic pneumonia, (c) chronic rheumatic arthritis. A cutting glued into my father's diary tells me she was buried two days later in Fairpark Cemetery in Newquay, a grave that was never referred to or visited when I was growing up, despite annual holidays in Devon.

I have a memory of my father telling me about 9 December 1943. 'What a day that was', he said, shaking his head. How could such a thing happen, he seemed to be saying, to have lost both remaining members of my family of birth on the same day. Yet he believed his mother never knew that Arthur had died and found some comfort there. I am chilled by the precariousness of all their circumstances, my grandmother's vulnerability and her family so far flung and all still in their 20s. It is easy for me still to see them as the very grown-up, capable people they appeared to be when I was a child. Looked at from my present age though, they are barely more than children. Yet separately, each of them had made the difficult war-time journey from East Anglia to North Devon. Then, with my father almost immediately confined to 'sick bay' by the RAF doctor, he was unable to look after his mother for 7 of the last 12 days of her life. This could only have intensified her worries about Arthur.

Had it not been for the war, my father may well have continued living with or near my grandmother—as Arthur had. Could they have averted the pneumonia to which she succumbed, particularly the hypostatic pneumonia that can result from being confined to bed, as she had been for the month before she died? From this distance the simultaneous and untimely deaths of my grandmother and uncle have an almost filmic quality, as if written into a drama about the 1940s. Yet the absences they generated became part of the life I was born into three years later, the post-war world where I grew up.

Neither Ella's nor Arthur's graves were ever acknowledged, their locations never passed on to me. Similarly I was unaware of a memorial to Arthur in the Langport branch of the Westminster Bank. He was one of five staff at that time, the only one to die in the war.

The memorial is fairly elaborate, the text standing out in bas relief with Arthur's name framed by decorative edging:

> In memory of the following member of the staff of this branch who gave his life in the Second World War 1939–1945.
> Arthur H. Manning

Although the Langport branch, like many small banks, is now about to close, I am told the memorial will be relocated to the Street branch in Somerset who will take custody of it.

Arthur also had an obituary in *The Westminster*, the bank's staff magazine. Under a formal photo of him in uniform, it refers to the deep regret of his colleagues at Langport, then detailing his career in branches of the bank and in the army and finally offering a kind of eulogy:

> Fond of outdoor pursuits, hockey, golf and shooting, he approached everything with great enthusiasm and was a keen member of Toc H.
>
> In the Bank he was very promising, able and efficient, always cheerful and willing to give assistance where needed. He will be sadly missed by his many friends and our sincere sympathy goes to his brother. His mother died before the news of his death was confirmed.

This information matches my impression of Arthur, though I was not aware of an active involvement with a Christian organisation. The roots of Toc H as a support for servicemen in World War One may have drawn him to it, following the death of his father. Equally it may be an organisation that the Drapers' School encouraged its pupils to get involved with.

In 1948, five years after Arthur died, my father wrote to Mrs. Lock. Arthur's golf clubs had been found in the cupboard at the Langport branch which is near a local golf course. The manager sent them to my father, asking him to contact Mrs. Lock about Arthur's other belongings that she had stored for him at Brick House. My father writes, asking Mrs. Lock to send them on to him, 'carriage forward'. Care is obviously being taken with these remnants of Arthur's life, but their distribution between workplace and lodgings heightens my sense of how ephemeral his life was, unrooted in a permanent home.

I think it likely that my father had met Mrs. Lock since his letter is more than just functional. He says:

> I am very happy in my job here, and we have a nice little house which is something to be thankful for these days. I don't know if I have told you that we have a small daughter … she is very full of life and certainly keeps us on our toes, but life would seem very dull without her. Incidentally she is called Jennifer.

How strange to find myself described in a letter sent nearly 70 years ago to someone I have contacted so recently. My father's route to his 'nice little house' occupies the next section of this chapter.

7.6 Enlistment

When Arthur was killed in 1943, it seems as though his life, as a son and a brother, a friend and a colleague, sputtered out soon after. I know so little about him from my father. With his mother dead on the same day, there was no aftermath in family conversations that I was party to. This contrasts markedly with the lives of the two men whose war-time experiences we describe in the final two sections of this chapter. So if we go back to 1940 and a letter sent to Jenny's father, we can pick up the threads of the first.

Among my father's papers, I find a 'letter' from Gilbert M. Williams, 'the Divisional Controller'. Undated and sent from a Bristol address, it is headed, 'National Service (Armed Forces) Act, 1939', and informs my father that 'you are called upon for service in the Royal Airforce'. He is told to report to the officer in charge of No. 2 Recruiting Centre in Cardington, Bedfordshire, on 21 June 1940. Kit will be issued, it tells him, but if he brings anything of his own it must not exceed 'an overcoat, change of clothes, stout pair of boots, and personal kit, such as razor, hair brush, tooth brush, soap and towel'. He must inform his employer straightaway of the date when he is required to report for service.

On 17 June 1940, even before my father reports to Cardington, his friend Donald wrote to my mother. At that point she was just his sister-in-law but living with her father in Cambridge, less than 25 miles from

Cardington. Donald begins by accepting my mother's invitation for him and his wife, Dorothy, to visit Cambridge that July: '… if everything is O.K. then, (everything seems very precarious)'. Then he gets to the point:

> My friend David (he is the dark one the snaps you saw, Dorothy said you always admired) has just been sent to Bedford to join the R.A.F there and as such a short way from Cambridge, we had the cheek to suggest he wrote to you about a visit in his spare hours. You see he's always been used to a home and I know a little of living away and how he would be only too glad of just someone to call on, to be in a home again even just for an hour or so, rather than barracks his only rest at all! Please try to forgive our nerve and if he does connect with you, you would be doing me an awful favour if you would see him. He is my oldest pal and when I was at Bristol he (& his mother) did just the same most acceptable (I can assure you) service for me and I have never forgotten it.
>
> He spent last Wed. afternoon and Sunday (until he had to return) with us and I can assure you he is a jolly good sort.

My parents' courtship took off within three months of the meeting that Donald had set up. On 11 September, my father wrote to my mother, saying 'remember I am just dying to see you again' and on 21 September declares:

> Forgive me for having to put in writing what up to the present I have found so difficult to say. "Lorna, I have fallen absolutely head over heels in love with you".

These are the first of the 46 letters he sent her between 8 July 1940 and 12 September 1944. He may have written more, since there are gaps in the sequence, but these 46 remain. Many of them juxtapose heartfelt romantic sentiments with accounts of guard duty in a pillbox or firing Vickers guns at enemy aircraft, or trying to smash rats with a spade. Often six pages long, their staccato quality partly reflects the fact that my father returned to them at different times and places. On 21 October 1940, for example, he wrote in intense detail about the depth of his love on the first two pages of his letter. Then on page three he says:

We have just had our first bit of real excitement here. The sirens went some little time ago, and we heard a few bombs fall away in the distance. Shortly afterwards a Dornier [a German heavy fighter plane] passed over, dodging in and out of the clouds, and we promptly opened fire. Unfortunately we failed to bring him down, but at least we let him know that he wasn't going to get it all his own way, and he certainly cleared off in a hurry, so of course we can't tell whether we scored any hits, although as you can imagine, the chap actually firing swore that he hit it.

Cliff and I were in the tent, and I was actually writing this letter, when suddenly we heard the Lewis Guns [machine guns] on the Gun Post not far away, start firing. Gosh! We grabbed our tin hats, and were out of the tent like a shot, just in time to see our fellows open fire. I popped into the Pill box and loaded the Vickers [a machine gun] just in case he decided to come back and fly over low enough for me to have a smack at him …

What do I make of this almost daily flow of writing? Clearly Ella, his mother, was writing and receiving letters just as frequently, from the evidence of her 1943 diary—whether sent by my father or his brother, my mother or other family members. What became of all these letters and where are those my mother wrote to my father? He often refers to something she said in hers, and I cannot find out why they have not survived. Perhaps my father had nowhere private to keep them—or perhaps he was not allowed to for security reasons. Maybe she worried that something of herself that was so personal could fall into someone else's hands. There are also unexplained gaps in the sequence written by my father, with only three remaining from 1943, for example.

In 1995 Tamsin Day-Lewis edited a whole collection of letters sent between service people and their families in World War Two. For many, she says, this was 'the most exciting dynamic period of their lives'. One letter writer insists that '[w]ar is a powerful aphrodisiac'. Day-Lewis goes on: 'Romance was quickly kindled: there was an urgency to get engaged, to marry, to have a child …'.[3]

My father's letters do become less animated towards the end of my parents' war-time correspondence, once they have been married for nearly two years, even though the same endearments recur. I wonder about an everyday life lived through the written word and how this might intensify emotional connection. I cannot remember my parents relating to one another in the way these letters suggest, even though they were quietly and companionably close, never rowing with each other.

Yet here in his letters my father is hugely emotionally articulate. Day-Lewis suggests that 'some writers clearly wrote to find out what they really felt … to make sure their loved ones understood how they felt about them, in a way they could never, outside the war, have spoken or written'. However, she also acknowledges that once the end of the war came into sight, 'the fresh set of realities – imponderables – began to dawn' and '[t]he reality of the reunion, so long desired, no longer seemed to be the uncomplicated, single greatest wish on the horizon'.[4] With my parents never more than a train or bus ride away from each other though, theirs was in some ways a very intense courtship, their letter writing fuelling a physical and emotional connection they experienced regularly if briefly—whenever my father had leave.

What else surprises me, though, is how often God is woven into my father's letters. For example, in response to something my mother has written, he says: 'I too feel, Lorna, that surely it was God's will that we two should be brought together like this', and he 'confesses' that he has been praying every night since he met her that she 'might be the one for me'. God also informs his understanding of the war itself. On 31 October 1940, he writes: 'if only this beastly war was over, but as it is, we must only hope and pray that our inevitable victory will not be long in coming. Although it seems very terrible to us peace-loving people, surely it is God's way of punishing the wickedness of the Nazi regime in this war between the Christian Faith and Paganism'.

These letters give me extended exposure to my father's voice as a young man—or at least the voice he used to communicate with my mother. They bear little resemblance to his diaries or indeed to the way I remember him speaking in later life. Both David and Arthur seem to identify as solidly middle class and entitled. When Arthur, for example, refers to 'an obliging rustic' and 'the old soul' staffing the grocery shop in Tregony in his Cornish walking diary, I sense a man who sees these people as different and probably lesser than him. My father, in his expressions of love for my mother, compliments her on how *sensible* she is, saying 'You know, I haven't much time for the modern girl with all her airs and graces and whose sole conversation seems to be "men", and what she can get out of them, but from the moment I met you I noticed the difference, and thought "Well, here at last I have come in contact with a really sensible girl"'.

My heart sinks a little when I read these sentiments. There is something amusing in my father's earnestness, but it sits awkwardly with me, making me wonder about my refusal to fit in comfortably with the family life he and my mother went on to create. What he says is, of course, very much of its time, and there are similar sentiments expressed in the letters that Tamsin Day-Lewis edits. That needs to be taken into account. But racism is also evident, particularly in letters written by Arthur and Donald, my father's friend. Both of them served outside Europe and sent home accounts of people from other societies that make disturbingly racist reading for contemporary eyes.

Meanwhile my father spent the six years between 1940 and 1945 moving between different air bases in Bedfordshire and Lincolnshire, always within a short distance of my mother in Cambridge. Indeed on 11 November 1941, he is on a charge for failing to return in due time from training courses in the Isle of Man. His diary reveals that he had been 'in the armchair' with my mother, a confession I find heartening but also unsettling since it disturbs my memory of him always adhering to the rules (Fig. 7.2).

In July 1941 he became a leading aircraftman, like James Gilmore, to follow. This was a training rank in the RAF and in August that year he was made a corporal. At that point he left RAF Cranfield, having completed aircraft recognition and 'gunnery' courses in the Isle of Man (though he tells my mother he 'already know(s) the Lewis gun inside out and has a fair knowledge of the Vickers'). He then returns to Cranfield but is posted to RAF Hemswell, in Lincolnshire, by the end of November 1941.

In January 1942 he is at RAF Ingham, also in Lincolnshire, not far from Hemswell, but his diary frequently refers to him being sent to different air bases in the area 'on attachment', for example, RAF Binbrook in Lincolnshire, primarily used by Bomber Command. His time is now filled by training courses, such as those in the Isle of Man, and then being

Fig. 7.2　David and Lorna Manning, Jenny's parents, as a young couple

sent to air bases in the area to train different personnel. In this respect, his contribution to the war was similar to James Gilmore's, both young men both providing the support necessary for Britain's air force, a key resource in overcoming the threat of a German invasion of Britain.

7.7　Enlistment and Training for the Normandy Landings

Arthur Manning and James Gilmore's wars overlapped by only a year. In what follows Carol recounts the story of her father's enlistment in 1942, up until he was about to take part in the Normandy landings in 1944. She draws on several sources of information: her father's war-time account of his RAF service between 1942 and 1946, supported and supplemented by an oral history that was recorded in 1984 by his grandson, Anthony Dolphin, her late sister's oldest son. The oral history project was part of Anthony's GCSE History, 'O'-level when he was 15.

Carol This was the first time I learned about some of Dad's more painful and distressing war-time experiences, although I knew that he fought in World War Two and was in the RAF. I was 36 and a mother, myself. His war record shows various key dates, but there is little detailed information available on the recruitment and enlistment of men from Northern Ireland.

In preparation for telling my dad's story I met several times with his brother George at his home in Coleraine, a town not far from where they were born. George told me that one lunchtime in early July 1942, Jim, as Dad liked to be called, and his two cousins, David and Bobby Gilmour, the sons of my grandad's brother and my great uncle, Robert Gilmour, decided to 'join up', having planned this while working together on the same farm in rural Kilrea, County Derry. I can only imagine that their motive was in part to get away from the drudgery of farming and to participate in what they would have seen as the adventure of war. They did not even tell their parents and 'ran away' to the recruiting office in Belfast. Dad's war record shows the date of his enlistment as 6 July 1942. He was 21. It also shows his occupation as that of 'Carter', which would have been someone who drove the cart on a farm—usually delivering hay. The equivalent farm occupation now would be a tractor driver.

Just as Jenny's grandfather left a memory of his war journey by train from Whitchurch to Aldershot on a postcard, so Dad described to his grandson Anthony the train journey through Irish countryside to Belfast and recounted that it was raining and that the train arrived an hour late. At that time, there was a local railway station in the nearest town of Kilrea to which they could have walked, but the station no longer exists. I assume that they had suitcases with them which they must have concealed somehow when they left the house and then at the farm where they were working. None of them had been to the city of Belfast before and indeed had not travelled further than their local seaside town of Portrush, a distance of just over 21 miles. As such, their local landscape was smaller, if anything, than the South Devon world Bert Manning inhabited. Dad recounted to Anthony how they found the recruiting office in Belfast only with great difficulty, joined up and then had a long wait before being told they were going straight to England. Archive photos of the recruiting office in Hanover House, Belfast, show long queues of Irishmen waiting to join up. Jim remembered that the news of going straight to England did not really sink in and how he became worried about not telling his parents that he had enlisted. The family did not have a telephone, and it is not clear how this news would have reached them. On reflection, it is highly likely that Dad's brother George, who knew of their plan, told their parents. On one of the occasions when I met with George to talk about this, he said that he had wanted to go with them, but at just 16 he was too young to enlist.

Dad's war record notes that he was educationally unsuitable for trade training, presumably an outcome of his poor education. Certainly, my dad was highly intelligent. On the same war record, his medical category is listed as Grade 1. Having enlisted, Dad and his cousins walked to Belfast docks with the other young recruit, as directed by the recruitment officers. Belfast docks housed the famous Harland and Wolfe shipbuilding yards where many warships (and famously the Titanic) were built. During the war Belfast, the most advanced industrialised city in the island of Ireland, also produced war tanks and planes. It was here in the dockland that they boarded a ship which James described as resembling 'two enormous sheets of rusted steel bolted together' and in which they crossed the Irish Sea to Liverpool. The journey would have taken 10–12 hours. James described how he prayed for a good crossing but his prayers went unanswered, and along with all the other recruits he had to manage seasickness because it was a very rough crossing. The Irish Sea is notoriously stormy, and Dad's abiding memory was of the pervasive stench of wet clothes and whiskey.

The timing of all of this suggests that it would have been the following day when they arrived in England. Landing in Liverpool, which he described as 'very dark and shrouded in mist', the recruits were told to make their way to a bus which then took them slowly through the fog to Padgate, an RAF supply centre and small RAF station in Lancashire. They spent seven weeks there being 'kitted out' and taught 'simple RAF etiquette'. According to his war record, this was '9 Coastal Command' where he was stationed from 14 July until 7 September 1942. This coastal Operational Training Unit, Number 9, was formed in 1942 to train long-range fighter crews. Later, Coastal Commands were to be overshadowed by Fighter and Bomber Commands.

Dad's war record is scant. Further enquiries through an ex-servicemen's association have shown me that most servicemen's records are similar, mainly because they relied upon unsystematic reporting at an individual level. Still, I am frustrated that there is a gap in his record from February 1944 to March 1946, the period leading up to the Normandy landings and during his time in Europe. According to his personal account, after arriving in Liverpool from Belfast, Dad was sent to Blackpool for 11 weeks of compulsory training, which he found to be what he described as both 'mentally and physically gruelling'. The recruits were billeted in hotels and guest houses along the sea front at Blackpool. Dad told Anthony that he thought about giving up and going home during some of the regular ten-mile marches along the sands from Blackpool to Morecombe. However, while he did not relish many of these extreme physical ability tests, it seems he did enjoy the rifle training and became an excellent shot. (As a child I remember visits to the fairground where he often won prizes! I was surprised and excited that my dad—who was so gentle—could shoot a rifle.) At the end of an 11-week stretch of this period of training, the recruits were assessed in terms of skills and ability and issued with the role to which they were thought to be most suited and a corresponding posting. Such RAF postings included the South Coast, Hereford and East Anglia and Stafford 16 Munitions Unit (MU), the latter being where Dad was sent. He was to be part of a squadron supplying fuel and munitions to the Second Tactical Air Force (2nd TAF) where he spent many months. At that time, Stafford 16 MU was described as a non-flying Royal Air Force station and was mainly an aircraft equipment unit.

Jim worked extremely hard at Stafford 16 MU, under strict discipline for the next 12 months, doing what he called 'hard labour'. He was registered as an AC1 (Aircraftman 1st Class) on 31 December 1942 and after the end of the war, on 31 December 1945, as a LAC (Leading Aircraftman). He described the hard work at 16 MU, manhandling converted train trucks into huge hangers and then loading them with ammunition, blankets and food. Presumably, this would be the nature of their task in Europe. However, because of the secrecy of what was about to happen with the Normandy invasion, the tasks and training during this time must have seemed pointless to the troops. Overall, this time comprised highs as well as lows, but Dad told Anthony that he found it tedious and was glad to leave Stafford. However, it was during his time there that he met my mother, Nellie Davis, a shopkeeper's daughter from Lane Head, Willenhall, in the Midlands. She had joined up and become a clerk in the Women's Auxiliary Air Force (WAAF) and was stationed at 16 MU.

While they were 'courting', as it was called then, my mother must have discovered she was pregnant with my older sister, and so my parents decided to get married as soon as possible. At that time, and for some time after, 'having to get married' was something to be ashamed of, and this conception 'out of wedlock' continued to be kept a secret from my sister Pauline until she was in her 40s and nearing the end of her shortened life. As a consequence of being pregnant, my mother had to leave the WAAF, which meant she had no alternative but to return to her parental home which she did reluctantly. Mum recounted to me many years later, how, despite her married status, her father disapproved most fiercely of her pregnancy and did not speak to her until after she gave birth. It was at this point that he became besotted with his granddaughter with whom he spent lots of time.

Talking to my cousin, Barrie Davis, whose father, Frederick, was the eldest child in the Davis family, he remembered my dad 'arriving on the doorstep' of his parents' home (his mother, my Auntie Doris and Uncle Fred), on Christmas Day, 1943, where everyone was gathered. At the end of December 1943, my mother would have been two months pregnant but was still unmarried and so most likely would not have disclosed her pregnancy to anyone in her family. Neither of my parents knew that Dad would be posted to Europe very soon.

In terms of the hasty marriage, Dad's war record shows that he was granted disembarkment leave on 6 February 1944. The record also shows details of his marriage to Nellie Davis in the registry office in Croydon on 5 February. This occupies one sheet of his two-sheet profile and also contains details of their daughter Pauline, plus his release date, and so must have been completed when he left the RAF. I have a copy of their marriage certificate and also a painting of them on their wedding day, copied by my nephew from a photograph. They are both wearing RAF uniforms, seated with just their top halves showing and both

Fig. 7.3 Nellie Davis and James Gilmore. Marriage at Croydon Registry Office, England. February 5, 1944

looking very seriously into the camera. Taking such a photograph must have been a service offered by the registry office, but one for which they would have had to pay. I know from my mother's account of the wedding that they had to get strangers off the street to act as witnesses. Further, they did not have a honeymoon and spent just one night together in Croydon (Fig. 7.3).

Now a married man, and an expectant father, Dad left Stafford and was posted next to Haywards Heath in Essex. He was assigned to the 309 Supply and Transport Squadron which was a support unit to the Second Tactical Air Force, which meant basically keeping the planes in the air. 309 Squadron was a Polish Squadron which was formed in 1940 in Great Britain as a tactical reconnaissance unit and was part of the Polish Government-in-exile in the UK. In 1942 it became a fighter Squadron flying Mustangs and Hurricanes in missions over France. It was part of the air defence of Great Britain and under Fighter Command which was a single command of all the RAF centres. Dad's war record shows that he was assigned to 309 RAF Squadron on 3 August 1943.

The 2nd TAF was one of three tactical forces in the RAF during and after World War Two. It was first formed in 1943 from units in Fighter and Bomber Command to establish a force capable of supporting the army in the field and was part of the intense preparation for the invasion of Europe. Dad's role would be part of supplying planes landing on temporary air fields in Europe. Here, in Haywards Heath in Essex, alongside the basics of warfare, camouflage and survival, men of the newly formed squadron were taught how to drive and live in a truck for long periods of time.

The squadron spent just a few weeks in Essex before being moved to Groombridge in Kent, where the troops were prepared for the Normandy landings and taught what to do once they landed. As told to Anthony, Dad's abiding memory was that the most essential part of the training was to remember 'speed is the key'. At this time, security was tight, and even the locals of what was then a small village were unaware of what was happening. Mail was heavily censored, and the men were not allowed to mention their location in any correspondence.

Next, Dad spent just over a week at Droxford, where the details of the landings were rehearsed before he and his squadron returned to Groombridge. Once there, he claimed that they felt much more confident in knowing what was going to happen and what would be expected of them. Eventually, they were given news that the date of the first landings onto the Normandy beaches was to be 6 June, with his unit leaving England on D-Day plus 3 and landing in Normandy on D-Day plus 4, which was 10 June 1944, one day before his birthday. While they waited, they undertook more intensive preparations. Security was stepped up, and no-one was allowed to write home because Operation Overlord, the code name for the Normandy invasion, had to be kept secret.

News of the first wave of landings filtered back to the troops and, on 8 June, Jim's squadron was transported to Portsmouth by train. He remembered the journey vividly because the train was crammed with British, American and Canadian troops, all with full kit and rifles. All the seats had been removed to allow as many men as possible onto the train with their equipment. Like everyone else, he had to stand all the way on the journey of nearly a hundred miles, which would have taken between three and four hours. On arrival at Portsmouth, Jim discovered that he had been assigned a Leyland Bullnose truck to drive—which pleased him because it was 'quick, responsive and one of the better trucks'. The Leyland Bullnose truck was one of the larger vehicles used in the squadron, and while it might have had the advantage of being more efficient, it required a decent road surface, and this would affect how easily he could stay with his squadron as they drove across Europe. Chapter 8 details Dad's journey across Europe—from 10 June 1944 to 17 September 1946 when he was demobbed and went home.

7.8 Seven Years of Change

The three men whose war-time experiences we set out in this chapter were clearly very different from one another, even the brothers, Arthur and David Manning. All three were involved in a *world* war, and for two of them this meant travelling to countries and continents they might otherwise never have visited. So the world opened up for them, and in the cases of David and James, so did the family lives we shared with them until their deaths.

That said, all three felt the power of the state to constrain and confine individuals, something neither of us have experienced. Donald Gould's letter at the start of this chapter expresses a sense of vital years of young life lost. And unlike a prison sentence, war-time service had no readily foreseeable end for these men. What did the requirement or the impetus to serve mean to them? Jenny's father wanted the war over but signed up to the idea that it was a holy war that would inevitably defeat evil pagan forces. James, as Carol describes later, went on to lose all faith in the rhetoric of nationalism and patriotism, instead recognising the pointless suffering it produced. Arthur may have been the most enthusiastic soldier, but his letters express loneliness and frustration at being so far from home for so long.

As ever we are both reading between many lines. In James' case he was asked directly by Anthony, his grandson, what had happened and what it meant to him. Carol too was able to elicit his recollections and his subsequent state of mind. His story is therefore told in a different language and form to those of Arthur and David. Their 'voices' are filtered through letters home and diaries.

As Carol describes though, there was a silencing of the distress James had suffered, as her mother directed the family's energies and attention towards the future and not the past in the years that followed. Similarly David brought little of the eventual loss of his entire family into the 'nice little house' where he spent the rest of his life. As authors we have found our way into experiences and environments remote from us in so many ways, yet they constituted the world we were both born into. As Carol says, finding that her father was a crack shot was both a source of excitement but also surprise, the skills of a serviceman spilling through a crevice in the post-war world. Jenny had exactly the same experience and wondered at her father's pride in a skill so at odds with the gentle domestic life he was living.

Notes

1. Winstone, Ruth. (Ed). 1994. *Tony Benn. Years of Hope. Diaries, Papers and Letters, 1940–1962*. London: Arrow Books Ltd.
2. Now Iran.
3. Day-Lewis, Tamsin (ed.). 1995. *Last Letters Home*. London: Macmillan. (P. 2).
4. Day-Lewis, Tamsin (ed.). 1995. *Last Letters Home*. London: Macmillan. (P. 4).

8

Experiencing the Horror of World War Two

The story of her father's experience of being an Aircraftman in the RAF 309 Squadron continues here as Carol describes what happened to him between landing in Normandy in 1944 and his discharge in 1946, more than one year after the end of the war.

Carol To set the scene for the extraordinary events that one ordinary man found himself involved in and because familiarity with a war which ended over 70 years ago is waning, I begin with the wider landscape of what was going on in Europe at that time and the key military operations that Dad was involved in. Although not taking part directly in front-line armed conflict, he played a crucial role within a supply unit that supported 309 Squadron planes by providing munitions, parts and fuel. There are gaps I cannot fill, however, between official accounts of the events he participated in and the partial record Dad left behind in his oral history. Joining the dots, as Jenny calls it, is not totally possible. It would be wonderful if Dad had written a detailed diary of everything that happened to him—but no such record exists. However, in presenting this overview into which I then fit his account, I find myself amazed by the accuracy of his recollections and how vividly he called to mind some of

© The Author(s) 2018
C. Komaromy, J. Hockey, *Family Life, Trauma and Loss in the Twentieth Century*,
https://doi.org/10.1007/978-3-319-76602-7_8

the detail, even to Anthony his grandson, nearly 40 years after the end of the war. It highlights to me how overwhelming it was for him and how it stayed in his memory until he died at the age of 70.

8.1 The Bigger Picture

The war in Europe took a significant turn when the Allied troops invaded Normandy in northern France, under the code name Operation Overlord, in order to liberate the territories occupied by the German forces. Between 1 April and 5 June 1944, in preparation for the invasion, Allied bombers increased their sorties across northern and western France. They were attempting to reduce the German forces' resistance to the invasion by targeting railways, bridges and roads and thus impeding enemy mobility. Of course the damage to roads also impeded the Allied advance through France and Europe, and this is why tanks were essential to both sides, not just in terms of the ground damage they could inflict with their guns but also in managing the terrain. The Allies also landed 155,000 soldiers by parachute to provide ground support behind enemy lines in readiness for the arrival of troops on D-Day. The highly secret Operation Overlord eventually took place on 6 June 1944 and involved three key phases: air landings, air and naval bombardments and seaborne landings. Fifteen countries were involved in the Allied invasion, but the troops were primarily American, British, Canadian, French and Polish. The five beaches used in the Normandy landings occupied a 50-mile stretch of coast and were code-named Utah and Omaha (American), Gold and Sword (British) and Juno (Canadian). The beaches subsequently allowed for the creation of an essential seaport where supplies to the Allied troops could be delivered—in the form of reinforcement troops and supplies. Mulberry Harbour at Arromanches was therefore an artificial harbour that comprised elements which had been pre-fabricated in England, towed across the English Channel and assembled in location, all in 12 days. Building artificial harbours was a revolutionary feat. Mulberry B (British) was nicknamed Port Winston; Mulberry A (American) had to be abandoned after a storm destroyed most of it. Mulberry B became operational from 'D'-Day plus 8, although work continued on it for some time.

The first day of the invasion was code-named 'D-Day', with 'D' simply representing the word 'day'. Preparations had been in process for at least two years, even though, as highlighted in Chap. 7, the troops involved had not been informed about it until very close to the event. Although the loss of life was great, there is no accurate record of how many people were killed and injured. Certainly in the air attacks in preparation for D-Day, it is estimated that 12,000 pilots died. Ever since the fall of France and the German occupation, there had been Allied bombing raids on strategic towns of course. The number of civilian deaths was therefore much higher than that for the armed forces, and even though they too had suffered many losses since 1940, the bombing in 1944 intensified just before and after D-Day and was particularly devastating. Indeed, in preparation during 1943 alone, 7458 civilians died on D-Day itself, however, Omaha Beach suffered the highest casualties with about 10,000 troops killed.

8.2 The Allied Advance

The city of Caen, 22 miles from Mulberry Harbour at Arromanches, was not captured by the Allies until 20 July 1944. The major German resistance at Falaise, 28 miles inland from Caen, referred to as the Battle of the Falaise Pocket, was finally overcome in August 1944 when 50,000 German soldiers were taken prisoner. Thereafter, progress was more rapid; the Allied forces crossed the River Seine, and on 25 August 1944, Paris was liberated. This marked the end of the Battle of Normandy, code-named Operation Overlord. The total casualty number for the Battle of Normandy is estimated at 425,000 Allied and German soldiers killed, missing or injured. Civilian deaths were estimated to be 20,000, with many towns flattened, including Caen. The Battle lasted for three months, much longer than anticipated, due to the strength of the German resistance.

The next major offensive was called Operation Market Garden—often referred to as 'a bridge too far'—which began a month later in September 1944. On 17 September, Allied paratroopers landed inside the occupied Netherlands, which Germany had invaded on 10 May 1940. Simultaneously, the advance of Allied airborne and ground force troops continued along the contested, armed front between German-occupied

Arnhem and Oosterbeck, with the British Second Army in the Eindhoven-Arnhem corridor.

The Allies' goal was to secure key bridges over the Lower Rhine to permit movement into the industrial Ruhr region of Germany, so avoiding the Siegfried Line, a series of German fortifications that stretched for 390 miles—from near the Dutch border to near the Swiss border. Due to a number of key factors—delays by the Allies, supplies that failed to meet demands, the underestimation of German resistance (whereas the 9th and 10th divisions of the SS Panzers were very strong) and several breakdowns in communication between various Allied groups—the British failed to take the bridge at Arnhem.

Accounts of Operation Market Garden highlight how the rapid advance on a broad front after Caen meant that supplies could not really keep up with the troops' demands. Dad recounted how congestion made it impossible for supplies to get through, part of his role being to deliver essential requirements to the air fields. The roads in the Netherlands, which were narrow in any case, were badly damaged by bombs. This held back tanks and heavy vehicles so that, along with the shortage of fuel that caused vehicles to break down, they became targets for air attack. Roads were also obstructed by burned-out vehicles that had been victims of such attacks and added to the congestion. Fundamentally, then, British troops could not get through to support the paratroopers in Arnhem. Further, although the German forces were in full retreat, and the Allies assumed this to be so, Hitler had ordered two senior officers to stop the retreat and organise resistance, most of which took place around Arnhem.

In the course of Operation Market Garden the Allies lost an estimated 15,000 to 17,000 men, mostly in the British First Airborne Division, who were killed, wounded or captured. In summary, analysts argue that Market Garden failed through factors that included intelligence failure, poor planning, poor weather and lack of tactical initiative. It ended in failure on 27 September 1944 when the Allied troops were positioned south of Arnhem with no bridges secured.

Subsequently, on 16 December 1944, German troops launched the Battle of the Bulge, also called the Ardennes Offensive, along a 75-mile front between Aachen, very close to the German border, and Triel, situated in northeast France and Luxemburg. The Ardennes territory comprises heavily forested, steep-sided hills and was therefore difficult terrain for ground troops. At the time this territory was being held by just six American divisions. In the winter of 1944, snow in this region was especially deep, but the German force was formidable, comprising 28 divisions, 10 of which were armoured—with over 1000 tanks. Hitler's plan to launch a surprise attack to take the Ardennes and then cross the River Meuse and retake Brussels and, more significantly, the Port of Antwerp came close to succeeding. The Allies were taken by surprise, and initially there was chaos and mayhem before US troops realised what was happening and got organised several days later. Montgomery sent reserves south to offer support and to forestall the German attack on the River Meuse, eventually defeating them in January 1945. Losses on both sides were high, with 120,000 German troops killed, missing or wounded and 89,000 Americans.

Then in February 1945, the Yalta agreement was signed between Churchill, Roosevelt and Stalin in which the Western Allies, represented by Churchill and Roosevelt, effectively abandoned support of Poland to Stalin's Russia. That spring, RAF and USAF aerial bombardment over Germany intensified, killing 25,000 people, the greatest loss of life being in Dresden. The town was seen as strategically essential to the German defence of the eastern front and the centre of communication; therefore, it had to be destroyed. Meanwhile, ground forces were being built up for crossing the Rhine, which was achieved in March 1945. Named Operation Plunder, this involved a series of co-ordinated Rhine crossings that began on 23 March at Rees and Wesel. To reduce German resistance, a massive assault was launched on Wesel during the day and night of 23 March, with guns fired continuously for four hours and supported by British bombers. Despite resistance by German forces, many crossings were made successfully on various floating bridges.

After these major operations, the Allied troops were able to advance through Germany towards Berlin, fanning out from the Baltic in the north to Austria in the south. At the time there was news of Russia being very close to Berlin. However, while Eisenhower and Montgomery were desperate to meet up with Russia, underlying conflicts began to emerge. Once the common enemy, Nazi Germany, was about to be defeated, long-standing tensions between incompatible ideologies, plus other issues of mistrust on both sides, made Allied military and political superiority over Soviet Russia a priority. It seems that the alliance only just held until the end of the war, with mistrust filtering through the ranks to the British and US troops on the ground. With the end of the war in Europe in sight, Western Europe and the USA began to grow concerned about how post-war Europe might be divided, both in terms of territory and influence. Indeed, a few months later, political and military power was one of the tensions that fuelled the competition in nuclear weapon technology—played out in the Manhattan project to build the first atomic bombs and which culminated in the bombing of Hiroshima and Nagasaki in August 1945. Some would argue the use of these bombs was a demonstration of military power and served several purposes beyond the defeat of Japan. Further, it seems that the post-war decisions that had to be made about the division of the spoils of war effectively soured relationships and culminated in the Cold War that was to last from 1945 until 1991.

A few months before the end of World War Two, in April 1945, the concentration camp Bergen-Belsen, situated in northern Germany and southwest of the town of Bergen near to Celle, was liberated. Effectively, it was clear to Germany that they were about to lose the war, and for various reasons, as I explain, the camp was handed over to the Allies who were close by. It was one of the first concentration camps to be liberated and thereafter brought to public attention. British camera and film crews, for example, recorded footage of the camp that was broadcast widely. Previously, between 1941 and 1945, several camps within Bergen-Belsen had been set up to house different categories of prisoner. Its first use was in 1941 when the camp had already been expanded from one that accommodated the workers who built it to contain Soviet prisoners of war. Its original purpose, however, had been to provide a 'special' camp for prisoners who could be exchanged for German citizens interned abroad. This 'special' camp was relocated to a separate area of Bergen-Belsen in March 1943. Then a month later, in April 1943, the Schutzstaffel (SS) took over part of the camp. The SS was a paramilitary organisation under the command of Hitler and the Nazi Party in Germany. Their takeover signified a change in the treatment of inmates, and its original purpose altered dramatically as prisoners from other camps were transferred there. People began to die in their hundreds every day from disease and starvation as overcrowding increased. The different sections of the camp were kept separate, however, and treatment did vary between them.

By December 1944 Bergen-Belsen housed 15,257 prisoners overall. From January 1945, thousands were transferred from camps in Eastern Europe, where the Russian troops were gaining ground and driving out German troops, so that by April 1945 the population had reached over 60,000. Indeed, during the final weeks of the war, evacuation transports from other concentration and extermination camps near the front line were also being sent to Belsen with many men, women and children taken there by over a hundred transports or on death marches. By then, the death rate in Belsen and in the transports and marches was high. Very close to the end of the war, the SS destroyed all of the camp's records to try to cover up what had happened there.

On 12 April, British forces in Celle, the nearest large town, were approached by the commander of the local German Army who requested that a neutral zone around the camp be established, and a 48-square kilometre zone was set up to allow British relief workers to enter. Fundamentally, this was to try to contain the spread of the infectious diseases endemic in the camp, given fears that it would spread to local populations and troops on both sides. Between 12 and 15 April, the first British soldiers entered the camp—and on 15 April the camp commander, Kramer, was arrested. Hungarian soldiers in the German Army had been sent to keep order during the transition period while the British troops took over the camp. The medical corps of the Second Army took control of the camp and put out an urgent plea for local troops to deliver fresh water and supplies since there was no food in the camp and the water supply had been contaminated. They also warned people that there was an epidemic of typhus in the camp—as well as typhoid, diphtheria and dysentery. Those people who were first to enter the camp noted the stench of rotting corpses lying around, the sight of piles of human remains, around 10,000 bodies in all, and living people moving slowly like ghosts, with an incredible silence, despite the numbers of people there. It is estimated that more than 52,000 prisoners lost their lives at Bergen-Belsen, 14,000 of whom died in the first few weeks after liberation. In May 1945, the camp was burned down and later opened as a concentration camp memorial.

On 30 April, Hitler committed suicide. Just over a week later, on 7 May 1945, at Supreme Headquarters Allied Expeditionary Force (SHAEF) at Reims in the northeast of France, the unconditional surrender of the Third Reich—called the Reims Accord—was signed. This did not totally satisfy Russia who were concerned about continued fighting, and in Berlin on 8 May 1945, a surrender document was signed covering all German forces, including troops in Eastern Europe. The war in Europe was officially over.

8.3 Personal Journey

My dad's journey from Portsmouth to Gold Beach in June 1944, up until he was demobbed in 1946, took place within the context of the unprecedented events I have been summarising. Here I describe what he went through personally, along with details of a journey I took with my partner, Peter, in July 2017, to retrace my dad's war-time experiences in Europe up until the end of the war. Partly, I hoped to recapture local detail by making this journey, but also I wanted to try to imagine what he experienced. Trying to get a feel for what it was like to be involved in war for those on the front line and those at home has involved much speculation. I was able to talk to my dad directly about how he felt about some of his war-time experiences, and visiting some of the sites of war has made it easier to imagine and contextualise his responses.

Listening to Dad and feeling the intensity of his experience of being in Belsen, as well as witnessing many of the archived images and listening to accounts in the museum, made it overwhelmingly apparent why the memory stayed with him, and, as he told me, reappearing every time he closed his eyes. In what follows, I present Dad's story alongside my reflections on it from my own more recent journey.

It was a frustrating experience for me in many ways. In part, checking the 'facts' was difficult because not all the events had been recorded and I have to accept that there are gaps that cannot be filled. For example, while there are detailed logs of 309 Squadron's flying missions in Europe and the main troop movement of the 2nd TAF, the daily events of parts of the squadron are not recorded. Further, there are many times when my dad and John, his gunner, who were driving a large supply truck, were separated from the main convoy of the squadron. None of that was formally recorded. At some point, and this was shortly after my return from Europe, I reframed my account not as a detailed history of Dad's war, but as a significant rendering of the extraordinary nature of war as it happens to ordinary people and how that can ripple through subsequent generations. Of course, my journey across parts of Europe was profoundly personal, and while I felt I was carrying him with me on the quest to try to uncover what happened to him, I was frustrated and upset at times that he was not with me physically to share it. I can only reflect on what he might have felt and still carry a deep sense of loss that he is dead. It was always my hope that when my father aged, I would have the pleasurable duty of caring for him. I am sure that taking such a reminiscence trip would have been something he would have wanted to do, and to share that with him would have been a great privilege for me to do so.

To begin again though, in June 1944, Dad was among the troops who sailed from Portsmouth to Gold Beach in northern France on the Empire Rapier. This was a huge cargo ship, commissioned by the British Ministry of War Transport and built in California (built in 1943 and scrapped in 1966). It appeared to Dad that there were only British troops on board. The ship creaked constantly, and he thought that the hold resembled a vast eerie aircraft hangar. Indeed, he described the creaks, groans and engine noise as merging into one 'giant vile scream'. This crossing in the Empire Rapier took from early morning on 9 June to midday on 10 June. Dad described how, on arrival, the huge doors opened slowly to allow in a rush of daylight and, squinting at the light, they drove off the ship onto steel landing ramps, leading to the wide expanse of Gold Beach. These landing ramps were later to be replaced by more permanent ramps as part of the famous Mulberry Harbour and part of the British sector. Jim described to Anthony, my nephew, how very nervous he felt on arrival at Arromanches. He recounted a vision of the beach as a black mass of fire and smoke, covered with tank tracks and the dents of thousands of heavy boots of troops. It is not obvious why the beach would be quite as Dad described it. There is not a great deal recorded about troop landings after D-Day, and so it is unclear why the remains of the damage from 6 June, D-Day, in the form of smoke, would still be visible, although the bombardment from the coastal defence forces had been intense (Fig. 8.1).

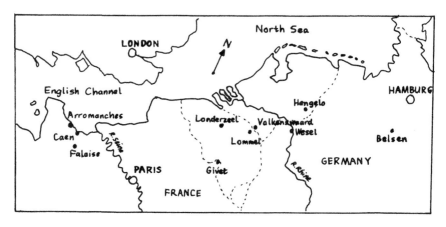

Fig. 8.1 Retracing Carol's father's journey from Arromanches to Belsen

Retracing Dad's steps with my partner in 2017, it is hard to imagine what such a beautiful area would look with such bomb damage (Fig. 8.2). In my diary of that journey I recounted:

Peter and I arrived at Arromanches – the hotel is on the sea front – and our room overlooks the beach and the remains of Mulberry Harbour. This is where Dad landed and onto which he and his mate John Craddy drove the Leyland Bullnose truck to make their way to Caen. It seems that today (2 July 2017) everyone in France is spending the day in Arromanches to take advantage of the sun, sea and sand. The overwhelming mood here is one of holiday fun, while the remains of Mulberry Harbour serve as stark and ghostly reminders of the massive operation to build a temporary harbour which could accommodate the supply route for all allied troops.

We strolled around the town, with all of the shops and cafes seemingly taking advantage of D-Day as a tourist attraction.

I can only speculate, based on what my Dad recorded in his oral history and from being in the setting, what it must have been like to be part of this event. I assume the troops knew that many had died on June 6th, but that their lives were safer for their own embarkment, several days after D-Day insofar as German resistance had been overcome at least on the landing beaches. Part of my motivation for this journey was by being in the same setting, I might be able to imagine what it might have felt like. However, my emotional speculation is limited and I can't seem to be able to imagine the feelings. I have no comparison to make with such an extraordinary event – and I am saddened by the cold detachment

Fig. 8.2 The remains of Mulberry Harbour, Arromanches, Normandy, France, 2017. Photo taken by Carol Komaromy.

I feel about my Dad's experience before I was born. I think I had expected to feel something more not just from being in the same place but also because I was very close to my father and often knew if he was upset, even at a distance, as he did when I was distressed. I can speculate, that even though the remnants of the Mulberry Harbours are still here, that the jolly holiday atmosphere, including people swimming around and diving from the remains of the Mulberry Harbour, makes this imagining impossible. As the sun sets, the structures take on a more sinister appearance as dark metal shapes in the orange sunset.

The following day we went to a cinema showing a film in 360 degrees of the D-Day landings and visited the associated museum. My diary record shows its impact on me:

Watching the film – showing footage on the D-Day landings – I felt very moved and tearful, quite overwhelmed in fact. Suddenly it all felt real. The sights and sounds were powerful. The footage and images, interspersed with speeches from various leaders, brought home the terrible devastation of parts of France as Allied forces made their way through Caen towards Paris. The look of terror on the faces of the troops as they stepped off the landing craft and witnessed the slaughter of their comrades made the horror of war more real to me. Suddenly, the camera focused on a tiny kitten crying in the rubble, and it seemed to symbolise both the horror and the threat to 'innocence'. I don't really know how I feel about the liberation – given my pacifist beliefs. I find war and violence horrific and morally indefensible, but I don't know what the alternative would have been. I'm reminded of Ghandi's quote, "Remember that all through history, there have been tyrants and murderers, and for a time, they seem invincible. But in the end, they always fall. Always."

In the museum, I was pleased to note that the Second Tactical Air Force, to which my dad's squadron belonged, got a mention. Also, Peter pointed out a map of the airstrips that were constructed, some of which Dad and his squadron would have been supplying.

There was no break in Dad's journey as, on landing, the British 'push' that was part of Operation Overlord began immediately. This was to include the capture of Caen. Dad's truck mate, John Craddy, was his gunner and had to stand with his head out of the top of the cab so that Dad mostly just saw John's legs. Even when John was not manning the gun, the roar of the squadron's engines was so loud that it made talking impossible. The congestion on the roads along the coast from the landing beaches increased, and gradually they had to slow down. Indeed, there were many days when they did not move at all but could hear fighting nearby. Jim disclosed that he was especially afraid at night because they had to sleep in the cab of their truck that contained high-octane fuel, munitions, bombs and airplane spare parts. Therefore, they were very vulnerable if fired upon. When stationary and at night, Jim and John took turns manning the gun in five-hour shifts. When the roads did accommodate large trucks, Dad and John were able to stay in the convoy with the rest of the squadron; however, this was not always the case. While their first destination of Caen was not far from Arromanches, it was not until 20 July 1944 that it was captured, having taken over a month from the invasion and lots of fighting before it was secured. Further, since Jim and John were in one of the bigger trucks, the heavy fighting and massive holes in the road often made it impossible for them to advance. To find a way around, they had to retreat back down the coast, away from the squadron, and then attempt to drive along small lanes, all the time worrying about possible land mines and getting lost. Dad recounted one such journey along a lane which turned into a track that ended up being a farm entrance. They followed the track for several miles until it got too dark to continue and had to spend the night in the truck. At dawn, they could hear traffic in the near distance and crawled into a ditch on the edge of a field from where, to their relief, they could hear English being spoken. They had stumbled on an American unit and announced themselves loudly in English. After being welcomed, they spent time with the troops, enjoying US rations, including chocolate and bubble gum—a first for them both. Although the American troops let Jim drive one of their massive Studebaker trucks, which were specially adapted Chevrolets, he was not impressed and claimed that he found them very slow and sluggish in comparison to their Leyland petrol truck.

Communication at this time was mainly by crystal radio, but radios and radio operators would have been within the main convoy. Therefore, while Dad and John would have been briefed on key destination points, they would have lost direct contact when separated from the main convoy.

Travelling from Arromanches to Caen on 4 July, I noted:

> It was helpful to visit the museum at Caen, which is totally dedicated to D-day. It brought home further, the reality of war and its destructive horror. Apart from the death toll and casualties, the terror on the faces of the troops shown in

the film footage, as in the cinema in Arromanches, conveyed something of the reality of the horror of war. We also visited the museum at Falaise which depicted the story of the civilian cost. It was the first time I fully appreciated that the Allies were deliberately – and often indiscriminately – bombing towns and villages in order to drive out the German occupying forces.

In my reflections, I note further:

I guess everyone must have believed what they were doing was right and trusted their leaders. Although, there is a comment from Dad's account in relation to 'Monty' (Montgomery who was in charge of the British troops) about beginning to doubt that their leaders knew what they were doing. While some of his account of seeing the devastation and, particularly distressed children, brings home his compassion and humanity, he does not openly make a connection between Allied bombings and the cost to civilians.

Eventually, travelling from Caen, Dad and John regained direct contact with their unit ten miles outside of Falaise. They joined them as they embarked on a series of complex air and ground raids, part of the Battle of the Falaise Pocket that aimed to drive out German, occupying troops. Jim and John's unit was heading east to carve a path for the Allies to cross the Rhine. Because their task was to prepare captured air strips for RAF landings, this meant taking supplies of fuel, munitions and spare parts to the air fields. Dad remembered the inhabitants of Falaise cheering as their unit went through the main streets. This was August 1944, and one particularly outstanding memory for him was the sight of slaughtered cows and horses in the fields outside the town, rotting in the heat. The foul stench and the buzzing flies turned their stomachs. It seems that the retreating German troops had shot the animals to avoid leaving the Allies any fresh milk and meat. In talking about Dad's account to my nephew, Anthony, after my July 2017 trip, he said that he remembered from the interview how Dad found the slaughter of animals particularly difficult to bear.

For Dad's unit, the move forward was hampered by German resistance, and it was not until US troops reached the British two weeks later that they could move on. The British 2nd TAF with 309 Squadron took advantage of the clear route ahead and thus made rapid progress across the northeast of France. The route involved crossing the River Seine, with hardly time to refuel before another call came for them to prepare an airstrip. Refuelling and loading their trucks would have been done at supply stations set up across the north of France. Jean-Pierre Benamou has written about the logistics of supplying troops during the Battle of France in 1944.[1] Everything from food to arms and tanks had to be placed in large accessible depots to meet the needs of over two million Allied troops. Fuel supplies were from a fuel line under the Channel from which fuel cans were filled and taken to supply stations. There were also various access points for fresh drinking water.

The continuous pace was tiring, but in approaching Belgium, and as a result of congestion, they were forced to stop at a small village 30 miles from Brussels called Londerzeel. As a result of Montgomery and Eisenhower's indecision about tactics, they paused here for nearly four days from 4 to 7 September 1944. Oblivious to the reason for the hold-up after such rapid progress, Jim and John worried that something had gone wrong. In his account to Anthony, Dad was amused that Montgomery blamed the troops for 'relaxing'. He realised in retrospect that it was 'dithering in high places that held it up'. Jim also recounted that while he held Montgomery in high esteem at the time, later he thought he was someone who was 'playing a big game with toy soldiers'.

Peter and I could not follow Dad's route precisely because his unit travelled back and forth, but visiting Londerzeel on 6 and 7 July 2017, I noted:

This 'small village', as it would have been in the 1940s, is now a medium-sized town. Presumably, it has grown because of its close proximity to Brussels and people's ability to commute more easily. Indeed, it resembles a large urban sprawl, but the area looks wealthy. However, the roads are in poor condition, which my partner tells me is a feature of Belgium. There is nothing in Londerzeel to show that troops were ever here. I've been given some email addresses of the local veteran's association, so I'll email them.

I think travelling some of the route in and around here helps me in getting the measure of the chaos and the war dragging on is an important feature and somehow being here makes it real. Perhaps it is just that the roads are in such poor condition and I have seen so much war-time footage that I can imagine his journey more easily.

The next phase of the advance began in September 1944 as part of the operation code-named Market Garden. It was one that eventually failed. When the squadron moved on through Brussels they were told that there was a hold-up at the Albert Canal (connecting Antwerp with Liege), and so they were diverted and told to try to cross the Rhine at Nijmegen in Holland. The resistance from German troops along the Dutch/German border meant that they were forced to stop at a small village called Valkenswaard in North Brabant. This was one of the first villages to be liberated in Holland on 17 September 1944, although it was not until February 1945 that all of Belgium was liberated. Dad recounted how he found the Dutch to be more genuinely friendly than the French and that he made friends with a couple who were teachers at a local school, called 'Mr. and Mrs.' Peel, as he referred to them (Fig. 8.3).

It was while they were here that the Luftwaffe began bombing raids as part of the response to the Allied troops' campaign, and Jim and John had to cower in the cab of the lorry as they flew overhead. They were terrified and convinced they would get hit and again face certain death, with the truck being full of high-octane fuel and munitions. Then they heard a massive explosion and peering out could see that a train had been hit at a

Fig. 8.3 A photo of Mr. and Mrs. Peel, Valkenswaard, given to Dad in 1944

small station nearby, fragments from which showered their truck. The station was burning, and the flames were 30 feet high while the train continued to explode. Next day they heard from Mr. Peel that the train was loaded with explosives. The RAF lost five men that night, but there were many more lives lost in this operation and in the RAF First Airborne Division. Dad and John moved on two days later and said sad farewells to their new friends. My diary entry for retracing the steps reads:

> *The visit to Valkenswaard was frustrating insofar as we found no trace of the station and no record of the train explosion – despite having found images on the internet of the event. All we could find was the old railway track, now used as a cycle path. There was a tiny stone memorial to the Resistance – but we visited the cemetery outside of the town situated in a wooded area and saw the graves of 250 British troops killed in the area during Operation Market Garden. Dad told Anthony that five of their squadron were killed the night the Luftwaffe bombed the train containing ammunition – but we could not see their graves. I left a message in the visitor's book. 'In memory of James Gilmore who fought and survived here in September, 1945.' I'm wondering if the apparent lack of recognition of what happened in September 1945 – with many troops held up in the area, represents a preference to forget the Occupation and the Liberation and indeed the war?*
>
> *Next we visited the Polish cemetery in Lommel, near Valkenswaard, where many who were killed during the Market Garden operation – were buried. The graves show some evidence of memorialization with some having poppies on the head stones and others having crucifixes on them. They contrast with the unadorned graves in many war cemeteries. Again, most died in September 1944. The final cemetery we visited in this area was also in Lommel, the largest war cemetery in western Europe for German soldiers. It is looked after by the German War Graves commission. The enormity and size of it is overwhelming – and evoked shock and a sense disgust in us both. The vision of so many graves and the young age of most of the men highlights the cost of this war on all sides. My own disgust is in seeing this level of slaughter as being in any way justifiable, as if 'enemy' slaughter is a necessary evil. There are 39,102 graves – and all you can see in this expanse are tombstones. Several thousand German troops buried here would have been killed in Operation Market Garden. It is interesting to note that rather than anonymising these dead soldiers by the uniformity and regularity of the headstones, to me they represent individual lives. This is true of all the war graves that I have visited over the years, and especially on this trip,*

but I see them as individual lives whose death has left their family in varying forms of pain and distress. On the grave stones with English inscriptions elsewhere, I have noted how some families have attempted to offer a compensatory message in order to make their sacrifice worthwhile and somehow mitigate the pain. As if that was possible.

The operation code-named 'Market Garden' had been a strategic move made by the Allied troops. The plan was to drop a massive force behind enemy lines to capture key bridges on the Rhine, including Arnhem and Nijmegen. Forced to stop many times, in a town the name of which Dad could not recall, he recounted one outstanding memory of making friends with a little girl that he and John found in tears by the side of the road. She was crying because of the noise of the trucks, and he and John gave her chocolate from their 'American survival box' and then took her home to her parents where they befriended the girl's family. The contrast with such a huge operation where the loss of life was so great and the fear of being killed was inescapable, makes this simple act of compassion very moving and gives a lie to the belief that emotional disconnection is an inevitable mental defence mechanism enabling people to survive.

This point comes up in the Russian author Vasily Grossman's account of Russia and Germany in World War Two. He argued that large-scale movements for the greater good of human society inevitably bring about bloodshed. In contrast there is 'everyday kindness'—'The kindness of an old woman carrying bread to a prisoner, the kindness of a soldier allowing a wounded enemy to drink from his water-flask, the kindness of youth towards age, the kindness of a peasant hiding an old Jew in his loft'.[2] This kindness, he says, 'is what is most truly human in a human being. It is what sets man apart, the highest achievement of his soul'.[3]

While American and Canadian troops were trying to clear the way ahead, the British slowly edged their way to the River Rhine. The German defences were very strong, and the squadron spent most of October 1944 stopping and starting and barely making any significant progress. Jim began to realise that the initial hopes of things happening at speed were not going to be realised and that the failure of Market Garden and the slow progress of the Russian troops in Central Europe meant the war was going to 'drag on for some time'. Indeed, between 16 and 25 December the US Second Armoured Division had retreated over 40 miles (Fig. 8.4).

Experiencing the Horror of World War Two 197

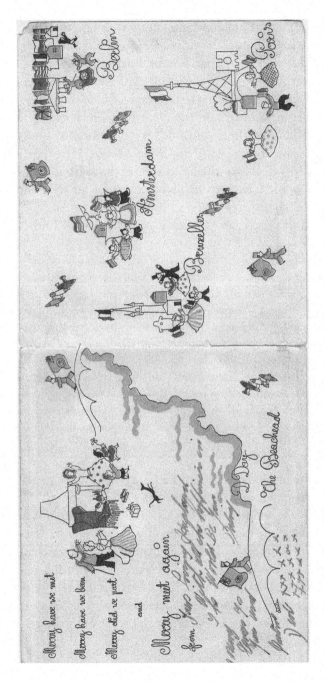

Fig. 8.4 A standard-issue RAF Christmas card sent from James to his wife and daughter, 1944

It is at this point that Jim and John, along with others of the squadron and as part of the Ardennes Offensive, were ordered to travel to Aachen, which is very close to the German border. But, because of the US retreat, they had to divert west to avoid the 9th Panzer division advancing as part of the Battle of the Bulge, one of the longest battles of the war. Retaliation by US Allies began in earnest in the New Year. Jim remembered a long drive to Givet—an American-controlled town in the Ardennes region of Belgium with a key bridge over the River Meuse. Here Jim and John spent a cold Christmas Day sitting in the truck, waiting for news from the front. Dad would have been involved in Europe for six months at this point.

We followed this route, and in Givet, on 5 July 2017, I noted:

Before leaving Givet – we went to the local war museum – which had film footage showing documentary accounts of the winter in the area and the Battle of the Bulge. It seems that the US Air Force bombed a local town by mistake. Of course, they bombed places where the German troops were holding out – and that would have killed civilians. There were many problems with the weather that affected the Allies' resistance to the Battle of the Bulge, in this case mainly US troops. The German offensive, deploying the Panzer division, was an attempt to reclaim part of Belgium and gain access to Antwerp. They used the bad weather to their advantage of the small number of US troops there – assuming it was difficult for the Allied troops to fly their planes. Further, many US and RAF planes were bombed on the small landing strips and thus unable to fly.

Dad recounted how January and February 1945 were extremely cold and how heaters were not allowed because of the glow they produced which would make them visible targets. Jim and John had to make for the Rhine but were unsure about where it was safe to cross. They headed northeast but lost contact with the squadron until they were nearly upon the Rhine. The Rhine crossings began in March 1945, and here they were told they had to use a Bailey bridge. Jim said it felt dangerous in the large Leyland truck, but in the end they crossed safely, their fears unfounded. Once across they found troops celebrating as some of the first to cross the Rhine.

It seems that the experience of the early months of 1945 was characterised by long periods spent waiting to move forward, and between 23 and 28 March two airborne divisions were parachuted in to clear the way behind enemy lines where they established a beachhead of 20 by 30 miles. Dad recalled how the race to Berlin was on and that they were in competition with the 'new enemy', the Russians, while, as he expressed it, they were all 'ordinary men who just wanted the bloody war to end'. As they advanced through Germany, they met little or no resistance. Dad remembered a town which he thought might be called Ochtrup that had been flattened by American tanks, where he and John saw people lying helpless in the rubble shrouded in foggy dust. They were not allowed to help the children in the streets who were clearly abandoned and distressed. This is something that upset him greatly. Ochtrup was not in fact the town, but there were many towns which had been flattened during the Allied bombing raids.

Retracing his steps, I noted:

On Sunday, we travelled to Hengelo driving from Londerzeel to this small town, which is north of Ochtrup. My research shows me that Ochtrup was not the town my Dad recalled being flattened by US tanks. He had queried the name – not being clear in his account – and while the 2nd TAF was in Ochtrup, this place was relatively unaffected by the war. Therefore, I decided not to visit. The drive takes us into Germany and then back into the Netherlands. The drive will have been in similar areas to where Dad was – he would have been around the border in the NL for several months. Wesel was a town that was flattened during the war, but I don't think this was the town Dad meant.

We crossed the River Rhine on a very large bridge at Wesel and speculated about whether he might have crossed at this narrower point. Accounts of the British 2nd Army crossing of the Rhine cite Rees, Wesel and Lippe as crossing points and so it could have been the same point the troops crossed in late March 1945. Unlike our secure crossing, Dad's was on a Bailey bridge and they were afraid it would not hold their large Leyland truck. We manage to drive down to the river bank and note large barges travelling along, indeed six barges are tied in two lots of three and being pushed along by another boat. The river is indeed very wide and it is very difficult to imagine how precarious it must have felt crossing such a large river on what must have seemed an unstable bridge. The photos of Bailey bridges show what a difficult feat it must have been to build them.

Jim and John drove on through the night and the next day and continued to see horrific sights of poverty, what Jim called 'the power of war'. Some civilians cheered as they passed while other threw stones and spat at them.

The next significant memory my dad recounted to Anthony was when the squadron had camped in dense woods in Lower Saxony, northern Germany, near to the town of Celle. This is close to the site of the concentration camp, Bergen-Belsen. Dad and I had never talked about what he saw at Belsen, although I knew from Anthony's account that he had been there. When he was dying and had taken on the appearance of a victim of starvation, wearing a permanent look of fear in his eyes, I asked him to tell me the story of going into Belsen. I realised that he might want to talk about it and that in doing so, it might somehow ease the burden. I arrived at my parents' home to find him sitting in the lounge. He had written everything down in preparation for my visit and went on to read it to me. It took him a long time and he had to keep stopping because he cried a lot. I had never seen him cry before. I also cried as I listened, but mostly I wanted to scream. This is what he wrote down and read aloud:

> One day, in April 1945, near Hanover, John and I and a small convoy of trucks were asked to complete a special assignment. We had to deliver Red Cross supplies of flour and water to a nearby camp, called a prison camp, which had been captured from the Germans and which was run by Hungarian guards.

This request would have been in response to an appeal sent out on 15 April for Red Cross relief to which many troops nearby had responded. Dad remembered that his heart sank at hearing the term, 'prison camp'. He said:

> The whole squadron was camped in the woods nearby and everyone was told they could visit the camp, but that it would be at their own risk because there was a typhus epidemic there in the camp.

They had an inkling of what they might see as some displaced people (as he called them) had wandered into the squadron's camp begging for food and eating from the dustbins. Some of the more recent arrivals at the concentration camp would have been relatively fit and mobile. He continued:

> We drove through an incredibly dense forest along a dirt track until me and John reached the camp.

Dad was totally unprepared for what he saw and the sights scarred his mind forever. As he reversed his truck into a muddy square in the camp, he caught sight of the prisoners. They were walking around a wooden barrack dressed in 'striped pyjamas'. He went on:

> They came towards the truck to scramble for a drink of water – their eyes bulged out of their bony skulls and they looked like ghosts, 'dirty ghosts'. I saw 'an old woman who was really a young girl and a toddler who was a child'. John and I were overwhelmed and didn't know what to say or do. They were in a terrible state – many just skeletons – and begging us to take them with them but we could not and they didn't understand why not. We could not understand each other and used signs to communicate. There were open graves, stacked dead bodies and open latrines with corpses of people who had died there. The awful stench of rotting bodies was everywhere.

He told me:

> We wanted to do something; to do our best to bring a little hope to them. We gave them cigarettes and *all* our rations. We were there for just 3 hours altogether. Then John, who had a wonderful Welsh singing voice, sang to them. And I remember how smiles appeared on their faces. We said goodbye to these smiling faces. We only camped nearby for 36 hours. I have often wondered what had happened there before the camp was liberated and what made the SS behave so terribly. Later we heard of all the other camps.

After a long pause, he disclosed that he still prayed frequently that those who were lucky enough to have found their way back to their homeland had found happiness. He said:

> During the war we had many a bad time, but Belsen stays with me as the worst experience. Even after so many years it is hard to forgive what

happened there and to the millions in other camps. I hope that the guilty were brought to justice. I often wonder if it is still standing for the world to witness.

After reading this account to me, I asked him how it affected him now. He said:

The worst part is trying to understand how someone could do this to another human being, trying to understand this cruelty. I tried to forget it, Carol, but I can't; the sight is there every time I shut my eyes.

Belsen was liberated by the British Army on 15 April, and Dad must have been there very shortly after that. The British Red Cross, who had put out a call for supplies, arrived a week after the liberation to co-ordinate the relief effort. Accompanied by the British Army were photographers and cameramen who documented the conditions that the liberators found at the camp—and so it became possible to see what my dad must have seen when he arrived there in April 1945. The photographs are archived in the permanent exhibition of Belsen kept at the Imperial War Museum. I attended the opening of the exhibition in April 1991 in place of my father who by then was dying and too ill to attend.

In retracing Dad's journey, we had arranged to stay near to Bergen-Belsen for a few days to allow plenty of time to visit the camp, now a memorial to those who died there (Fig. 8.5). My reflections of the visit on 12 July 2017 were:

Seeing the sign posts to Bergen-Belsen on the way here from the small hotel we are staying at was very sobering. I remember the densely wooded area from before when we both went to the 50th commemoration of the liberation with AJEX, the Association of Jewish Ex-servicemen and Women group, in 1995, and I remember how very upsetting it was. It's difficult to believe that it is 26 years ago. Dad died in December, 1991 before the commemoration. The weather is cooler and I'm feeling better for it having suffered with lymphedema in the heat as a result of the Melanoma surgery on my leg and the removal of lymph nodes. Also, I share my dad's Irish pale skin and freckles and find intense heat difficult, as did he.

Fig. 8.5 Individual graves in the grounds of Bergen-Belsen, Memorial. Photo taken by Carol Komaromy, 2017

We spent a long morning in the newly built (2000) permanent museum which has an incredible amount of detail and also film footage of the history of Belsen. I was struck by the silence even though there were many visitors at the museum. It seemed appropriate and respectful. It was raining very hard so it was a good decision not to visit the external site of the camp area, which is huge, and to leave that and the various mass graves until tomorrow. In any case, it would have been exhausting to do it all in one day. I didn't feel as upset as I did the first time I visited, and I expect it was because I was more adjusted to what to expect. However, the sights of the burials in various archive films were still overwhelming in the lack of dignity afforded to people's remains and how they were treated like unwanted waste; which in some ways they were. The SS had tried to bury as many bodies as possible, before the camp was liberated, but thousands remained in open pits when the British Army Corps arrived and many were piled high around the camp and others just lying on the ground where they had died. One piece of footage of a woman who was in the nursery at the time, showed her describing how, being left to their own devices, counting the corpses, stacked like logs, was a game the children used to play. I found her story horrific but her honesty refreshing. Horrific because this could have become a normal part of life for children. But while, for some, the horror was 'normalised' and part of that reality, it is almost impossible to imagine the scale of the suffering. Also, I had forgotten that Belsen is where Anne Frank, who symbolises the Holocaust in many ways, died after being transported from Auschwitz.

We're both surprised to see Mala on film talking about the importance of being open about what happened and seeing it as her duty to talk. (Mala was someone who survived Belsen and whom I had taken to meet my dad before he died). The question remains of how local people could either pretend ignorance of what was happening or appear to condone it. There were accounts of this in the museum. Some people said they had been told that there were good reasons for people being detained there while others found it difficult to condone such treatment, whatever they might have done. Of course, after the liberation when they saw the scale and reality of what had taken place, they could not accept it as being deserved by anyone, no matter what their crime was. Some recounted how on seeing children, who had to be 'innocent', they realised something terrible had happened.

Whatever one thinks or reads about Belsen, the sight of what happened changes things. To be there and experience it with all of his senses definitely changed my dad's view of humanity – in seeing what some people are capable of doing. I find it heart-breaking that someone so kind and compassionate as him would have learned about the possibility of such inhumanity and then going further into Germany and seeing the suffering – especially of children – to learn firsthand the reality of war. He certainly struggled to justify the inhumanity. That is why I think he saw potential danger in so much and constantly warned my sister Pauline and I of the dangers 'out there'.

On Thursday, 13 July 2017, we made our second trip to Belsen and walked the many miles around the camp. We noted the mass graves and some individual ones – some were memorials to the people who died after the Liberation.

The harsh reality is that each day, after the Liberation, people continued to die in their hundreds. Certainly, in the immediate aftermath of the Liberation, the need for fresh water was a priority, hence the urgent call from the British Red Cross to all troops nearby. Managing the effects of starvation was the biggest challenge alongside controlling the spread of typhus and typhoid. However, despite all efforts, 14,000 former camp prisoners died during the first three months after the liberation.

We visited the locations of the various camps and went to the original entrance where Dad and his small convoy would have entered the camp. The main entrance to the museum had been relocated further along the road and this, the original main entrance area, seemed comparatively unvisited.

When we walked along one side of the camp, close to where the Polish prisoners of war had been held, and next to a wooded area, I experienced a very eerie sensation. My skin seemed to be crawling and I wanted to get away. I made myself stay and continue – but it was very strange. My explanation is that I had somehow embodied part of my dad's experience of being there. The sensation is a milder version of what I felt entering the camp for the first time in 1995, when I walked in beside an older Jewish woman who had returned to try to find her mother's grave. She had been there as a child with her mother, and my memory is that her mother had died just after the liberation. She was with her grandson and suddenly stopped and said she could not enter. He and I helped her to continue. It was then that I was struck by a searing pain in my legs – as if my skin was being burned.

This particular area was fairly quiet with only the occasional visitor – but we could see that in the distance in the main car park, many more people were arriving by coach loads and in cars. The camp was surrounded by dense forest and birdsong was evident from the surrounding trees dispelling the myth that there are no birds in the camp, or at least, that non fly over the camp.

On the way back quite near to the back entrance to the museum we saw a red deer in a small clearing – it was a cheering sight Indeed, almost joyous and roused in me a feeling of hopefulness in contrast to the site of the community of dead people and the knowledge of the suffering they had endured and, subsequently, a feeling of helplessness.

On the way out, I wrote a message in the Visitor Book. It was about the impact of what Dad witnessed and in his memory of the camp and his meeting with Mala, who was a child in the nursery and had typhus at the time of the liberation and who befriended him at the end of his life.

Dad's convoy moved on towards Hannover, noting how the further north they went, the greater they found pro-Nazi sentiment. When they reached Hannover, they found it to be what he described as 'eerie' and a 'city of dust and rubble'. That evening some of the men, including John and Jim, went to look around the city where they found a whole warehouse full of clothes, watches, cameras and new stockings which they loaded into various trucks and took back to the squadron. He did not explain what happened to these 'spoils of war', or why they took them away, but I can assume they might have been traded for other things or kept by the troops. On 30 April 1945, they learned that Hitler had shot himself, marking what they considered to be the end of the war, although the war did not officially end until 2 September 1945.

From Hannover, John and Jim began the drive to Hamburg. On the approach, they were hit by a burst of enemy shells, highlighting that the war was far from over. Jim hastily turned the truck around and John started firing the gun. As they sped by a disused factory, a shell skidded off the bonnet of the truck and exploded. Jim and John leapt out of the truck but fortunately it did not explode as they feared. However, Jim's face was a bloody mess. He had sustained shrapnel wounds to his face and shoulder and was rushed to the Red Cross Hospital in Hamburg where he had surgery to remove the shrapnel. His war record shows that he was admitted to 53 RAF Hospital on 4 June 1946. There is no discharge date. This date does not fit with the chronology of events in Dad's oral history account, and I think it was a recording mistake and the year should have read 1945.

After two weeks' rest, he was allowed to go home on leave. For most of the war, Jim had to sleep in his truck every night and longed for a comfortable bed. But when he journeyed from Calais to Dover in a filthy boat, he contracted impetigo—a skin infection—from a dirty blanket. He went to visit his wife, Nellie, and meet his new daughter, Pauline, travelling by train and then bus. My mother told me that this was an emotional reunion. Dad was not in a good state, although he had no permanent physical scars from the shrapnel wounds. The time was short before he had to return to Europe and make the long journey to Berlin where his squadron was carrying out a supply programme for the Americans and Russians there. There is nothing in his war record of his leave dates and no mention of leave. If it is the case that he took leave after his injury, then Pauline must have been just under two years old. However, it is more likely that he went on leave in July 1945 making Pauline about a year old. According to my mother's account, he arrived late at night when Pauline was asleep, and in the morning Pauline rushed to him and called him 'Daddy'; so she was clearly walking at least a few steps and talking. And of course, my mother would have told her that this was her daddy (Fig. 8.6).

Fig. 8.6 Studio photograph of Nell with Pauline taken in, Wolverhampton, 1946

When Dad returned, Berlin was in turmoil and there were rumours that pro-Nazis were hiding, refusing to believe that Hitler was dead. He went to the western, American sector where buildings were still ablaze and children were running around the streets searching for their parents. Not only were they told not to help the 'enemy', but they were given orders to supply only American troops and not the Russian ones. However, Jim met a Russian soldier who traded his watch for some food and cigarettes. He remembered how exhausted the Russian troops appeared to be and how limited their supplies.

The final part of my dad's account lacks detail about the period up until he was demobbed, but it must have been late summer. Probably this was because the focus of my nephew's oral history was the experience of war and once the war in Europe had ended, events would have seemed less relevant to him. What I do know is that from Berlin he drove to Kiel in northern Germany where he spent a lot of time at an airstrip to which hospital supplies were delivered. I can only speculate that he must have been delivering them to field hospitals in the region.

Dad mentioned that the squadron travelled to Schleswig and Flensburg on the Dutch/German border. In Flensburg there was plenty of time for the squadron to relax.

Further, Dad told Anthony that, for the rest of the year, time dragged on until December 1945 but that there were great celebrations on Christmas Day—the first war-free Christmas for six years. The squadron had a big Christmas dinner in an ex-German Army barracks in Husum, Germany.

The next recorded part of Dad's account concerned the summer of 1946 which was very hot and Jim and other members of the squadron were given permission to go to Copenhagen—which Jim remembered fondly as being a 'marvellous city'. He spent a year in service beyond the end of the war in Europe before finally being demobbed in September 1946. He never met John Craddy again. He had many photos of Belsen, but he said that he had lost them on the train on the way home. At the end of his account, his comment to Anthony was:

> I never had any doubts that we would win, but would be lying if I said I was never frightened. We never expected any reward for what we did.

The extraordinary events that took place in the war in Europe are difficult to imagine, even when visiting sites of fierce fighting and of imprisonment. Exploring the history of the war, chasing war records and accounts, as well as visiting various key landmarks, has helped fill some of the gaps in the detail of my dad's experiences. Sometimes, though, it feels as if there are more questions left pending than are answered. The detail of key battles is well documented, but trying to trace so individual a journey as that undertaken by two men who were part of a large squadron has been difficult. As I already said, I wanted to be able to record what it might have felt like for Dad and its impact on his life subsequently. Certainly, set against a backdrop of so many war dead, a lot of survivors would have felt lucky to be alive, and this was an emotion that I heard my dad express. He often compared his life to others and thought his was less significant insofar as he did not consider his contribution to be worth much. However, those who survived had a heavy burden to carry. Part of that burden, for Dad, was finding a way to look forward while coping with sights burned onto his memory that clearly hurt and haunted him until he died. The person who returned from the war must have been a different person to the one who went there as a young man from rural Ireland. It is clear to all who knew him that it did not damage his ability to care, but it certainly made him anxious about the safety of those close to him.

As I go on to explain in Chap. 9, what happened after the war demonstrates that while he did not expect any reward, times were far from easy and surviving in post-war Britain was a challenge.

Notes

1. Jeanne-Pierre Benamou. 2014. *10 Million Tons For Victory, 1944 A fantastic Armada*. Bayeux, France: OREP Editions.
2. Grossman, Vasily. 2006. *Life and Fate*. London: Vintage Books. (P. 392).
3. Grossman, Vasily. 2006. *Life and Fate*. London: Vintage Books. (P. 393).

9

Growing Up Post-War: All Over Now?

Throughout this book we have been resurrecting worlds in which we played no part. In this chapter, however, we introduce our personal recollections s of growing up in the shadow of war. While they share commonalities insofar as they are rooted in the broad social context of a victorious Britain looking to an optimistic future, they also reflect the diverse economic circumstances of those who survived. Further, we each occupied different positions in the family which inevitably affected our experiences of home life so close to the ending of war. In particular, the accounts highlight the impact of war on our parents' circumstances. Their economic situations were rooted in social class and undoubtedly affected our aspirations, but more striking is the way that silence played a role—so that what was not spoken remained unacknowledged—but continued to exert a powerful influence. In contrast to that silence, these accounts are a form of speaking out in order to make sense of, and make public, the impact of war on ordinary lives such as ours. What we also shared is our experience of being born into situations where the gendered division of labour was the norm. Our mothers provided the full-time childcare and carried out the domestic work, while our fathers were the full-time breadwinners. Further, our mothers were not affected by the war itself to the same extent as our fathers, but they were affected by the social, historical and personal context of military conflict. As our accounts unfold, they highlight how deeply some divisions in society were entrenched, but also how the immediate post-war generation was set to enter a new era. We seem to have straddled the shift that heralded social welfare reforms, educational opportunities and feminism. While we might not have been clear about what we wanted out of life—we were clear about what we did not want.

For Jenny the two world wars which provided the context for the lives and the deaths of her grandfather, Bert Manning, and his son, Arthur, were over by the time she was born. Had she started life five years earlier though, her grandmother and her uncle would still have been alive, Ella in her early 60s and Arthur in his late 20s. Britain would already have been at war with Germany for the second time in a century. However, by June 1946 when she arrived, people in Britain had already experienced ten months of 'peace'. Yet as Carol's account demonstrates, not all servicemen and servicewomen had even been demobbed. Two years before Carol was born in 1948, how did the recent war manifest itself in the world Jenny came to know?

Fearing coastal bombing raids, Jenny's widowed maternal grandfather, Meredith Watling, had moved away from Great Yarmouth where he was living with his daughter Lorna, Jenny's mother. He bought a very small, newly built, two-bedroom house in Cambridge where Lorna committed herself to sharing his home and providing his domestic care. After Lorna married in 1942, David, her new husband, moved in with her and Meredith—and went on living in that house until his death in 1996. The alcove in her parents' bedroom at the front of the house accommodated Jenny as a small child, but until Meredith died in 1955 there was nowhere for a second or third child to sleep. Aged 40 by this time, Lorna was wary of giving birth to a child with Down's syndrome, a potential risk for older mothers, with the result that Jenny grew up as an only child. How much the absence of siblings contributed to her early shyness and lack of confidence around other children is hard to say, but visits to her parents' relatives and friends, as well as exposure to other children, were experiences that she felt poorly equipped for.

By contrast, Carol had an older sister, Pauline, already born in 1944 while James, her father, was still fighting the war in Europe, not being demobbed until 1946. It seems that her father's return heralded a new phase in her parents' lives. The pain of separation and the fear that James might be killed were over. However, the promised happiness of setting up home together in James' native country of Northern Ireland was short-lived as the post-war unemployment situation in Ireland and Nell's second pregnancy, with Carol, meant they had to return to England and what turned out to be a difficult situation. Here Carol relates their immediate post-war history.

Carol After being demobbed, James persuaded Nell to move to Northern Ireland and to live there with his parents, and this is what they did. My maternal grandfather, Frederick Davis, was very upset about the fact that Nell was taking his granddaughter, Pauline, from him and told her he would never forgive her for doing so. My mother quoted his words to her: 'I don't care about *you* leaving, but I will never forgive you for taking that girl away from me.' Clearly his words stayed with her for many years. I never met him but, as I described earlier, he was a rigid and unforgiving man. James and Nell must have travelled from the West Midlands by bus, train and boat to Belfast, via Liverpool. It would have been a long overnight crossing and one my father no doubt would have recalled from the time he enlisted and travelled to England. The details they shared with my sister and me about their life in Northern Ireland are sketchy, but what is certain is that initially they lived with James' parents in Kilrea, County Derry, sharing a small cottage. It is here in Kilrea that James managed to find work as a farm labourer for Mr. Hugh Barr, who owned a farm called Gold Plough Farm in Coleraine, County Derry. It was one of the few options available. As Chap. 4 describes, my memory of my grandparents' cottage from childhood holidays in Ireland remains vivid. There was one large downstairs room with a peat fire in the corner on which were placed pots and pans for cooking. My grandparents did not have a range, but instead there were hooks from the inner chimney breast for hanging cooking pots and a stand over the fire for the kettle. Next to the window overlooking the lane were a table and chairs and a very uncomfortable two-seater sofa near to the fire. This is where people mostly sat. My memory is that there were just two bedrooms. There would always be a pot of tea brewing on the fire, producing very strong black liquid that I hated. I remember that Granny drank a lot of tea and at meal times dipped her bread into it, a habit that Nell told me she found disgusting.

Nell often complained to me that James' mother, her mother-in-law, Margaret, did not like her because she was English and because she wore make-up. However, she had a good relationship with James, her paternal grandfather, introduced in Chap. 2. He was always very warm and friendly to her. My memory of Granny Margaret, also introduced in Chap. 2, was that she was a little strange and what might be called eccentric, ever at odds with her husband, James. She was very tall and slim and liked to be teased and made to laugh by 'her boys'.

Eventually, as a reaction to tensions between my mother and Margaret, my parents told us that they moved into a very small cottage that was owned by the Barr family and had only basic amenities with mud floors and no running water or electricity. As with most dwellings at that time and in rural Ireland, lighting was via oil lamps and cooking on an open peat fire. Indeed, as Chap. 4 describes, none of my father's family had running water or electricity in their homes until the 1970s. Water had to be collected for their cottage from the pump one mile away. My mother often recounted fondly that she had two dogs who accompanied her to fetch the water every day and how happy she was, finding this simple life idyllic. It seemed that this was mostly because they had their own home for the first time.

In October 1947, Nell became pregnant with me, and this made James' situation of irregular farm labouring employment and very low wages more difficult and the need to earn a regular income more pressing. Sadly, the economic situation in Ireland at the time meant that work was very hard to find and, despite living very frugally, James had to face up to the reality that they could not remain in Ireland. He went to Wolverhampton in England in the spring of 1948 to find work and drove a trolley bus there to earn enough money to pay the fare for the whole family to return to England. He had acquired the skill of driving a large vehicle from his war-time experience with the Leyland heavy lorry.

While away in England, through one of his work contacts, James had found lodgings in Bloxwich, Wolverhampton, where the whole family could stay. In May 1948, my mother, Nell, eight months pregnant with me; my father, James; and sister, Pauline, boarded the boat back to Liverpool and travelled from there to the West Midlands. I was born in a lodging house on the evening of 11 June, delivered by a community midwife. The woman who owned the house was called Dolly, and my mother told me how she insisted that my mother should bottle-feed me and 'not mess about with breast feeding'.

By then my father was securely employed as a trolley bus driver, but working lots of unsocial hours. He had to cycle to work to drive the first trolley bus at 5 am, or work very late and cycle home after the last bus. This meant Nell was alone with us as young children a lot of the time. Within the first year my parents moved into a rented room in a house owned by a widowed man called Mr. Hartnell, who was a spiritualist. Later, Pauline and I were told stories about how the house was haunted. Also, how, if my father was working late, my mother would be invited to join Mr. Hartnell in the sitting room in the evening. Apparently, in the middle of chatting he used to stop the conversation to announce his wife's presence. My mother told us he would suddenly raise his hand and say, 'Shh, she's here! Can you feel her?' Nell told us that this terrified her even though she colluded with him by pretending she could feel the late Mrs. Hartnell's presence. There are other joint stories from my parents about how they thought that their bedroom was haunted—for example, how the bedroom door, which they locked at night from the inside, would be unlocked in the morning and other tales about the candle not lighting until the third attempt.

Sadly, it seems that accommodating a small family was not easily tolerated by Mr. Hartnell, who my parents described as old and frail. During the day my sister and I had to 'be kept quiet', as my mother told us, because he did not like the sound of noisy children. I have speculated as to whether this was the root of my silence later as an elective 'mute'. My sister, however, appeared not to be affected in this way and continued to be outgoing and gregarious throughout her relatively short life. Eventually, Mr. Hartnell's daughter decided that her father should sell the house and he gave my parents notice to leave. Although they already had their name on a waiting list for council housing, in post-war Britain the lists were long, and they were advised by a work friend of James' that if they allowed themselves to become homeless, they would be housed as a matter of urgency. This meant that Nell sent Pauline to live with her grandfather, Frederick Davis, while she took me into the workhouse in Wednesfield, Wolverhampton, to be with her. I was 18 months old.

Women were not allowed to keep their children with them in the workhouse, and so I was sent into its nursery section. Nell had to work hard all day, mostly doing heavy cleaning, and was not allowed to see me. When I was an adult and a mother myself, probably bemoaning the lot of motherhood to her, she tried to explain to me how hard her life had been in comparison. That was the first time she had disclosed the account of the workhouse to me. The aspect of that experience which seemed to upset her most was how one day a more senior resident took pity on her and helped her to see me, but only through the nursery glass door. Mothers seeing their children was against the workhouse rules. What Nell saw disturbed and upset her. While all of the children were playing together, I was standing on my own, well away from them and with my back to them. She told me that it was at that moment she knew that something was 'wrong'.

After two weeks, my parents were rehoused in a new, three-bedroom council house in Bushbury, Wolverhampton, which meant that the family was reunited after this short but traumatic separation. James had been able to stay in a lodging house. For him, continuing to earn a wage was a priority. My parents managed to buy what was called utility furniture—and gradually furnished the house. I remember how they kept this furniture all of their married life. At about the same time that Nell disclosed to me the circumstances of being homeless, she also told me that when they moved into the new council house, she began to have 'fits', as she called them, and heard voices that told her that I was an evil child and she should destroy me. She recounted how I used to watch her very carefully with a look of fear on my face and how she had to sit on her hands to stop herself from responding to the voices' commands and harming me. I have no memory of this—other than a sense of something awful happening and a fear of my mother that stayed with me for most of my life until her death in 2009.

Pauline and Carol inherited the difficulty of their parents' financial struggle which persisted throughout their childhood and beyond, both in its material and emotional form. This meant that any unforeseen financial demands created anxiety. By contrast, Nell's sisters and brothers had all married into situations of financial security which meant they owned their own homes and the menfolk (either brothers or brothers-in-law) were securely employed. Therefore, Carol's parents were unusual in never owning their own home. Her paternal grandfather, James' family too were secure in owning their own homes, despite their modest roots. However, while Carol's family lived in council (social) housing for most of their married lives, Nell did not identify with the working classes. This affected who Carol and Pauline were allowed to play with and how they were expected to keep up appearances—both through being well dressed and by the house being kept spotlessly clean and tidy. Making a mess or playing with 'rough' children on the estate was forbidden.

This financial struggle was not so evident in Jenny's memories of growing up. Her family's relative security, sharing a house owned by a grandparent, evoked different recollections. These, however, were no less anxiety-filled but perhaps more characteristic of an only child. For her, the aftermath of war is evident both in the times she spent alone and the more daunting requirement to interact with other children. The unused pages of ration books, for example, a material legacy of war, provided her with entertainment during bedtime hours spent drawing on the spare paper and tearing out the perforated coupons. It was 1954 before all rationing ended, but as particular categories of food or clothing became more available, not all the coupons were needed. Outside her house, further material evidence of the recent war included air raid shelters in other children's gardens—damp, unpleasant corrugated-iron enclosures, or, more daunting still, steps down into an earthy cave of some sort. Going inside these shelters was something one child would dare another to do. Jenny did her best to avoid this kind of situation. As well as shelters in people's gardens, she recalls that along the River Cam, a short walk from where they lived, concrete gun emplacements hunkered down in the waterside grass, visible for years to come.

Jenny Other reminders of the period immediately before my birth sit like snapshots in an album, redolent with atmosphere but lacking readable context: the eerie wail of a siren which my parents told me had sounded whenever there was an air raid (why it continued to sound is unclear), the wall that divided the stairs from the hall. My parents and my maternal grandfather had huddled against it during raids in the belief that it would hold up when the rest of the house was in ruins. The occasional sound of the siren and the improbable image of my family feeling safe in the hall were fleeting reminders of what had just ended. Yet my dreams were frequently populated with enemy aircraft, the terror of death hurtling in from above, a strange juxtaposition with my belief that heaven was just up there, evidenced by the haloes of sun at the edges of evening cloud that I assumed was radiating from the heavenly host.

Alongside an awareness of the threats and deprivations of a war just over, there were pointers towards what later turned out to be a short-term future where health and social care would be provided by the State: free nursery education from the age of three, early days in school with boiled milk in Bakelite mugs and cod liver oil. And then the 'bulge' as post-war baby-boomers, like Carol and Jenny, crowded into primary classes of more than 40 children, all waiting for space at a junior school. Such facilities were wasted on Jenny who found nursery school overwhelming, always standing at the window waiting for her mother to collect her. When the percussion instruments were put down on the floor, the hurly-burly rush for the drums was too much for her. All she got her hands on were the two sticks to bang together. Finally, she managed to give the nursery staff the slip, escaping the playground and heading off down the driveway through the trees and out to the gates. Had she been more decisive she might have made it, but she was unsure which direction led to home and remembers dithering until a large hand clamped her shoulder and she was returned to the fray—a hesitation she still regrets. Eventually her mother was advised to keep her at home for a bit longer, a recommendation prompted by the afternoon she spent walking round and round one of the school dining tables saying 'No' repeatedly, before retreating underneath it and falling asleep. When she later joined the first year of infant school, the boiled milk and cod liver oil seemed manageable by comparison with the isolating wilderness of the nursery school.

By contrast, Carol grew up with the story of her illnesses before reaching school age, one of those oft-reported family accounts. Aged four, she had an axillary 'cold abscess on a swollen gland' and was referred by the

GP to New Cross Hospital, Wolverhampton, apparently in need of urgent surgery. This type of abscess concerns a tuberculous lymph node, and, on reflection, it is possible that Carol contracted this from the workhouse nursery. Nell frequently recounted to Carol how she had to rush home from the doctor's, pack a case and take two buses to get Carol to the hospital urgently, where she was admitted to Isolation Ward 21 in New Cross Hospital and operated on that day. It seems that although her condition was considered to be urgent, no ambulance was called. However, the surgery was declared to be life-saving—and so without the NHS, Carol might have died.

Ironically, the workhouse where Nell and Carol had been housed over two years previously stood in New Cross Hospital grounds as a fearful reminder of the recent pre-NHS days. The workhouse symbolised an ideology of the undeserving poor, alongside a hospital representing the new social order of entitlement to health care that was universal and free at the point of delivery. As such, it highlighted a political tension that persists within health and social care today.

Carol has no memory of her father visiting her in New Cross Hospital, although her mother did so daily. Visiting rules were strict at that time. The open and free access that is encouraged today was considered inappropriate or even harmful then. Carol's mother told her that she was considered to be a very good child because she was silent and did not cry during the whole hospital stay. Her memory is one of terror. Seeing bars on the cot and bars on the window suggested another type of danger to her. Perhaps she was dangerous and had to be locked in. The hospital stay held other dreadful memories that were dominated by fear; some staff members were unkind, and her refusal of food meant that on occasions she was forced to eat. Further, she was alone most of the time in a large room which housed a cage over a fireplace on one wall. Carol imagined it to be covering the legs of a patient in the next ward intruding into the room.

Carol I think that this is because I could hear the other patient screaming in the room next door—and being terrified by it. I must have been told that she was in a wheelchair. It seemed appropriate that patients would scream because some of the nurses were cruel, and I remember not wanting to eat and one nurse forcing rice pudding into my mouth with what seemed like a very large spoon. Further, I was shouted at for wetting the bed at night. This hospital stay and being in isolation with only occasional visits from my mother was where I located my own personal trauma which connected so powerfully with the Robertson films.

The Robertson films,[1, 2] used in counselling training, later highlighted the trauma that is caused to young children when separated in hospital. James and Joyce Robertson filmed young children in hospital to evidence the impact of the separation from their mothers—and worked with John Bowlby, famous for his psychological theories about attachment and loss.[3]

After two weeks Carol was discharged. She retains a very vivid memory of her mother bringing her a new red coat and shiny black patent shoes to wear home. She and her mother stood in the ward sister's office while Carol was dressed in the coat and shoes. They seemed to be a type of reward for having survived and would certainly have involved financial sacrifice. The ward sister was full of praise about how 'good' Carol had been; here again, being quiet was equated with being good.

Many years after that, Carol's father, James, apologised for not visiting, something that he had felt guilty about and which played on his mind. He told Carol that he could not bear to visit because of his hatred of hospitals brought about by his war experiences and further, that in the German hospital where he was treated at the end of the war, the nurses were unkind to him. Carol's frightening sense of isolation can be seen to compound her earlier trauma when she was confined to the workhouse nursery. When she later went to school, she found that too was a wretched and miserable experience. The institutional setting with its interior gloss painted brick walls, its smell of polish and food, its rigid routines and its strict teachers cast her back into a place of terror where she felt lost and powerless. She chose not to speak in the first few years—and remembers being 'tested' on a couple of occasions in junior school which, on reflection, must have been because they suspected that she had some sort of learning disability. The tests she later recognised as IQ (intelligence) tests.

9.1 Home Life

Although of different types, both Jenny and Carol experienced an everyday life of domestic routines. For Jenny the daily life of the three adults she grew up with at such close quarters was largely made up of predictable events: meals around the drop-leaf table with table cloth, mats and the full panoply of cutlery, much of which came from her grandmother Ella's home, scheduled breaks for morning coffee made from the sticky brown liquid in the Camp bottle, and afternoon tea once the adults had had their 'rest' on the settee after lunch. So fixed was the routine that when Jenny married Bob in 1967 and he offered her impromptu cups of coffee in their flat, she felt startled and uneasy. But that time-structured pre-war domestic world was just beginning to fracture as Jenny grew up. Women were beginning to work outside the home, and the new white goods of the 1950s made running a home something that could be managed more flexibly, aided by private ownership of cars and other motorised vehicles. As a small child, however, Jenny would go with her mother on the daily shopping trip to the local Co-op, the two of them standing in long queues in a shop that only later became self-service. The butcher's next door was where Jenny waited outside for her mother, intimidated by the blood and sawdust, the crashing of the chopper into hunks of animal. On the wall outside the Co-op there was the slot machine where her mother bought her box of ten cigarettes every day, and on the way home, they would shop at the greengrocer's high-sided cart with his horse munching in its nosebag.

Like many women in the 1950s, both Nell and Lorna smoked, and though Lorna regarded smoking as an extravagance and limited her daily consumption to a single packet, health issues had yet to be associated with tobacco. For Nell smoking was a reward for all her hard work, and she did not consider it to be extravagant. While smoking was about to be recognised as extremely dangerous to health, it was then common even for health workers to partake during the 1940s and 1950s. Carol remembers the GP smoking during consultations. For parents of that time, though, fresh air, cleanliness, the avoidance of damp and, in Jenny's parents' words, 'moderation in all things' were key to staying well.

In terms of domestic work, the washing was a major feature. Apart from the bedding, which was sent to the laundry, Lorna did her washing in the kitchen sink every week, using a mangle, always feeling the pressure to get the wet clothes hung out as early as possible. The washing line would be wiped down first, perhaps a reflection of sootier air at that time, and items were pegged carefully to achieve maximum billow and therefore speedier drying. If they came in damp, there was always the clothes horse, centre stage in the small living area the family shared. And then the airing cupboard beside her parents' bed provided further security against damp clothes. For both Lorna and Nell, residual dampness was seen as almost life-threatening, and both mothers would hold items to their lips to test for its presence. Nell frequently issued warnings of 'catching one's death' from damp clothes.

While the washing dried, Lorna hoovered, took a carpet sweeper and a beater to the rugs and maintained a complex hierarchy of fraying clothes and sturdy brushes that shored up distinctions between the relatively 'clean' or 'dirty' floors and surfaces she laboured over. This hierarchy of cleaning cloths is echoed in Carol's memory, with a range of distinctions made between what was used for what purpose. Handkerchiefs were boiled, and the Dettol was always visible in the cupboard under the sink. Today Jenny still finds it hard to breathe deeply through her mouth when running or cycling, so systematically was the fear of germs ingrained in her. For her mother it was unthinkable to allow Jenny to go to Saturday morning 'minors', the screening of films for children. In her mind the small children who clustered together in the warm dark spaces of the cinema were hugely germ-ridden.

Like Lorna, Nell did not have labour-saving devices and many tasks required a lot of heavy work. However, sending larger less manageable items to the laundry was a province of the rich, although later it seemed to be more common in middle-class families. It would be many years before Carol's parents could afford a washing machine and the whole of Monday was devoted to washing. They had a boiler with a gas burner to heat the water—and in which white clothes, 'the whites', were boiled. Just as for Jenny's mother, handkerchiefs were particularly germ-ridden items that were boiled in a separate pan, kept specifically for that task. For both our families, with memories of a pre-NHS era, avoiding illness was essential.

Without a washing machine, everything had to be rinsed in the kitchen sink and the clothes rung through a mechanical ringer. Helping with the washing and turning the handle on the ringer was one of the ways Carol was allowed to help. Occasionally, she was permitted to scrub shirt collars before they were boiled. However, it seemed to be a tokenistic way of involving her, and the risk of being scolded for doing things incorrectly, accompanied by an exasperated tut and an 'Oh, give it here!' exclamation, was a constant threat. Many of 'the whites' were starched, as were the collars on shirts and blouses. The required starching of clothes is now relatively uncommon, and while it was important to look smart with a stiffly starched collar, it seems the damage to one's skin from constant chaffing was a worthwhile sacrifice. When the washing was hung out following the same strict rules as Jenny's mother—on a pre-cleaned washing line and catching the wind for maximum drying capacity—other clothes queued in the washing basket ready to be hung out after 'the whites' were dry.

Then it was time to clean the kitchen and prepare the supper. Tuesday was the ironing day—when, like Lorna, Nell aired clothes in the airing cupboard after hanging them on the clothes horse by the kitchen electric fire. Cottons needed to be made damp again if the creases were to be successfully ironed out. Both of us have retained the skills of effectively hanging out the washing to achieve the greatest drying capacity, and we cannot help feeling proud of our skill. Carol, though, was not allowed to hang out anything other than the rags and dusters when all else had dried. On a Monday, Nell made supper from the leftover Sunday joint, while an anxious eye was kept on the weather. If Monday was wet, it would be deemed a very difficult day. Nell would be in a bad mood because washing had to be hung out indoors, and the rest of the family were afraid of upsetting her further and provoking her wrath. It seemed keeping her 'in a good mood' was an endeavour in which the family joined forces most of the time. However, Carol's sister Pauline would stand up to her occasionally and in return would be told off and sometimes slapped. It was some years later that Carol discovered why she felt such profound terror of her mother, and not just wariness.

Carol I have wrestled with the extent to which I should disclose examples of my mother's frightening behaviour. Making private histories public entails an ethical dilemma for all researchers, and even more so when it is about one's own family. In his chapter on absent fathers, Martin Bashforth[4] quotes Annette Kuhn who has argued that families strive to keep secrets from the rest of the world and also will lie to each other or just not talk about things. This 'social pressure towards concealment' might not even be conscious.

Through psychoanalysis though, I came to see how I had spent a lot of my childhood watching my mother and trying to detect mood changes. In some way, at an emotional level, I felt responsible for my mother's anger. It may be inevitable that the anger of one's parent(s) should feel personal—especially to very young children. I can only speculate about how my mother's war experiences, accompanied by her severe sense of humiliation when condemned by her father, Frederick Davis, for getting pregnant before marriage, plus her separation and shame when she gave birth to Pauline, caused what must have been some sort of psychotic breakdown. It seems likely that the circumstances surrounding this pregnancy served as a trigger.

The memory of Nell I have decided to recount contains the seeds of my deepest terrors. They resonate with the killing of innocent beings which has been one of the stories in this book. So shocking was this particular event that I checked her memory's veracity with my sister shortly before her death. This is what I remember. When I was five years old 'my' big black fluffy cat had six kittens. I was beside myself with joy at the sight of them. Sadly, Mom was really angry about the arrival of the kittens. One day when the kittens were about a week old, mom made Pauline and I sit at the kitchen table to be taught what she called 'a lesson'. I remember she was very stern and I felt frightened. She had the kittens on the draining board and had wrapped them in a duster with a knot tied at the top. They were meowing very loudly which added to the terrifying tension. She then plunged the kittens into a bowl of water to drown them. One of them put up an enormous struggle and escaped—running around the kitchen in its drenched state. I ran after it and caught it—thinking I had saved it—but Mom snatched it off me and drowned it. She shouted at me, 'I'll teach you!'

I remember sitting there and crying silently, overwhelmed by a feeling of helplessness. My memory is that Pauline, who was much braver than me in standing up to her, was just shocked and silent. When we were told we could go and play and were out of earshot, Pauline called her a lot of names. But at the time she did not protest. I think we were both frozen with terror.

I have no memory of telling anyone about this until I went into therapy. My therapist connected the act to my mother damaging the helpless part of me and how it could not be a punishment for what I had done. I do not think I told my dad although he must have known what she had done. I certainly never discussed it with her. I still don't know what sort of lesson she was teaching us. A more recent insight is that I was a dreadful inconvenience in that they could not really afford another child. Years later, as a teenager, I declared with a lot of anger that when I had my own home I would fill it full of animals. I think she made a sarcastic comment about how dirty it would be.

9.2 Fathering

Whenever possible, Carol tried to be with her dad. This was a period when it was unusual for men to spend so much time with their children. Both her parents had wanted a son, having chosen the name Colin it seems, and Carol was his token son—but she was delighted to comply in occupying this role and accompanied him to football matches, went out with him on delivery trips, helped him in the garden and joined him on walks. For this she earned the label of tomboy. Indeed, Carol adored being with James and his consistent loving kindness and gentleness compensated for her mother's unstable mental state.

Money and its lack was always a feature of life for Carol's family. James' wage was low even though he had changed his job from being a trolley bus driver to being a van driver and earned a slightly higher wage. Before his succession of old cars that frequently broke down, James had to cycle to work. He ritualistically handed over his wage packet every Friday as soon as he came home from work, and Nell divided up the money into different tins and envelopes for such expenses as rent, food, electricity and savings, something Jenny also remembers her mother doing. Nell would then give him what she called his 'spending money'. He used this money to pay for the football pools, a pint of bitter after work, a weekly ticket to the football match at the Molineux, in Wolverhampton, and one packet of ten cigarettes to smoke at the match. Nell spent her money on cigarettes, smoking ten a day, like Jenny's mother, her weekly visit to the hairdresser and make-up. Needing new clothes and having to buy school uniforms were big sources of anxiety and required special savings and sometimes had to be paid for on hire purchase. Carol remembers clearly the shop where they bought their school uniforms, Ward and Whitehouse, and how proper the two women shopkeepers were and how they offered weekly repayments. Despite having certain new items, she also remembers how most of her clothes were those handed down from Pauline and how she hated the way she was told she would 'grow into them' if they were too big.

The environment of dutiful housework was one Lorna and Nell adhered to resignedly. It provided the backdrop to Jenny's private preoccupations, the solitary life she lived crawling about behind the furniture, the long light evenings she lay awake in her bed, the walk-in cupboard put aside for her toys by the back door. Like Carol, Jenny took little part in real housework but was aware that other children—perhaps those whose mothers 'went out to work'—were often required to run errands and at times step in when their parents' grip on the family's needs slackened. As a result, Jenny grew up without feeling competent to tackle adult tasks: lighting a match, filling a hot water bottle or, when attempting her childcare badge as a girl guide, putting a child to bed and telling it a story. Carol remembers Nell's possessiveness about her domestic expertise, deeming Carol not competent enough to do things to the right standard and not really wanting to teach her how to get it right. Nell's attitude of martyrdom in terms of her domestic toil was reinforced by being the only person able to do things properly. It was as if her small domestic domain had to be given a greater level of status to make her position in the home feel more worthwhile. Nell was one of the women whose labour was no longer required post-war. If a woman's place was in the home, then a married woman and mother's place was definitely so.

Despite funds being very tight, every year, Carol's family went to Ireland for two weeks, planned to coincide with the 14 July Orange Day parades. They stayed in rural Ireland outside of Kilrea, with James' sister Gladys, her husband (big) Billy and their two sons Ronnie and (little) Billy, who was deaf and non-speaking. One of the holiday rituals was to visit the Kilrea War Memorial which had Dad's name listed on it. At one point during his service, he (and John) had been reported 'missing and believed killed'. They were separated many times from the convoy and this was one of them (Fig. 9.1).

At some point this annual ritual changed, and her family graduated to hiring a car and going to seaside places in England, mostly Devon and sometimes North Wales. Staying in guest houses meant having to stay out of the house all day until tea time and struggling to find things to do when it was raining.

When Carol started secondary school, Nell got a job as a dinner lady. She loved going out to work and earning a wage, albeit very small—and seemed to flourish in her new-found independence. She achieved the dual role of being a mother and working outside the home because the hours were shorter than the schoolday. She seemed to love the camaraderie of her work colleagues. However, Nell still let her family know that she was carrying a heavy burden—doing what social scientists call the double shift—but she did not want to be at home all day any more. Indeed, she continued to work part-time in various jobs until James stopped working due to ill health in the 1980s.

So we grew up protected from the dangers that were thought to exist outside of the domestic space. Independence for each of us took different forms. This level of protection and the low expectations to be anything other than *good* seem to have propelled us into the world where we were determined to 'see for ourselves'. Jenny recalls how, when her mother was in hospital having abdominal fluid removed as a result of her ovarian cancer, she was telephoned at work to say that they were discharging her. Then aged 20 and with her father away on a day's training, she cycled the three miles home during her lunch hour, gathered what clothes she hoped were appropriate, and cycled with them to Addenbrooke's Hospital so that her mother could be dressed ready to come home. Lorna was genuinely astonished that Jenny had been able to take responsibility for her.

Fig. 9.1 The war memorial in Kilrea where Dad's name appeared when he was recorded as 'missing believed killed' (Taken by Carol Komaromy, 2017)

Not unlike Nell, Lorna, it seems, felt deeply constrained by the demands she placed upon herself to prioritise housework, stifled by the mantra she repeated, without irony: 'Duty before pleasure'. Gardening, knitting and sewing, home décor and, more than anything else, painting and drawing were the activities she wanted to give her time to. Was this the reason that she 'suffered with her nerves' and from time to time would not get up in the mornings?

Jenny For Mum, the legacy of her parents' quarrelsome marriage and the death of her mother not so long before I was born is difficult to ascertain, but Mum's friendliness and her singing in the house and the local shops—'Vilia, oh Vilia', 'The Anniversary Song'—intersected with an angry desperation that I somehow learned to galvanise by being untidy, late and generally unwilling to fit in with an orderly way of life. I remember my mother's eloquent footsteps, hard on the floorboards, as every morning she brought me up a jug of hot water to wash with, knowing that I would linger in bed until it grew cold. Why was I such a difficult child, never softening or mellowing towards either parent, only moving into a formal kindness towards my dad after he was widowed?

Equally frustrated by not being able to express her talent, Nell used to sing along to the radio—in a beautiful operatic soprano voice—which Pauline inherited. Sadly, James and Carol were deemed to be unable to sing and told to mime on the occasions they attended church together. However, years later, when a young mother herself, Carol joined a small local choir and discovered she had a decent contralto voice. The joy of music and the delight in listening to the operatic voice was something that Carol later recognised to be a precious inheritance. As we both mine the memories of the impact of the war on our childhoods, we have the benefit of hindsight and education to make sense of who we were conditioned into becoming and how we have resisted the duties and constraints that our parents enacted.

9.3 Social Life

Jenny When I think about the relationships that were important in my father's life once the other three members of his immediate family had died, it is his love for my mother that stands out. As I grew up my parents were very much 'good companions', going out arm in arm for 'a walk round the river' (see Chap. 7), teaming up to lay new lino or build a cardboard chimney breast over the electric fire. My father's diary entries are coy but suggest a huge excitement and pleasure at meeting someone who was quite clearly a demurely beautiful woman. The inscriptions in the books of poetry he gave her speak of his 'deepest love' (Fig. 9.2).

Fig. 9.2 David and Lorna Manning walking by the river

For both of us, our extended family was also a part of growing up, symbolised for Carol by visits to relatives in Bloxwich in the West Midlands and holidays in Ireland. Carol's family lived some distance away, although there were many of them in close proximity, six aunts and uncles and Grandma Davis. Family dinners—a midday meal—and teas involved two bus rides and getting dressed up in her Sunday best. Pauline and Carol had godparents too, and visits to them involved attending Sunday school and having to pretend to be familiar with Methodist religious rituals after prior warnings from their mother not to show her up. Carol remembers hating Sunday school but also that her godfather, Uncle Fred, used to tease her—so that she felt shamed and embarrassed, rarely, if ever, finding his jokes at all funny. Pauline was more robust and outspoken and likely to be the one who stood up to such teasing.

It seems that in Jenny's immediate family it was difficult for any of them to find any privacy, and Jenny recalls how for the first 13 years of David and Lorna's marriage her grandfather slept on the other side of the wall against which their bedhead rested. In addition, as she already described, between 1946 and 1953, she slept in their room, in the curtained-off alcove over the stairwell. Her parents' privacy as a couple was further constrained by the size of the house itself. Maybe this explains their 'walks round the river'. Beyond this, there were friends who visited for tea, rather formally, colleagues from Robert Sayle, where both Jenny's parents had worked. And, as with Carol, there were visits to her mother's relatives: Will, Lorna's brother, and his family in Colchester, her two great aunts and their families who lived in or near Cambridge. Once or sometimes twice a year, Jenny and her parents travelled to Devon where they stayed with Dorothy, Lorna's sister, and her family, sometimes joined by Will, Lorna's brother, and his family. More than this, though, visits to the Devon relatives, 'Don and Dorothy', took David back to the landscapes of his boyhood, the seasides and harbours, the moors and farmyards that feature in photos of him together with his mother and brother, sometimes with an uncle, aunt or cousin from his father's side. By then Donald was his brother-in-law as well as his boyhood pal. Only Donald shared his childhood memories of Ella and Arthur, of London House and the places they played in as boys.

As described already, though, David's early life had been lived out in an institutional setting. He was used to fitting in with other people, accustomed to living within personal boundaries that allowed him some kind of privacy and autonomy. In adult life, many of his friends were either work colleagues or fellow participants in his work-based leisure activities. Facilities for table tennis, amateur dramatics and sailing were all provided by the John Lewis Partnership, to which Robert Sayle belonged. His evenings were often taken up with painting scenery for the next production at the theatre in the Cambridge Masonic Hall, or with rehearsals for plays that he took some small part in. Just as was the case with table tennis (see Chap. 6), Lorna was often unhappy about the amount of time this all required and made him aware of her feelings—even though explicit rows were unheard of.

For her part, Lorna rarely went out socially, except to visit the great aunt who lived nearby and a local friend she was close with for a while. Institutional relationships were something she feared, the risk of 'getting drawn in'. Though spiritualism was a strong interest of hers, along with Christian Science, she never went to church, suspecting that she would somehow be required to take part in its regular activities. As Chap. 6 describes, even a three-mile bus trip into town was something that made her anxious and agitated, a challenge she had to muster strength for.

David, by contrast, was especially at home as one of a group that came together for a shared purpose: staging a play, winning at table tennis, crewing a yacht. Similarly, his primary friendship group at the end of his life was the Cambridge branch of the Ramblers Association. As he neared death, one of his walking colleagues ruefully recalled the time when he had been 'King of the Cambridge Ramblers', organising walks, visiting locations to check their suitability. Alongside this, the sense of belonging he derived from the John Lewis Partnership was lived out through visits to 'pensioners' and the role he played within the Partnership's ongoing social care for its former employees. It is perhaps unsurprising that his loyalty to the Partnership, his sense of pride in its values and principles, was close to reverential. For him, membership of an institution of some kind was where he derived his sense of self and felt most at ease, reflected in his concern to follow the rules: 'What's the drill?', he would ask when faced with some new outing or activity.

9.4 Leaving Home

How Jenny's parents envisaged her future she is not sure. Along with finding their routines irksome, she also resisted doing homework. Since she had passed the 11+ examination and spent seven years at a girls' grammar school, her father imagined she would go to university. But not only the homework but also the social environment of her secondary school was consistently painful for her. In every classroom the side desks were filled with girls in strict friendship pairings, a central aisle being occupied by a large group of 'popular' girls—well into rock 'n roll, boyfriends and backcombing. If friendship wavered within any of the pairings, girls could find themselves horribly isolated, something that constituted a permanent threat. Lorna saw only more of the same misery for Jenny if she went on to university. For Jenny, so long in the exclusive company of girls, the need to establish a relationship with a boy who might become her husband and father her children was imperative. But living in Cambridge she saw very few female undergraduates—and indeed the contemporary presence of women in the colleges she would pass every day on the way to school still startles her. At that time, then, university promised few opportunities to make a start with building a family. And teacher training college, the only alternative to nursing offered then, was simply a short route back into the schools she was eager to escape from.

While having a sister might have provided the ideal companionship, during childhood, Carol and Pauline simply did not get on. The contrast between them was played out in their behaviour at home. Pauline was very talkative, earning the nickname of Polly Parrot, and enjoyed social contact. Carol was described as someone who rarely spoke except when she had something to say. Lacking in confidence, she remembers spending her time trying to please her mother, while Pauline, less fearful of Nell, seemed happy to look after her own interests and never offered any help in the house. Despite her profound confidence, Pauline stayed at home until she married her sweetheart, Michael, who she met at the age of 15 and courted for seven years. Childhood was shorter at that time, and Pauline left school at 15 and took on a hairdressing apprenticeship in Wolverhampton. However, such independence was limited. Paid a very low wage, Pauline had to be supported at home during that time.

By contrast, Carol could not wait to get out of the home that felt like a prison. She left school at 16, gaining only three 'O'-levels, French, English and Art. On reflection this was partly as a result of doing minimal revision and homework and partly as a rejection of all that school represented. To survive the trauma of school she had transformed from being an elective 'mute' and a silent, freckled, ginger-haired girl at infants and junior school to the school clown at grammar school. Humour had been central to managing the hardships of family life and, despite difficulties, seemed to sustain everyone as James had the gift of being able to make people laugh. Later, Carol would see this as a way of making the unmanageable manageable. Nell could be in a good mood when she loved to laugh a lot or very angry with something or someone who had upset her. Being able to predict her moods was a skill that Carol developed. Mostly as an observer, throughout her childhood, Carol had harboured a passionate desire to relieve suffering and so decided to leave school to become a cadet nurse. She did this from 16 and then at 18 went to Stafford Mental Hospital to do her mental nursing. Carol recalls how both parents were upset at her decision to enter the world of 'mad' people instead of doing a 'nice' job. It seems that her rejection of such niceness and her newly found independence had more profound causes. As she recalls, it was time for the baby of the family to take control of her own life and help others to do the same.

Beyond their mother's excessive concern with respectability and what that constituted, Carol and Pauline grew up with her constant warnings about not 'getting into trouble'. This meant not getting pregnant—a reasonable but ironic warning from Nell whose life had changed so dramatically by falling victim to that fate and paying a heavy price. Carol's fleeting aspirations to go to art school were squashed. Not only could they not afford to support her to stay on at school until the age of 18, but they considered art schools to be dens of looseness and drug taking. They had seen the hippies of the 1960s as disreputable people to be feared, added to which was the apparent impossibility of ever getting a job afterwards. After all, respectability was *everything* in Nell's eyes who thought you could make a judgement of men's characters by the shine on their shoes and women by the state of their net curtains. James was happy to go along with Nell's wishes and do what she wanted. The contrast between them in terms of how they judged people was striking. Carol put away her wild fantasy and, claiming that she hated education and studying, went into something that offered useful and practical skills. The obvious contradiction that not only was she entering another institution, but also would have to study hard and take many exams, did not occur to her. She saw herself as someone who could conquer her fears and make the world a better place by relieving suffering. So it was with a missionary-like zeal that she entered the world of work.

It was many years later, when Carol had her own children, Debbie and Nick, that work had to be fitted around childcare. When she then became interested in ideas and began to study with The Open University alongside paid work and housework, Nell would give her the occasional lecture on neglecting her duties—it seemed to the house and her husband but not the children. It was to Carol's amazement that Nell told her later that she considered her to be a really good mother.

As Chap. 1 sets out, Carol became a trained mental nurse, a general nurse, a midwife and a counsellor. Encouraged by her second husband, Peter, she decided to do her MA full-time, securing a place at Warwick University to study Sociological Research in Health Care". Carol wanted to bring together the skills from her time in the NHS with the critical thinking from her degree. The more she studied, the more critical she became about the way that patients and particularly women were treated—and she still wanted to be able to make a difference. At a psychoanalytic level it could be argued that she was still trying to make up for the damage done to her parents by suffering and prejudice.

9.5 Bringing the Threads Together

The meeting of two people from different families often yields strange anomalies and juxtapositions that require idiosyncratic accommodations. No-one in Lorna's family of birth had died in either war, even though both Will, her brother, and Donald, her brother-in-law, had been in the services. Yet as Chap. 7 describes, she brought the worries and insecurities of a troubled childhood to the marriage when she met David, a person who had never experienced family closeness with another man. The family Jenny grew up in, then, was anything but large and rambling. Instead, within a tiny enclosed world of three adults, all of whom were very 'grown-up' in their mode of living, Jenny felt somehow excluded. She suspects that this was more than anything a product of their protectiveness towards her. For them, the world they found themselves in may have felt risky. Neither of her parents had a hinterland of 'family back home', a secure reference point in the past to which they could turn. In their small, crowded house, it was difficult for Jenny to find a significant space to grow up into. Maybe, like some kind of dog that shakes itself, that turns and turns restlessly in its bed, jagging against its surroundings, she tried to make some room for herself, to make her presence felt and be on a par with 'the grown-ups'.

9.6 The Impact of War

These two accounts have explored some of the significant aspects of our lives as two women growing up in post-war Britain and the impact of war upon our lives. They have focused on those features that can be articulated in terms of broad social structures such as class, age, gender and location, all of which intersect with the specificities of our separate personal circumstances. You could argue that the most profound impact has been a gendered one. Our mothers were the full-time carers located at home with limited personal time. They provided a model of womanhood that neither of us wanted to emulate. Their main role—of being a good mother and a good housewife—centred on cleanliness and avoiding the tyranny of dirt and germs and, associated with that, the judgement of others. It is not clear how they might have been better equipped to provide us with a different world view, but it seems to both of us that they were only just about managing to cope with their own emotional states. They certainly communicated a sense of frustration about not fulfilling their potential, combined with a sense of martyrdom and duty. Both suffered from various anxieties and did not seem to have the resources to get help or to help themselves. Their mental state was not talked about openly in the family, and the expectation was to get on with life. On one level they were lucky to have survived the war and to be married to someone they loved and who cared for them. While it is clear that we each noticed that all was not well, their emotional upheavals remained unquestioned.

In his account of his mother's severe depression, Alan Bennett[5] writes about the shame associated with mental illness, its hidden nature and its impact upon the whole family. Indeed, he sees his father's death as attributable to the stress of having to cope with his wife's 'madness'. This is something Carol recognises very clearly.

Carol It seems now that Dad's death was, in part at least, due to living with such a difficult woman whose paranoid psychosis was left untreated and suppressed for so many years. His frustration and anxiety seemed to be turned inwards, potentially a cause of his ill health.

Yet the attitude that prevailed and one which was conveyed to Pauline and me was to keep our feelings to ourselves. Tears and 'histrionics' was frowned upon by Nell. Indeed, reflecting the common wisdom of the time, Nell had told James to stop talking about his war-time memories of Belsen and other sights to the extent that he never spoke of them until Pauline's son, Anthony, invited him to do so. Ironically, we could both see that our mother was not coping and suffered what I now understand as paranoid delusions.

It was several years later when I trained as a counsellor and underwent psychoanalysis that I began to better understand the psychodynamic aspects of my own traumas and those of my parents. Rather than hiding unresolved emotions and being doomed to continue to repeat unhelpful patterns, I had the advantage of being able to access one of the 'talking therapies', in this case Kleinian based. Even though in the 1990s therapy no longer carried the same taboo, my mother, still alive and unaware of my therapy, would have been horrified at what I was paying and how long and how frequent therapy needed to be—had I told her. But it was not just negative emotions at home that had to be restrained; it was positive ones. I cannot recall any show of affection between my parents in front of me. There were signs that they were very close—sleeping like spoons in their bed and once the shocking sight of a condom in the toilet, not flushed away. On reflection, I never really understood how Dad tolerated my mother's unpredictable moods. It was certainly the case that her emotional needs and her views dominated his own needs, so that he always made light of his concerns and needs. At some level, perhaps he thought he deserved it—perhaps he felt guilty in some way. At the end of retracing some of his steps in Europe and seeing things for myself, I am in awe of his ability to cope with the trauma of war so well. And his ability to be mostly silent about what he saw, while my mother constantly reminded us of her burden and sacrifice. While I admire his tolerance, I still feel frustrated and sad that he did not seem to have a happier life.

It was when Jenny left home and encountered boyfriends from very different backgrounds that she began to recognise the distinctiveness and also the limitations of her childhood home.

Jenny Like Carol, I was brought up in an environment where the impromptu expression of emotion, even in the privacy of the home, was ignored as a kind of embarrassing breaking of ranks. When I first met Bob I was astonished one evening when a game of Monopoly we were playing with Gilman, his flatmate, and Gilman's girlfriend erupted into a row between the couple. Gilman's girlfriend shouted at him tearfully and rushed out to leave the flat. Rather than ignoring what my parents would have seen as an intensely awkward moment, Bob got up and took hold of the girlfriend, coaxing her into staying. For me, being able to drink coffee whenever I wanted, along with the prospect of kindness rather than coldness when I was upset, seemed like a very welcome prospect.

Despite Carol's many reservations and ideas about travelling, we both assumed that it was our destiny to marry and have children, one which we fulfilled. Further, it was a time when there was a danger of being left on the shelf. That said, we were aware that marriage and motherhood would not define our entire identity. We had witnessed the frustrations of our parents and complied with or resisted the constraints they placed upon us. We had other aspirations. Even so, as Jenny says, for her finding a man to marry and have children with was imperative. In childhood, she had to find a space in which to live—quite literally—in a cramped home where she had no right to her own space, while Carol, whose freedom was limited by her mother's control, resorted to a silent world where she might limit the harm by keeping quiet; seen but not heard. Unlike Jenny, Carol vowed never to marry and wanted to travel the world not just with missionary zeal but *as* a missionary. She had ambiguous feelings about God and a particular dislike of the church, but nursing could give her a passport to freedom.

We both devised a form of escape from settings where we were not offered the freedom in which to grow. Our physical needs were met—but our emotional needs seemed to be overshadowed by other factors. For Carol, the fun and freedom she experienced with her father was something she escaped into rather than feeling it was a legitimate part of her life. At any moment, she could be told she was not allowed to do things. After all, her mother ruled the household. For Jenny, it was the closeness of her parents that seems to have left her feeling excluded, the odd one out as a child among three adults.

The contrast between the roles of our individual fathers is quite striking. James had been severely traumatised by the experience of World War Two although it was not all bad and parts of the experience were liberating and exciting. Further, he seemed to learn about what was really important in life. For example, he and John Craddy were very close, and their friendship sustained them through difficult times. As Chap. 8 describes, James recounted stories of being really upset by the sights of distressed children and not being able to rescue them, especially in Germany, while earlier on there were some children he was able to help and befriend. Throughout his life, until he died at 70, he continued to be protective of children—and was a huge favourite of his four adoring grandchildren. Carol cherished him all of her life and still feels terribly bereft without him over 26 years later. For Jenny, it was not until after her mother had died that she had to establish an independent relationship with her father. This sense of obligation was exacerbated by her marriage within months of her mother's death and an associated sense of guilt at leaving her father to live alone. She remembers announcing her engagement to an older family friend a week or so after her mother had died and the friend saying 'You're only getting *engaged* aren't you?'

9.7 The End of Family Life

When Nell and James were finally free of the burden of children, young grandchildren and debt, they were liberated. A small win on the football pools enabled them to buy a new car and take holidays abroad. They developed a group of new friends when they took up ballroom dancing. James was not that keen on the public performance of dancing but was happy to see Nell having so much fun. This liberation from the constraints of relative poverty and family responsibilities lasted only a few years, and it felt like an unjust blow when James got cancer at the age of 68. The condition was terminal by the time it was diagnosed, and he spent the last few months of his life trying to make sense of it all. Part of the emotional pain he suffered related to the images of Belsen he carried within him. With the help of Peter, her partner, Carol located a survivor who agreed to come and meet Dad. Her name is Mala Tribich, and Carol feels that her visit, together with her husband Maurice, was helpful. In a letter, dated 8 October 1991, Mala wrote in acknowledgement of his part:

> For me, James, and all those brave men and women who fought in the Second World War, have a special place in my heart. You have contributed to making the world a better and safer place, perhaps not as good as we would like it, but I dread to think what it would have been like had Britain and the allies lost the war.

Carol Dad survived for 14 months after his diagnosis. He wanted to be at home and only visited the hospice for pain and symptom management. Mom found it a struggle to care for him, even with the help of the hospice community team and community nurses, but was determined to keep him at home. I visited as often as I could and stayed there occasionally. Gradually Dad became less mobile and his pain was difficult to manage. By the end he was on a phenomenal dose of 7000 milligrammes of morphine daily via his 24-hour syringe driver. He stayed compos mentis until the end. I had asked him to promise me to let me know when the end was near as I wanted to be with him, and he told me he would if he could. On the morning of 1 December 1991, I woke at 5 am, knowing that this was his last day.

As I was leaving home, my mother rang to tell me that the night before he had asked permission to die—would it be alright with her? And with Carol and with Pauline? She told me she had said 'yes'. Mom went on to tell me that he toasted us in water. I told her I knew it was going to be that day and was just leaving. He had somehow let me know. I arrived mid-morning—after a journey I had made hundreds of times—thinking that at least the M6 would be clear, because it was Sunday. During the drive, I reflected how on 11 November 1991, I had sat beside my dying father, who was at home in bed, to watch with him the Remembrance Day memorial service on TV. It was a tradition for him to watch the service and one I have carried forward as an act of memorialisation of him. He viewed it all very keenly that day and when it ended he let out a deep sigh. It was a particularly poignant moment because he was very close to the end of his life and knew that he would not see the next Remembrance service. I asked him how watching it made him feel and to my great surprise he said, 'We were conned. They promised us a land fit for heroes and they lied'. His tone was one of resigned bitterness which was not characteristic of him—ironic wit was more his style. On reflection, it seemed that now that he was dying he did not need to conform to the prevailing script that underpinned remembrance and its dominant discourse of meaningful sacrifice—although to be honest, I had never asked him how he felt before. But, throughout my childhood and into adulthood, I knew that he had been proud to be part of the liberation of occupied Europe. He was not anti-war. As an adult I had campaigned against nuclear weapons, and my anti-war sentiments seemed to upset him and probably offended him.

That final day, Dad was alert and seemed to be noting everything that was happening around him. I had things I wanted to say. I managed to say just two of them. Fundamentally, I told him that I loved him and did not want him to die but wanted his dying to be over. I also asked him to forgive me for the times I was unkind to him. That afternoon, a few people came to say goodbye. My partner came with the children (and dogs)—my sister came with her husband and even my ex-husband, Stuart, came to say goodbye. He had always been extremely fond of Dad. My memory of the day is taking time out from the deathbed vigil to help with refreshments but spending most of it with Dad. He tried to say things to me but I could not make them out, which was really upsetting to me. The Methodist minister came to see him at about 7:30 that evening and told him that while we did not want to lose him, it was okay for him to go now. Shortly after that, at ten past eight, I sat on Dad's bed, this time holding him as he was dying, one arm around him and the other holding his hand. Suddenly, he snatched his hand away from mine, noisily ground his teeth, contracted into a convulsive-like movement and let go of life. The thing I had dreaded most had happened. This scene was to haunt my dreams for years.

A few years later, in 1996, Carol's sister Pauline died quite suddenly. All attempts to resuscitate her failed. The suddenness of her death was a shock to everyone, despite the reality that they had known her condition was life-limiting. Nell Gilmore outlived James and Pauline—surviving to 84. For the final year she lived in a care home run by Jehovah's witnesses, having converted to that religion in the last few years of her life. It was a religion she liked in that it offered her certainty, especially in relation to right and wrong and the afterlife. It seems that when she was alone one day and the Jehovah's witnesses called she welcomed them to her home and embraced all that they offered her. When she was a young mother she had considered taking up the religion, finding the beliefs emotionally comforting. However, because she did not feel able to go from door to door to try to convert people, she left the faith. For the last few years of her life she took great comfort from the support they offered and likened them to her 'true' family. She tried very hard to convert Carol and was saddened to fail in this quest. Eventually, Nell was diagnosed with dementia and paranoid psychosis. Her end-of-life trajectory resembled many in the research Carol had undertaken on the end-of-life care for older people.[6, 7, 8] She was in and out of hospital for at least two years before being transferred to a care home. While she was in hospital, Nell showed signs of extreme paranoia and was convinced the hospital ward staff were plotting to harm her. When she could persuade the staff to let her use the phone, she rang Carol and whispered the details of the plots against her by the staff. These thoughts followed the same pattern she had expressed many times to the family involving the details of people turning against her and plotting harm. The private state of mind she had worked so hard to conceal within the family became public and could no longer be denied. Carol found visits to the care home difficult, and she experienced feelings of sadness, anger and guilt in equal measure. As her dementia progressed, Nell seemed to recognise Carol, but was clearly out of touch with reality. On one of the final visits, she asked Carol if she had ever been married. Many times, during those final years, Carol wanted to stop seeing her and resented the fact that she had been left with this complex and difficult woman. The extreme pain of ambiguity—both love and hate—within a framework of guilt and duty was emotionally exhausting.

In brief then, both of us have experienced a sense of duty, of responsibility to family. This can be a privilege, as Carol hoped would be the case if her father had lived on. But equally we have both known it as a burden. Family structures shift with death, and different members take up new roles and responsibilities. This book, in some ways, is a reflection of our joint sense of a duty of care to the people who brought us up and to those others who, in their turn, brought up our parents. We have tried to make sense of it all and in Chap. 10 recollect what this has required of us in the past two years, what we have contributed and what it is that we are taking away into our own futures.

Notes

1. *A two-year old goes to hospital.* 1951. Produced by James and Joyce Robertson.
2. *Going to hospital with mother.* 1958. Produced by James and Joyce Robertson.
3. Bowlby, John. 1969. *Attachment and Loss.* London: Pelican Books.
4. Bashforth, Martin. 2012. Absent Fathers, Present Histories. In *People and their Pasts. Public History Today*, ed. Paul Ashton and Hilda Kean, 203–222. Basingstoke: Palgrave Macmillan. (P. 216).
5. Bennett, Alan. 2005. *Untold Stories.* London: Faber and Faber.
6. Komaromy, Carol, Moyra Sidell and Jeanne Katz. 2000. Dying in Care: factors which influence the quality of terminal care given to older people in residential and nursing homes. *International Journal of Palliative Nursing*, 6, 4: 192–205.

7. Komaromy, Carol. 2002. The Performance of the Hour of Death. In *Palliative Care for Older People in Care Homes*, eds. David Clark and Jo Hockley, 138–150. Buckingham: Open University Press.
8. Komaromy, Carol. 2003. The needs of relatives and other residents when a death occurs. In *End of Life in Care Homes*, eds. Jeanne Katz and Sheila Peace, 87–98. Oxford: Oxford University Press.

10

Endings and Beginnings

Throughout this book we have been asking how the two world wars have affected family life as we have known it and in what ways this has shaped our consciousness. Our response to these questions has not been a straightforwardly causal explanation. And that is part of the challenge, or enigma, of a past that is recent yet has become rapidly obscured. What we have been able to offer is a reflexive account of the *process* whereby we have excavated and brought to life the people we grew up with or whose memories we grew up with but about whose pasts we knew little. Although the extraordinary events we revisit in this book were still unfolding in the decade when we both were born, they soon became muffled or marginalised as our families took on the optimism of 1950s Britain. Winning the war and building a new, more equal society led us and our parents to look forward rather than back. So there remains much about our families that we do not know and cannot bear witness to. If that information and insight were accessible to us, this would have been a far, far longer book. Instead, what has been important for us is the process of engaging or reengaging with what we half remember, or what we hoped may be there in the old diaries and photographs our families left behind. As this period of writing comes to an end, we recognise the new or reanimated relationships we have forged with those family members. And yet we are also returning them to their pasts now that our present tasks are almost done, whether they involve searching the internet, reaching out to distant living relatives or straining our eyes over tiny pencilled diary entries. Most of the people in this book are dead and gone. We will miss the everyday intimacy of our time spent in their company, of knowing them through our writing.

10.1 L'Osteria Restaurant, London

Since we met at the University of Sussex in 1995, we have had many conversations about our families and their relationships with us. Carol already knew Jenny when David, her father, died in 1996. Jenny was around when Carol's sister died that same year and also when Carol's mother moved into residential care, leaving Carol with challenging visits and the task of maintaining some kind of relationship as Nell became increasingly physically disabled and confused. Our conversations across these years provided the starting points for much of what we have written here.

Then in the spring of 2015, when Carol had recovered from illness sufficiently for us to meet for a meal in London, she talked about her plan to write something about her father's journey across Europe to Belsen, something she had long wanted to do. She said she thought we could work together on a project about both our fathers and their war-time experiences. She was thinking in terms of a book. That is when the research and writing began, a project that has now nearly come to an end.

Our conversations on these matters also extended to friends, former colleagues, family members, often in response to the small-talk enquiry, 'What are you up to at the moment?' If we answered, 'Writing a family memoir', there would be an assumption that only one family could be involved. How could a family memoir encompass two different families of at least three generations? We too had to address this question, even though we were aware of the common ground we shared within a broad historical landscape of military conflict and post-war hardship and hope. And after all, surely the work we had contributed to Death Studies was as much collaborative as individual. No professional academic works alone.

Even single-authored pieces are littered with references, the traces of the author's wider community.

10.2 The Rutland Arms, Bakewell

On 27 September 2015, once the holidays were out of the way, we met up again, for a weekend at The Rutland Arms in Bakewell, Derbyshire, to decide how we were going to approach the book. Outside the sun was shining, and we joked about being stuck indoors when we could be out there possibly having fun. Going shopping, or just visiting tourist sites, for example. There seemed to be an unspoken recognition that we were 'duty-bound' types and not inclined to frivolity. As Chap. 9 has described, a Protestant work ethic where duty always came before pleasure had been instilled into us from childhood onwards. Where we differed, however, was in the large amount of material that Jenny had gathered in preparation for the joint project compared with the small pile of papers that Carol had. We recognised immediately the danger that the book could replicate this uneven level of documented detail—what, in our research capacity, we might have called visual and textual data. As Jenny brought out photo after photo—in the well-ordered albums that recorded her ancestor's lives—Carol sat enviously clutching just a few family photos and her nephew's handwritten account of her dad's war story. This discrepancy left us wrestling with the fundamental question of how we were going to make sense of these very different legacies in a way that gave equal value to the lives of both our families. In addition, we shared an imperative to find out more about the experiences of relatives caught up in the two world wars but wanted to do this in ways that captured the quality of their lived experiences. More than this, we wanted to provide readers, among whom we counted our children, with a sense of how our parents' and grandparents' experiences had impacted upon us.

The concept of recovery, discussed in Chap. 1, was helpfully roomy. As a frame for our different histories it had space for healing but also for retrieval and recollection. It nicely encompassed our distinctive agendas. But any book, however theoretical, still has to tell a story. The traditionally linear form of the western book sets it up for a trajectory, a journey between what may start off as very loosely related ideas, events and emotions. So how could two women and eight dead people become a single story? Would we have to find a form that inevitably separated them out into different chapters or even sections? Surely a story needs a more coherent shape than that. It was the chronology of the twentieth century itself that eventually provided us with an easily navigable form within which to locate the feelings, remembered events and stories told to us by others. There was room for us both, for our photos and letters and documents, for the history of Europe and its wars. These have been the constituents of what we have produced. In finding the shape and texture of our story, we have come to understand our families and their circumstances in ways that eluded us previously.

10.3 Form, Content and Style

If we had found a form that we could begin to work with—and each of us brought to it the memories and memorabilia from which to generate content—there was still the question of style. The core issue that inspired us to write was the distancing and silence that surrounded earlier trauma and loss. Born so close to the deafening screams and sirens of a global war, we nonetheless grew up in emotionally incomprehensible or muted worlds where our parents' immediate histories were either kept deliberately secret or effectively made off limits. As Chap. 1 explains, our response to these circumstances was a felt need to write in a far more direct style than we were accustomed to. In life writing, we had a model of texts that crossed genres and mingled dominant histories with marginal, neglected or hidden areas of experience. If we were challenging the marginalisation or obfuscation of trauma and loss, we needed voices that were more immediate and personal than those we were comfortable with as academic writers. Again in Chap. 1, we refer to Alison Light's expressed hope that her *speaking* voice would anchor the reader as she—and they—moved through time.

Where possible then, our story is told through a single, shared voice, a joint 'we'. Intercut with this are passages which reflect the specific experiences of one or the other of us, written in our own distinctive 'speaking' voice. Here, in this chapter, we also include extracts from the diary Jenny kept while working on the book, writing with a more informal quality still. And where there is much that we share, then that single *shared* voice has been used to present either 'Carol's' or 'Jenny's' versions of an experience or event. There are few models for texts of this kind, for writing that is both collaborative *and* individual. In this respect our project has been a form of experiment that we have done our best to make accessible to our readers.

10.4   John Lewis, Birmingham

What has it been like for us, working together these past two years? It helped a lot that we had so much shared research activity behind us. We knew each other's strengths and limitations, and we knew, crucially, that we would both deliver, regardless of other pressures on our time. In that all-important dimension of any collaborative work, we knew we could totally rely on each other.

As we each uncovered and shared more fragments of information, what emerged were all kinds of continuities and synchronicities. These snippets, often just sparse words or dates or numbers, nonetheless worked on our imaginations, particularly when so much had been left unsaid and was therefore unknowable. In the absence of words, dates can reveal poignant coincidences, rather in the way that the inscriptions on gravestones tell stories simply through the alignment of dates when husbands or wives died, the ages at which children perished.

So, for example, it was only after Jenny 'joined the dots' of her father's life that she came to see the continuity between his parents' lives as drapers, his own childhood as a boarder at the Drapers' School in Croydon, his adolescence as an apprentice draper at Baker Baker in Bristol and subsequently his long years of employment in the carpet and bed departments of the John Lewis store in Cambridge. The shop was known as Robert Sayle when Jenny's father worked there, but its membership of the John Lewis Partnership was a source of great loyalty and pride for him. Robert Sayle, the man, like Bert, Jenny's grandfather, had also been born into a farming family. He too went to work for a wholesale draper before opening his own business in Cambridge in 1840. His list of merchandise resonates with that sold by Bert and Ella: linen drapery, silk mercery, hosiery, haberdashery, straw bonnets.

It seems appropriate then that when we held regular meetings in Birmingham in 2016 and 2017 to discuss this book, we chose the John Lewis café, a venue easily accessed via the splendour of New Street station. A coincidence perhaps, but there were also the synchronicities of birthdays, mentioned in Chap. 4; three of the key people in this book were born on 11 June—Carol, her father and Jenny's grandfather. And the inadvertent timing of Jenny's visit to Amiens which was precisely 99 years after her grandfather died there and almost exactly 46 years after her son, Gareth, was born. Croydon, too, is a place where David went to school and where Carol's parents married. It is also where Carol's first husband, the father of her children, was born.

If nothing else, our sensitivity to these coincidences, continuities and synchronicities has arisen out of a long process of assimilating scraps of information, of meshing historical and auto-/biographical material[1] to better understand what a relative's experience of their circumstances might have been.

10.5 Death Studies

It may seem that now in retirement we have been more than ready to turn our backs on the rigours of academic writing, its conventions and excluding terminologies. For the reasons set out above, this is partly the case. And yet this book also draws on the spirit of our academic research. For many years we set out to discover what happens when everyday continuities are upended, when horizons expand in ways that bring trauma, terror and loss as well as adventure. As academics we also sought to embrace these areas of life by *understanding* what we had observed or been told about by research participants.

In other words, we have not shied away from working in the somewhat taboo areas of death, dying and bereavement, instead choosing to explore the potentially uncomfortable truths that are the stuff of Death Studies. As we discussed in Chap. 2, it is an area of scholarship and professional practice that grew up in response to the sequestration or hiding away of death in the twentieth century. Yet more recently, talk of death, along with new death-related practices, has proliferated.[2] For example, in May 2016, in email correspondence, Jenny noted the prevalence of what could be called amateur autobiography—the practice of genealogy. She saw it reflected in the popularity of the TV programme *Who do you think you are?* and its pre-occupation with dead forbears. After half a century of seeing off the dead in a perfunctory fashion, of sequestering them in rarely visited cemeteries, we now seemed to be digging them up, metaphorically, and creating personal networks of ancestors. This raises the question of what tasks we implicitly allocate to those to whom we are connected yet may never have met.

We can stand back and observe this shift and its reflection within Death Studies' research, but Carol knows from her own psychodynamic work that the *motives* we attribute to our research can be a million miles away from the real, irrational driving forces. What Freud would call polymorphous and perverse unconscious driving forces are more likely to underpin what we do. So coming to the end of this particular quest demands a different level of honesty. 'Making a difference', based on a deeper understanding of other people's lives and deaths, is an easy justification for conducting the research we have done. But responding to our own deeply unconscious needs might reveal a very different motivation. The unconscious *choices* we make are always tightly censored, and revealing them can leave us shocked and aghast.

Carol I was amazed to find in my own analysis that my motives for doing things were quite different to those I retrospectively afforded to them. I had to look at the wider patterns and choices in my life to stand any chance of making my choices conscious and changing the patterns. In other words, to realise that I was not destined to continue making the same unhelpful choices.

So what do we think we have been doing in Death Studies? Carol argues here that the silence around the death and trauma of World War Two instilled in her a deep desire to uncover what was really going on.

Carol So many things were concealed—but in a way that I knew something was going on. My mother's illness. My father's profound grief. And all those vulnerable children and people he had to leave behind and could not help were a profound burden to him and one he was not ever allowed to share until the end of his life.

On one level Carol has been trying to find out the truth—and that quest has continued on the pages of this book. But also on her father's behalf, she has been trying to make amends for the terrible harm that was done to ordinary people by those in power. Jenny's motivations for undertaking work on death and dying—and for extending it in the present project—are similarly rooted in her historical and familial history. Retirement, for her, meant attending to a number of tasks she had reluctantly sidelined while still employed. Among them was looking at and reading the documents and photos that remained after her father died in 1996. As Chap. 2 describes, they had been quite literally shelved on the top of her various sets of bookcases. Immediately after his death, she did start to look at the loose photographs, pulling them out of the boxes they had been stored in. They risked getting dog-eared, and this prompted her to make her family album, a time-consuming task that was difficult to combine with her job. It put her off doing much more with the rest of her legacy at that point. But she still felt an obligation to it.

Jenny In fact I feel an obligation to many material things: unworn clothes that go into my wardrobe but rarely come out; lovely books that just sit on my shelves, unopened; beautiful notebooks with nothing written in them; broken things waiting to be mended, unfinished things waiting for completion. I make promises to myself and promises to them. That their day will come.

For her father's documents and photos, their day came when we had that meal together in London. Within Death Studies, Jenny belongs to a school of material culture theorists who argue for (and also about) the agency of objects, for their capacity to exert demands upon us, to afford us possibilities.[3] So if it seems that she has simply tidied up her inherited documents and photos, that is misleading. They were already quite tidy, up in their wicker basket above her shelves. But they wanted more than a safe haven. They had lives inscribed in them. But not lives that would open themselves to her straightforwardly or necessarily reward her for the time and effort spent reading what remained.

Jenny I would be allowed to know only so much and not be allowed any questions at the end. Because the whole lot of them had gone off and left me. Worse still, they had left me with snippets that were dwarfed by the grand scheme of a whole life and family connections. So why should I bother? How would it be to turf out everything? I could do that, now the book is done. And then I would feel alone, untethered, unrooted. Plus, I would have betrayed my father and his family by trashing their stuff, dumping my tiny residue of their lives. They would want to mean something to me as I would want to mean something to my children when I die. I would not want to be tidied away. I would want to intrude on my children and grandchildren's lives, despite my belief that 'now' is what matters or what matters now is what matters. But when there are no more 'nows', that is different.

10.6 Journey's End?

Writing about the play and film *Journey's End*, Martin Blocksidge, teacher of English, describes it as the claustrophobic story of soldiers waiting for action in a World War One dugout: 'ordinary plain people caught up in extraordinary events over which they had no control'.[4] This has indeed been our focus throughout the book, one that began precisely with the impact of World War One on Jenny's family. As we too reach our journey's end, where has the process of research and writing left us, and how has it affected our relationships with the family we have been worrying away at?

It has been a long journey into the past, and we have both been trying to access information beyond memory that has involved a struggle to verify dates and events. We have been both key informant and researcher, making connections with surviving and deceased persons, including family members who have been the gatekeepers of family stories. For Carol, the process has involved embodying the past and reordering accounts of what happened when and to whom. For example, how her grandfather's illegitimate status had been previously attributed to her grandmother. It has all resulted in changed relationships with missing persons and a better understanding of them. Certainly it has been a kind of quest to repeatedly attempt to make sense of our own family legacies, a quest that has involved an emotional and physical progression. In what ways, though, has it changed us, and to what extent has it altered our relationship with the missing persons in our lives?

Carol I have been struck many times in my reading of his biographical work by the way that Alan Bennett manages to portray his family with such accuracy and compassion.[5] Overall, I have found him to be forgiving, while in contrast, I have experienced a range of emotions about the constraints and narrow-mindedness of my early home life and upbringing. In the process of writing the book I have come to disclose examples of the horror of my mother's mental state. That process, of explaining why my mother might have suffered from mental illness, has not eradicated the resentment I still feel about the crippling nature of her unpredictable moods which meant having to be constantly on my guard. The extreme fluctuation of stifling affection and incomprehensible cruelty that seemed to be so damaging to my sense of self-worth and my confidence while growing up is difficult to forgive. It is interesting to note that in my drive to find out why my mother was as she was, I studied psychodynamic theories and underwent analysis on myself, always feeling it was too late and too daunting to save my mother, but intensely driven to understand the reasons why I was as I was. In the process of recording aspects of my life in this book, I have had to revisit some of the memories that stand out from my childhood. They have included 'good' and 'bad' ones. It has also been possible to offer an explanation for why my parents behaved as they did to each other and to us, their children. Such speculation has felt like a burden at times—but also it has been a luxury to explore in this book, something not readily afforded within academic writing.

Jenny On my table is the wicker basket I stored most of their stuff in. It is empty but I do not want to put everything back into it, to be forgotten about. I want to make their documents into a book, another book, with plastic pages, a ring binder that I can dip into and browse all their materials. I will have opened them up properly then, for scrutiny. Anyone could take that ring binder off the shelf and help themselves. That too seems wrong. But they cannot have it both ways, the dead. Or can they? Think of relics, their joint exposure/concealment. People have venerated them, invested them with healing powers, but most of them are housed in elaborate caskets, largely out of sight. In 2009, the relics of St Therese of Lisieux went on tour in the UK. I visited them in the Carmelite Monastery at Kirk Edge in High Bradfield, just outside Sheffield. The residue of the saint was doubly distanced by an elaborate gilded casket and then by a glass case. We 'pilgrims' filed past, pressing the palms of our hands on the glass, imprinting it with our lips. Have I been doing any more here in these pages than filing past my relatives, opening my hands and lips but only to the surface of the glass, a question that calls to mind Joseph Cornell's boxed, glass-fronted collages (see Chap. 2). My dead family are still layers away. Maybe they need to be. Or maybe I need them to be. I do not wear my family jewellery though I have enlarged and framed my grandmother's photo and hung it on my wall, as well as some photos of my mother as a child. But all these are behind glass too, even though my grandmother extends her cheery smile and fabulous dress sense to me as I walk past every day.

Reflections such as these, coming after months and months of close engagement with particular individuals, have led us to imagine what they would make of our final work.

Jenny These relationships are the places I live for hours on end, most days. I might think of them as illusory or fabricated. I am attributing qualities and experiences to them that there is little evidence for. But is that not what happens in all relationships? We do not know people terribly well when they are alive, but operate within a set of assumptions. Arthur is so beautiful and I suspect good fun. How sad that I cannot know him as he walks around the southwest of England with a reckless disregard for maps or booking accommodation. Was he reckless in the war? Was that why he didn't survive?

This intensity of involvement means that we have both had to make all kinds of ethical decisions along the way. It has not just been a matter of trying to recover something of what has been lost. There is also the issue of what to hold back and whose interests we should, morally, be protecting.

Carol I am fairly clear that my mother would have found it unhelpful, even overwhelming, to dig up the past in this way. Even though she often reminisced with Pauline and me about the past and the war, it was a story of the fun she had in the WAAF as a single woman away from home and the trauma of her pregnancy, separation and trying to cope financially. I am less clear about how Dad might have felt. I am fairly certain that he would be horrified that I have made public things that, in his view, should have been kept private, mostly by disclosing my mother's mental state, its damaging effects that he worked so hard to mitigate. However, I think he would have been flattered by how much I valued what he did and secretly proud that his story was told as one that represents the ordinary airman.

Now, after two years, Jenny finds herself asking these questions directly of the absent members of her family.

Jenny So what do you all think now, you ghosty ashes and bones, all in your separate graves: Topsham churchyard; Cambridge crematorium gardens; Fairport Cemetery, Newquay; Sangro River Military Cemetery, Italy; Villers-Bretonneux Military Cemetery, France? What do you make of the work I have done on your behalf? I think you would be pleased that I devoted so much time to you, that I have treasured what you left behind. I think you would forgive my intrusions into your diaries and letters. Why would you want your thoughts and feelings, your adventures and your country rambles to be discarded, to go to landfill? I will look after you all and do my best to hand you over to the living members of your family. What have you got to lose now, if other people read what you wrote? I trust them to read it respectfully, as I have.

And what do I want back from you? That is also part of my reluctance to file you away or jettison you entirely. I am still waiting and hoping that you might hold out your arms and lips to me. Talk to me about yourselves and tell me what I mean to you, that you love me, are proud of me. That is never going to happen but I wish it could. What is the point of all this family reserve, this turning away or inward? All I can do is consider the lives you all lived on the edges of two horrendous wars when being born was a dubious blessing.

Finally, here, we acknowledge the regrets that have surfaced in the course of our project. It has been sad for Carol to think about what her mother's life might have been like without the mental anguish and paranoia she had to manage. At the end of her life, as her memory began to fail and with it the essential features of her identity, she became increasingly angry and frustrated.

Carol I remember standing at her bedside when she was dying and feeling terribly sad that I did not feel loving towards her. Her two grandsons (my nephews) were there, and they were able to show her great affection.

Jenny echoes this sense of an opportunity she was unable to take, in diary writing two years after the beginning of our project.

Jenny Both Arthur and David are now young men I have sets of feelings about. I really do want my dad to have something special happen to him—I want him to have a girlfriend or at least be drawn that way. I really do not want him to be lonely. I care about him, as a young man. And I am drawn to Arthur. I also feel sorry that I did not look after my father lovingly in the way that his mother did—I want her to care for me but I have let her down by not being loving towards her son.

10.7 Legacies We Take Forward

Born in 1946 and 1948, respectively, we came into the world at a critical military and political juncture. Within months of the war ending in Europe on 8 May 1945, a landslide victory for the Labour government meant that the extensive social reforms proposed by Sir William Beveridge in 1942 could be brought into play. At this time of transition, the differences between life pre- and post-war were constantly being born in on us, as were the conditions of life in Britain compared with what close family members had so recently experienced overseas. Growing up on the edge of so momentous a global event as World War Two left us with a sense of excluding boundaries between different times and places. This notion of boundaries, both symbolic and physical, became a key theoretical resource for us academically. It is also relevant here as we look at the detail of what it was like to be born just after the end of World War Two. We have argued that our parents looked forward to a future of peace and how the price of that peace was depicted as the great sacrifice made by those like Jenny's grandfather and uncle who died and never came home. We have dared to look over the edge of that time to see what managing that divide meant for those who survived. Jenny has told the deeply sad story of what it meant for her grandmother and her father. In this sense, we have been exploring the cost of survival. For Carol's parents there were dangerous boundaries, some of which were crossed with dire consequences, for example the extreme poverty that led to their homelessness and which intensified the trauma that Nell experienced and that increased her paranoia.

On the one hand, then, we were lucky to arrive at the end of the last world war and to grow up in a time of optimism and hope that things could be done differently. And they were. And we did. Becoming senior academics was beyond anyone's imaginings, but we did it. There were opportunities for us to study, despite both being mothers at the time. And there were permanent jobs for us too, with pensions. There was good health care, contraception, babysitters and husbands who expected and encouraged us to do more than just make them a home to come back to after work. No one required us to wear corsets, stuff mushrooms or keep quiet and carry on.

But there were challenges that came with our greater independence and freedom, and the fragility of the benefit system we inherited should not be overlooked. Nor indeed its restriction to particular groups within society. That said, we are grateful for what we have carried forward from our pasts. Both of us inherited aspects of a way of life that turned on routine, habit and hard work, on letting nothing go to waste. Arguably, without that commitment to graft, to 'doing things properly' and seeing them through, no amount of opportunities could have provided us with the careers we have had. This book documents our families' very different histories, but in Chap. 9 the similarities of our upbringings come to the surface, the values our families shared despite very different circumstances. Neither of our childhoods was particularly happy. Carol's was shot through with terror as well as fun, love and humour. Jenny's was cramped and gloomy with limited confident connection with a wider world of family and friends. But these experiences too have tempered the ways we have lived, helped us to trust that with patience and hard work all manner of problems can be overcome.

Apart from the contrast between her parents, Carol is convinced that she could have made so much more of her life if the home philosophy of 'being true to your roots' and 'making the most of what you've got' had not been such dominant messages. Ambition was not something to be proud of—it was better to know your place. Jenny similarly recalls the pride with which David, her father, would assert, 'I'm not ambitious', when talking about his job selling carpets and later beds. Carol remembers attending a lecture by Jonathan Miller in her early 30s at the Institute of Psychoanalysis in London. His introduction made it plain that he was born into a home and family that gave him much more than a head start.

Carol It was striking how different his start was from mine. The accolades of what he had achieved were impressive, but I remember thinking, well I'm not surprised with *that* start in life!

Carol is also convinced that she could have made much more of herself had she had more intellectual stimulation at home—and if she had not hated most of her time in school. When she did discover the joy of education later in life, she felt as if she was in a race to catch up, going on to have a successful academic career, feeling totally committed to improving health care through education, and encouraging others to enjoy learning as much as she does. She said at the outset that her recent illness has given her a sense of urgency and also brought to the fore what is important to her.

Carol I realise I do not really have any regrets. I did as much as I could do to the best of my ability, and I have memories of the times I made a difference to people. I have been able to connect with people in many ways, and I have met lots of really inspiring and committed people, and Jenny is one of them. Further, even in the darkest moments, I have been able to see the funny side of things. And I have had lots of fun. Whatever else I have inherited from my family, I am a survivor. Core to that survival is a sense of humour.

As a parent, Carol feels she has a strong and loving bond with her two children. Indeed, they are the most important people in her life. She would love to have been as good a parent as her father, a tall order, but in Kleinian terms, perhaps she was 'good enough'. Her dad taught her that kindness and humour were essential to living a good life.

10.8 The Personal and the Professional

Neither of us envisages our conversations being brought to a close any time soon. While making decisions about how to finish this book, we are also exchanging news about another 'next generation', the Death Studies post graduate students we have been lucky enough to supervise. The contributions of people like Kate Woodthorpe, Julie Ellis, Therese Richardson,[6] Hong Chen and Caroline Pearce are partly our own legacy for the future of a reflexively informed sphere of research. The field is in their eminently capable hands now, and we are consistently impressed by their capacity to generate new theoretical ideas, as well as to organise and develop a community of scholars and practitioners.

This meshing of the professional and the personal, or rather, their indivisibility, is evident in one final example. When Jenny was exploring the process of ageing through the prism of footwear, it was Carol's recognition of the theoretical relevance of her very personal experiences of looking after her mother's body when she died that provided an important starting point for a key article from that project.[7]

Carol,[8] in her 60s, described how her mother, Nell, had changed from someone who hated 'old age', was very concerned with her appearance, obsessively busy with housework, to someone inactive and disconnected from life. Nell continued ballroom dancing into her late 70s, managing high-heeled shoes with ease and style. Her deteriorating mobility and frequent falls forced her to wear 'sensible' shoes. Carol said, 'when she died, Debbie, my daughter, and I went to the care home to clear the room. We had to choose her clothes for the coffin and the outfit we chose was smart – but still glamorous. We looked at the shoes in the wardrobe and agreed that Nana could not be seen dead in them! In a department store, we found just the right ones – they were extremely elegant, not too high, looked expensive (indeed they were) and something she could wear to a dance. We declined offers of trying them on and giggled about how – as long as they were big enough – it didn't matter. Buying the shoes gave us a real sense of achievement as if we had done something really important that we knew she would have loved'.

Notes

1. See 'the historio-biographical approach' in: Hockey, Jenny and Allison James. 2003. *Social Identities across the Life Course*. Basingstoke: Macmillan. (P. 59).
2. Hockey, Jenny. 2011. Contemporary cultures of memorialization: blending social inventiveness with conformity. In *Governing Death and Loss. Empowerment, involvement, and participation*, ed. Steve Conway, 27–36. Oxford: Oxford University Press.
3. discussion article. 2007. *Archaeological Dialogues*, 14, 1: 1–16.
4. Blocksidge, Martin. 2013. English Association First World War Bookmarks 2. https://www2.le.ac.uk/offices/english-association/publications/bookmarks/WW1/2JourneysEnd.pdf. Accessed 08.01.2018.
5. Bennett, Alan. 2005. *Untold Stories*. London: Faber and Faber.
6. Therese died, sadly, soon after graduation in 2012. Her thesis formed the basis of the following article: Richardson, Therese. 2014. Spousal Bereavement in later life: a material culture perspective. *Mortality*, 19.1: 61–79.

7. Hockey, Jenny, Rachel Dilley, Victoria Robinson, and Alexandra Sherlock. 2014. The Temporal Landscape of Shoes. A Life Course Perspective. *The Sociological Review*, 62.2: 255–275.
8. Pseudonyms were used in the published work.

Index[1]

A
Ancestors, 29–30
Anthropology, 4
Association for the Study of Death and Society, 17n1

B
Banking, 130
Bashforth, Martin, 109, 224
Batchen, Geoffrey, 27–29
Batten, Richard, 74
Battles
 of Amiens, 84, 85
 of Britain, 152
 of the Bulge, 182–183, 198
 of the Falaise Pocket, 192
 Passchendaele, 84
 Operation Market Garden, 181, 194–196
 Operation Overlord, 190
 Operation Sealion, 152
 See also World War One; World War Two
Benamou, Jean-Pierre, 193
Benjamin, Walter, 29
Bourke, Joanna, 30, 73
Bradley, John, 98
Brooks, David, 52

C
Cannadine, David, 55
Cornell, Joseph, 23–25

---

[1] Note: Page numbers followed by 'n' refer to notes.

D

Day-Lewis, Tamsin, 166
Dead, the, 246
    objects of, 33, 36–38, 50, 89, 161, 248, 252, 255
    war, 88–92
Death
    animal, 56, 225
    bed, 240, 257
    fear of, 48
    making sense of, 48, 51–59
Death studies, 1, 6–7, 49, 250–251, 260
Drapers, 113, 117–119
    apprenticeships, 131–134
    identity, 114, 249–250
    school, 110–119
        gardening, 117
        prizes, 118–119
        punishment, 113
    shops, 69, 107

E

Education
    higher, 2, 51, 233
    in Northern Ireland, 100, 120
    post war, 218
    school, 233
    See also Drapers, school
Employment, 214

F

Family
    deaths, 11, 31–33, 40–44, 160–162
    kinship, 26
    siblings, 143–145, 163
Farming, 66, 74, 99
Funerals, 40, 42

G

Geertz, Clifford, 53
Gender
    domestic division of labour, 221–223
    employment/careers, 227, 258–259
    identity, 225
    widowhood, 106
    women in war, 73
Genealogies, 39, 100
Ghosts, 48, 54
Gibson, Margaret, 38
Graves, 41
    headstones, 94
    See also Military cemeteries
Grossman, Vasily, 196

H

Hallam, Elizabeth, 54
Hayward, John A., 88
Health, 135–136, 161, 219–221, 227, 239
    childbrith, 215
    mental health, 224–225, 229, 236–237, 242, 254, 256
    pregnancy, 214
    smoking, 221
Heirlooms, 33, 34
Hockey, Jenny (publications), 5, 8
Holocaust
    Bergen-Belsen, 184–185, 200–205

survivors, 44, 240
Homelessness
   workhouse, 216, 219
Howarth, Glennys, 54
Hudson, Pat, 75

I

Ingold, Tim, 56
International Death, Dying and
      Disposal Conference, 1, 2
Ireland
   domestic life, 99, 212–215
   employment, 99
   famine, 97
   history of conflict, 96–98, 121
   See also Education

K

Komaromy, Carol (publications), 6
Kuhn, Annette, 224

L

Laqueur, Thomas, 91
Leisure
   Cadena Café, 132, 135
   cinema, 132
   hobbies, 117, 232
   holidays, 227, 231
   sketching, 136–138
   walking and cycling, 123, 128, 138–141, 232
Letters, 37, 76–78, 82, 84, 91–93, 145, 148, 155, 164, 165
Life-writing, 16–17, 246, 248–249

Light, Alison, 21
Lloyd George, David, 70

M

Marriage, 233, 238
   birth outside, 100–101, 173
   courtship, 141–143, 165–166, 173, 229, 233
Memorialisation, 106, 162
Memory
   selective, 28–34
   traumatic, 209
Military cemeteries, 90–95, 195
   visiting, 90–93, 105

N

Nursing, 2, 48, 87, 234

O

Oral history, 34

P

Parenting, 36, 42, 43, 109, 226, 260
   father/daughter, 225, 239
   mother/son relationship, 134–136
Prior, Robin, 85
Psychodynamic interpretations, 3, 8–9, 114, 224, 237, 251

R

Recovery, 11–14, 247
   recollection, 11–14
Reflexivity, 7–8, 245

Religion, 50–57, 94, 121, 167, 242–243
Remarque, Erich Maria, 26, 79, 85–87
Remembrance Day, 37, 241
Representations
  of family, 62–63
  of World War One, 25

S
Simic, Charles, 23
Smart, Carol, 12, 23, 27
Smith, Jenny, 69
Social class, 36, 103, 113, 167, 258
  poverty, 214–216, 225–226
Steedman, Carolyn, 27

T
Taylor, Lou, 63
Terdiman, Richard, 27
Terraine, John, 83
Time
  awareness of, 114–116, 128
Timeline, 2

V
Van Emden, Richard, 109–110
Van Gennep, Arnold, 128

W
White, Bonnie, 74
Wills, 80
Wilson, Trevor, 85
Winter, Jay, 7
World War One
  clearing stations, 85, 87–88
  Imperial War Graves Commission, 90
  National Registration Act, 71
  orphans, 109–110
  recruitment, 71–72, 74–75, 101
  Royal Garrison Artillery, 73, 82
  siege batteries, 82
  training, 73–82
World War Two
  air raid wardens, 127
  Blitz, 131, 132, 152
  Egypt, 153–155
  Enlistment, 169
  history of, 108, 148–151
  home front, 217
  Iraq, 156–158
  Italy, 159–160
  Normandy landings, 175, 179–180, 188–190
  Second Tactical Air Force, 172–173, 190, 192, 196
  training, 170–171

CPSIA information can be obtained
at www.ICGtesting.com
Printed in the USA
LVOW13*1917190518
577815LV00011B/88/P